MARTY GLICKMAN

MARTY GLICKMAN

The Life of an American Jewish Sports Legend

JEFFREY S. GUROCK

WASHINGTON MEWS BOOKS

An Imprint of

NEW YORK UNIVERSITY PRESS

New York

WASHINGTON MEWS BOOKS
An Imprint of
NEW YORK UNIVERSITY PRESS
New York
www.nyupress.org

Library of Congress Cataloging-in-Publication Data
Names: Gurock, Jeffrey S., 1949– author.
Title: Marty Glickman : the life of an American Jewish sports legend /
Jeffrey S. Gurock.
Description: New York : New York University Press, [2023] |
Includes bibliographical references and index.
Identifiers: LCCN 2022054708 | ISBN 9781479820870 (hardback) |
ISBN 9781479820887 (ebook) | ISBN 9781479820894 (ebook other)
Subjects: LCSH: Glickman, Marty, 1917-2001. | Runners (Sports)—United States—
Biography. | Sportscasters—United States—Biography. | Jewish athletes—United
States—Biography. | Olympic Games (11th : 1936 : Berlin, Germany)
Classification: LCC GV1061.15.G55 G87 2023 |
DDC 796.42092 [B]—dc23/eng/20221116
LC record available at https://lccn.loc.gov/2022054708

This book is printed on acid-free paper, and its binding materials are chosen for
strength and durability. We strive to use environmentally responsible suppliers and
materials to the greatest extent possible in publishing our books.

Manufactured in the United States of America

10 9 8 7 6 5 4 3 2 1

Also available as an ebook

For Charlie

CONTENTS

Marty Glickman on his broadcasting perch at Madison Square Garden.
Credit: https://sportsbroadcastjournal.com.

INTRODUCTION

Sportscaster, Olympic Athlete, American Jew

IN the 1960s, fall Sunday afternoons were prime time for the fans of the New York Giants, who tuned in their radios from their homes or their cars to Marty Glickman's play-by-play descriptions from Yankee Stadium. During this era the National Football League (NFL) blacked out television broadcasts of home games to promote stadium ticket sales. Unless a truly devoted fan was prepared to trek at least seventy-five miles from Gotham to Upstate New York or to Connecticut to catch the event on local stations, Glickman was their go-to guy. Even then, as they sat in front of "fuzzy pictures," some fans stuck with their stronger radio signals to pick up the "Voice of Sunday" from New York City. So it was on September 21, 1969, that the Giants were down thirteen points to the visiting Minnesota Vikings with only five minutes left in the fourth quarter before the home team rallied. Led by quarterback Fran Tarkenton, Big Blue scored one touchdown and was driving for the winning tally as the clock wound down to the two-minute warning, a brief pause in the action. During the tension-filled time-out, Glickman showed uncommon concern for the safety of his listeners in their automobiles. Aware that his histrionic announcing might cause drivers to lose control of their vehicles and crash, he implored, "Now folks if you are driving, I suggest you pull to the side of the road because you are liable to endanger yourself." Groups of motorists on Westchester County's Saw Mill River Parkway dutifully followed Glickman's instructions and stopped their cars on the side of the road. Miles away, drivers stuck in a traffic jam on Brooklyn's Flatbush Avenue weaved their way across multiple clogged-up lanes to safety. Such was the reach of Glickman's lung power across the highways and byways of the metropolis. For his legion of gridiron listeners, Glickman's accounts "seemed to ease the frustration inflicted by the then-strict NFL rule. Even if you couldn't see the action Glickman's rapid-fire delivery never let you feel cheated." Some fans who could not secure tickets to the home games "never knew what the stadium looked like" except from their favorite announcer's descriptions.[1]

This would not be the only time Glickman's radio devotees followed his commands. In 1971, again in the closing moments of another hotly contested game, he called upon fans to show their allegiance to the Giants from afar by opening up their windows and shouting "Go Giants Go." Some years later, in the movie *Network*, a fictionalized and outraged New York television anchor, Howard Beale, would demand from his studio that his viewers at home stand up, open their windows, and shout, "I'm mad as hell and I won't take it anymore." In real life, Glickman's request did not horrify his listeners, who were just hopeful that their efforts would help their team as they rose dutifully to make their own public statements. The cheers reverberated from apartments and tenements all over the city and out of the rolled-down windows of automobiles. Fans in Yankee Stadium, who were listening to their favorite announcer while watching the game in person, joined the chorus of supporters. Glickman later would discover that over at Queens' Shea Stadium, where the New York Jets played, ticket holders "started yelling too." At those critical moments, the vaunted code of announcer objectivity, which Glickman generally observed, was ignored as he successfully led the cheers of the New York sports community. "With a voice that possessed the toughness of the sidewalks, the speed of spaldeens and the richness of egg creams," Glickman readily embraced this status as the sports voice of Gotham. He declared himself "as much a New Yorker as a New Yorker can be."[2]

During wintertime, Glickman was, from the club's inception in 1946, the voice of New York Knicks basketball. From his booth on a platform on the mezzanine level, about twenty feet above the floor of Madison Square Garden, the mecca of American indoor sports, his well-chosen and creative words, delivered in a "staccato, concise and clear" style, reflected his firm belief that "the listener ought to see the game the same way the spectator in the stands sees the game." In setting the scene, he went so far as to detail what color uniforms opponents were wearing. In describing the action on the hardwood, he "set basketball terminology" as he provided listeners with a "geography of the court." His audience could almost "see" the "keyhole," "the head of the foul circle," or "the corner" or "mid-court line" as he painted action images of movements and plays. In his vocabulary "dribblers" took "high arching shots" into the basket with a "swish," his best-known onomatopoeia. Or they "drove across the lane down to the hoop" after receiving a pass from a teammate who "fed" him from the "pivot" or "banked in" a "fast break" basket. In his classic roman à clef novel *On the Road*, Jack Kerouac, a legendary voice of the 1950s beat generation, has Dean Moriarty—the fictionalized persona of his travel companion, poet Neal Cassady—groove to a "Garden" broadcast: "Man, have you dug that mad Marty Glickman, announcing basketball games-up-to-midcourt-bounce-fake-set-shot, swish, two points. Absolutely the greatest announcer I have ever heard."[3]

Radio critic Don Freeman, gesturing toward the announcer's directions to his captivated audiences, noted that it was clear that "Marty issues such statements with the inherent sense of frolic of a man who knows what he is reporting is merely a boys' game played by young men. But he is serious too as befits the true professional at the microphone." Documentarian James L. Freedman, who directed an HBO film to posthumously honor his hero before a national viewing audience that included those who, in his view, had not been privileged to hear Glickman's voice, heartily agreed. For him, Glickman represented "the purity of sport, a primal feeling when you first had a catch with your dad, that's what emanated from Marty's broadcasts." Brooklyn-born historian Peter Levine, speaking for thousands of boys and girls of his generation in Gotham, has reflected similarly, "Marty Glickman was the voice of my youth."[4]

Though Marty Glickman broadcasted to New Yorkers of all backgrounds, age groups, races, and ethnicities and aspired to find fans well west of the Hudson River, he was also the most Jewish of announcers, a rarity when he started his on-the-air career even in the largest Jewish city in the world. He would allow that "even on the air, I have no hesitancy about using Yiddish phrases to depict the action." His Jewish lexicon went beyond terms like *meshuga*, *kvetch*, and *chutzpah*, which many of his Christian neighbors regularly used and became part of English dictionaries and New York street vocabularies. Words like *farmatert*—Glickman's English translation was "dead beat," as in "he really looked beat out there"—rolled off his tongue often to the bemusement, if not confusion, of his non-Jewish color commentators who complemented his play-by-play accounts with their analyses of the action. At those moments, sidekicks like former Giants linebacker and West Virginian Sam Huff, whom Glickman characterized with affection as an "often garrulous, very bright hillbilly," were silenced for a spell. But the word choice synthesis was a source of pride to his Jewish listeners, as one of their own integrated sports reporting with their ancestral roots at a time when so many others hid where they came from. For Glickman, such digs into Yiddish phraseologies, which he drew from his bilingual background—even though the use of English was preferred at home—provided a subtle way for this American broadcaster to express himself as a "cultural Jew." This self-definition reflected an enduring pride that he had in his ethnic background, though it was one of the risks that he took in hoping to make his mark among more than just his devoted fans in New York City.[5]

As his more than half century of broadcasting ended in 1992, Glickman harvested inductions into a myriad of sports and broadcasting halls of fame across the country, ranging from the announcers' wing of the National Basketball Hall of Fame in Springfield, Massachusetts, to local formal tributes in his hometown, including recognition from the National Jewish Sports Hall of Fame on Long Island.

Thus, if sports—as they most certainly do—constitute fixtures in the popular culture of Gotham and the nation, Marty Glickman was among its brightest lights in the metropolis across the five decades following World War II. He was as much an iconic sports figure in town as Willie Mays, who was often pictured playing stick ball with neighborhood kids in the streets of Harlem after games at the Polo Grounds, the Knicks' sartorially resplendent Walt "Clyde" Frazier, who graced the Garden, and the Jets' Broadway Joe Namath, who loved the city's nightlife with Gotham's beautiful people and whose football games Glickman also covered on the radio from Shea Stadium in Queens.

To this day, men and women, who are now oldsters, still remember Glickman's calls and use his words to brag about their own feats in pickup games all over New York. When such an attenuated athlete makes a particularly difficult basket, he might exclaim, "Good like Nedicks," just like Glickman had shouted out, back in the day, the name of one of his sponsors when a shot from one the home team's favorites went through the net. At those moments, recollections and recitations of Glickman's word pictures provide warm memories of youthful days well spent in the city's gyms and playgrounds. While Marty Glickman passed away at age eighty-three in 2001, his voice endures among those who will always be his fans.

Beginning in the mid-1980s, a second dimension to Glickman's life attracted audience attention among sports people and a wider general public both in New York and nationally. It was at that point that he began to speak openly and candidly about an anger and sadness that remained with him for much of his adult life. His enduring pain was rooted in his experience of being snubbed as an eighteen-year-old track star during the 1936 Summer Olympics in Nazi Germany. Prior to that dark moment, Glickman had been privileged in his youth to not experience much in the way of anti-Semitism. Growing up in a predominantly Jewish neighborhood, he was exempted from the prejudices and discriminations that circumscribed the lives of so many Jews of his era and rarely heard ethnic slurs on the streets of Flatbush. At James Madison

High School, as a good student and an outstanding sprinter and football player, Glickman was with his own kind within an overwhelmingly Jewish student body. As a collegiate freshman, though enrolled at Syracuse University, an "out-of-town school" that was far from free from anti-Jewish trends, Glickman was spared the canards and marginalization that other Jews endured because he was an athlete who brought sports-based honor to the institution and its legions of fans. His presence on campus as a budding football and track star, however, did little to improve the lot of other Jews at Syracuse. Improving their numbers and status had been the fantasy of the group of Jewish alumni who recruited Glickman to their alma mater at a time when quotas were very much in play. Glickman integrated well within a Christian majority. Even as he was aware of "differences," he generally fit in with young men and women whose backgrounds were so different from his erstwhile Brooklyn neighborhood. Glickman had nothing to say about discrimination toward others on the college campus. He kept his eyes fixed on achieving his goal of Olympic stardom as a member of the U.S. track team's upcoming games in Berlin and was not attuned to the Jewish groups that called for a boycott of Hitler's games in protest against Nazi anti-Semitism. These voices were outside of his earshot.

But then came what he called "the meeting" in the Olympic Village in August 1936. Though he had secured a coveted spot representing his country, the coaches of his country's track team curtly told Glickman that he was to be dropped from team for the 4 × 100 meters relay race, a featured event. Despite his athletic pedigree, which he had spent his entire young life developing, and his earned position, he was sidelined. He was certain that he was egregiously excluded because some American Olympic officials did not want to embarrass Hitler should a Jew end up standing on the victory platform. This unanticipated blow to his hopes and expectations hurt him deeply as he sat alone in the stands. The best possible face that he could put on this unexpected development was that he would triumph four years later at the next Olympics. World War II chilled that dream. The wound would reside within him for many years to come, even as he endeavored, and success-fully committed himself, to move on with his life. Sam Stoller, his often-forgotten fellow Jewish teammate who was also banned from the race, found it extremely difficult to transcend this offense. It would undermine Stoller's life.

When the sidelining took place and for long thereafter, Glickman did not publicly confront the decision makers and tar them as Jew-haters. Though certain in his heart of hearts that prejudice had de-terred him, he did not say, for all to hear, that his enemies within U.S. Olympic leadership were anti-Semites. Indeed, for several decades after the 1930s, as he built a career and dealt with other forms of prejudice that undermined his quests for success, he held the story of Berlin 1936 close to his chest. He had every reason to believe that few people were interested in his story. Even his own children were kept unaware. One of his sons would allow that his father's quietude was somewhat reminiscent of how so many mem-bers of what has been called America's Greatest Generation were often silent about their own trying, if in their cases victorious, times.

However, beginning in the 1980s, close to a full half century after the Berlin Olympics, when Holocaust memories became part of American Jewry's consciousness, Glickman was drawn into that ongoing conversation about the cataclysm as he was living within a new era among American Jews. At this point late in his life, many Jews, of a different generation from his own and more comfort-able in their skin as Americans, were responding without reserva-tions against anti-Semitism, past and present, within and beyond America. Within this accepting atmosphere, Glickman articulated his feelings about prejudice, toward himself and others, without a second thought about how his story would be received. He was then keen to publicly recount time and again the humiliation he felt in 1936—and the painful memories that he had long kept inside—due to American Olympic officials keeping him from com-peting in the Berlin games in sympathetic deference to the feelings of their Nazi friends who sat in the stands at the Olympic Stadium. He no longer spoke of "politics," an ambiguous term that he had occasionally used to characterize how and why he was ousted in favor of a coach's protégés who were inferior runners. Now he asserted without reticence the anti-Semitism he experienced.

The consummate turning point for Glickman, when his silent period ended, took place in 1985 when he was invited back to Germany as part of a memorial track meet in honor of Jesse Owens. This great African American runner, who garnered four gold medals, had almost single-handedly exposed the fallacy of Aryan racial supremacy through his track triumphs. Then, the "rage," the "bitterness" that long welled up inside of him came to the surface. An emotionally riven Glickman "spewed out anger [he] didn't know still existed." He wondered to himself, though he really knew the answer: "How could they keep an eighteen-year-old kid from competing. . . . They kept my dream from me."[6]

Some ten years later, Glickman was again invited back to Berlin, this time to watch his favorite football team, the New York Giants, play an exhibition game. Still not free from his earlier "anger and frustration" as he sat in the same stadium where Hitler had once presided, "a feeling of sadness" enveloped him as he peered at a pillar with the names of the 1936 gold medalists, a memorial that did not bear his name. Realizing that he was still alive and both his enemies as well as most of the Olympic champions of a half century earlier were dead, he "became aware of [his] mortality . . . and there was a feeling of completion. . . . This time there was a feeling of coming full circle." Glickman would assert that "the Olympic story ended."[7]

Not exactly: while Glickman would on occasion muse regarding "the irony about the medal that should have been mine but wasn't . . . how many [other Olympic] relay runners can anyone name," the telling of the sad saga of Glickman in Berlin 1936 was not over. Indeed, the discriminatory act was destined to be replayed and projected as part of a far broader historical narrative. It came to be seen as a symbolic prequel to the Holocaust. Along these lines, most notably in 1996, the United States Holocaust Memorial Museum created an exhibit titled "Nazi Olympics: Berlin 1936" at its D.C. institution. This array of pictures and documents eventually traveled the country as part of the organization's ongoing effort to educate, and to graphically illustrate to the public, the horrors of the destruction of European Jewry. They could use the story of Glickman as an entry point for a conversation about the troubling antecedent circumstances that soon led to this catastrophe. The museum hosted this special exhibition again in 2008, demonstrating that the significance of sports transcended the simple question of who might have won or lost a match. Participation or exclusion in the world of games was understood as metaphorical for understanding how a minority might be viewed and ultimately oppressed and attacked in an aggressively racist society.[8]

An edited version of Glickman's four-hour testimony, placed on public display, was a very important feature of the project. The long version was archived for future scholarly use. There he detailed fully his life and perspectives. His words were an important way for him to teach, to aid the next generation of Jews and indeed the world in becoming more fully aware of the problematic critical years that immediately preceded that terrible period of Jewish history. The sportscasting icon now became a desired contributor to the worthy effort to preserve Holocaust memory even if the actual destruction of six million Jews did not begin until the Nazi invasion of Poland three years after the Berlin Olympics. Glickman agreed with this central periodization and was always sure to submit that what happened to him, at his very unhappy moment, should not be compared to Kristallnacht in November 1938 or the destruction of European Jewry beginning in September 1939. However, in focusing on Glickman, who was turned away from an athletic event by those who despised his people, a profound message was projected that the same pernicious elements of hatred, aggression, and complicity among anti-Semites, and disinterest among bystanders who might have spoken up on his behalf, represented more than just the unhappy fate of an athlete within the confines of a stadium. Rather, his experience presaged the story of how the Nazis, their allies, and the world community would behave on the largest scale toward Jewish victims during World War II. The exclusion of Glickman and Stoller placed these Jewish athletes outside the community of sports. Soon thereafter their people would be damned as the world's consummate outsiders.

The two narratives of Glickman, as a sportscasting icon within the pantheon of sports and popular culture and as a victim of anti-Semitism at the 1936 Olympics, have been fully documented in literally hundreds of newspaper and magazine articles and in several documentary films. Through his autobiography and his published and unpublished interviews, Glickman also contributed so much to what is known about this legendary public figure. But at no point did he contemplate the broader significance of his entire life story as a twentieth-century American Jew. Perhaps it is too much to ask of Glickman—a man of action far more than reflection who kept many of his deepest thoughts and feelings to himself—to have seen beyond his own memories.

This volume sees what its protagonist could not. It projects Marty Glickman as far more than just a notable figure in sports media history and a nice guy who mentored many in a very competitive industry and who as an athlete eventually admitted publicly to the trauma that had long haunted him. Rather, this book, out for bigger game in a different arena, roots its comprehensive account of Glickman's life within the sweep of the twentieth century's American Jewish saga. It details a life of multiple challenges, frustrations, and achievements and places in high relief the quests for professional success and social acceptance that characterized his career. As it would turn out, the Olympics would not be the only time Glickman had to cope with sidelining as a Jew, even to endure what he would call "Jewish anti-Semitism." Metaphorically, through this full-length examination of the life of one well-known American Jew's experiences, over eight decades, the prejudicial and cultural obstacles that were common to thousands, if not millions, of fellow Jews of his times as they strove to make it in America are identified and contextualized.

Second-generation American Jews like Marty Glickman, especially those who grew up in New York, the largest Jewish city in
the world, began their lives in neighborhoods where they could
believe that the whole world was Jewish even if there always were
some gentiles around. They were located in comfortable cocoons
of their own ethnicity where everywhere they turned they bumped
into their own kind: on the streets, in stores with Yiddish signs
on the frontages, in public schools, at work, and in synagogues.
Although occasionally some noisy anti-Semites might show up in
their neighborhoods, their nasty canards against Jews did not really affect their lives.

However, those who ventured away from their homes to parts of
America that were not their own discovered that notwithstanding
their ability to speak, dress, and act, not to mention play sports,
like all other Americans, there were distinct barriers to achieving
economic success and social acceptance. Though their problems
with integration paled in comparison to the racism that African
Americans always faced wherever they lived, these Jewish children
of immigrants were a minority group with limitations on their advancement. The crisis point for Jews might be the time they attempted to enroll at elite and restrictive colleges and universities.
Alternatively, troubles might have ensued when they sought to rise,
beyond entry levels, in their chosen occupation in fields where few
Jews were employed. For some, they found out how different Jews
were when they sought to live in tony towns. At worst, there were
overt anti-Semites who opposed them and projected Jews as existential threats to this country's future. But more often the word on
the gentile street was that Jews just did not fit in. The problematics
of exclusion for second-generation Jews in the educational, employment, and residential realms did not end for American Jews
until decades after the Second World War.

Given these obstacles, some American Jews of the interwar period
abandoned all associations to their past, hopeful that their special
talents would carry the day. They certainly did not challenge those
who would limit them and were thrilled on the occasions when they

were admitted to Christian preserves. Anglicizing their names was one sign of their quest to belong among the gentile majority.

Many more sought a middle ground as Americans and as Jews, striving forcefully for integration based on their merits while retaining a residual connection to their past. They did not divorce themselves from their community and might have harbored some resentment toward those who "passed" out of connection with their people. On a day-by-day basis, those who retained an affinity or residual affection for their heritage spoke a different cultural dialect when interacting with their fellow Jews, while in most instances coming across differently to gentile colleagues. In the best of circumstances, they shared their linguistic affinities with their Christian friends. However, since they did not feel fully at home in America, these second-generation men and women were reticent, until late in their era, to dispute their haters or even take on those who just did not like them. They did not call out anti-Semitism or for that matter racism in all its incarnations as a social and political blot upon America. Large-scale activism and outward expressions of group loyalty awaited the rise of the next generation of Jews who were fortunate to live in a more tolerant and accepting United States. Marty Glickman's story illustrates many of the complexities that faced his generation of Jews and is the gravitas of this biography, which is far more than a sports or media book.

I wish to believe that Marty Glickman—broadcaster, athlete, pop-culture figure, mentor, and teacher to many—would have liked that this book serves an educational role in emphasizing the truth that the exploration of sports experiences has always been more than who won or lost a game and hallowing heroes but more crucially about whether a striving participant is allowed to play society's games, on and off the court. The journey into the life of this once-outstanding American Jewish sportsman who became an esteemed and iconic media personality, as well as an important representative second-generation American Jew, begins with the saga of his immigrant family within the neighborhoods of New York after World War I.

1

RUNNING THROUGH THE STREETS OF THE BRONX AND BROOKLYN

THE Glickmans were much like most New York Jewish families in the 1920s and 1930s, with one notable difference. Both Harry and his young son, Marty, loved athletics and were awfully talented at games and sports. The decade after World War I was a time of substantial economic prosperity that spurred residential movement for tens of thousands of Jews who had begun their American lives in the great Jewish quarter of the Lower East Side. While many immigrants who started to achieve in America stepped away from the legendary enclave before the Great War for improved residential locales like Central Harlem above Central Park in uptown Manhattan or north to the South Bronx or over the East River to Brooklyn's Williamsburg and Brownsville, in the 1920s, for immigrant and especially for second-generation American Jews, a string of newly constructed areas beckoned throughout the city. One of the city's prime locales for prosperous Jews was Flatbush, considered a new part of Brooklyn. Just a few years earlier it had been dubbed an underdeveloped "suburban" locale. The neighborhood's Jewish population rose in the 1920s from 16,000 to 56,000. The Glickman family took part in that ethnic relocation.[1]

For all the excitement of being able to afford to reside in a new and better place, relocation out of the Lower East Side brought with it a social and cultural challenge. Despite its squalor and poverty, there was nothing quite like the downtown quarter, which brimmed with a palpable warmth as Jews felt connected to one another on an ongoing basis through their synagogues or transplanted Old World societies or through meetings within radical social institutions. They also congregated culturally through their newspapers, coffeehouses, and theaters or even just passing by one another on the streets as they walked to sweatshop factories where most of their fellow workers labored. Although there was a discernible decline in religious observance as new secular, social ideas permeated the "ghetto," as it was called, there was nothing comparable in America to the expressions of sincere Jewish life when the High Holiday season came around. However, on a day-to-day, week-by-week basis, only a few old-timers strictly adhered to Judaism's ancient codes and resisted Americanization. A commitment to past ways was largely lost on youngsters, especially when they moved away from their parents.[2]

Jews on the move out of the Lower East Side, and on the make economically, had the option of totally abandoning their ancestral connections. Although there were some areas that barred Jews, most notably Queens' tony Forest Hills Gardens, home to the U.S. Open tennis championships, the majority of new middle-class neighborhoods in the city were available to them. Individuals who chose to settle on gentile streets were quite anxious to feel that they belonged and would not be caught dead speaking a word of Yiddish. They also worked on eliminating their Jewish-accented English when they spoke. Some might even went so far as to change their last names to help them rise in the wider world. However, given the choice of many available locales, most Jews who relocated decided to settle among their own ethnic group. In these Jewish areas, Irish, Italian, and German American children of immigrants lived next door to them. There were almost no African Americans around in what was a racially segregated city. While some non-Jewish adults harbored mean thoughts about the Jews and some youngsters shouted insults leading to street fights, neighborhood anti-Semitism, at least in the 1920s, was not nearly as problematic as it had been in earlier decades. The early postwar period was an era of good times. Moreover, where Jews resided, generally they were the largest group in the vicinity. They were comfortable where they lived.

So ensconced and content, these Jews created sometimes consciously and often unconsciously "a world of [their] own," an "orbit of community." They were not especially worried about how they spoke, even if their children came home from the public schools, which almost all Jewish youngsters attended, and told their parents that they were instructed to speak like Americans did. They dwelled together in the new buildings, worked together at comparable trades and occupations, and considered the sidewalks of the newly built avenues where kids and their parents hung out like Brooklyn's Ocean Parkway and Eastern Parkway to be the centers of a vibrant, informal social life. As far as the practice of Judaism was concerned, with the inevitable passing of those within the older generation who had held on to the past, in most neighborhoods careful adherence to, or even interest in, strict observance became increasingly uncommon. In the 1920s, second-generation American Jews who were proud of their faith—and with the money to prove it—financed large synagogues and hired young, ambitious rabbis to promote Judaism. However, their sanctuaries, some of which could seat a thousand or more worshippers, were almost always empty, except on the High Holidays. Even then, more people stood outside the synagogues than prayed within. Many young men did not set foot in a local house of worship after their bar mitzvah—a social and somewhat religious rite of passage—until their wedding day, when they married a fellow Jew who had also grown up in their predominantly Jewish enclave.[3]

Besides regular synagogue attendance, one of the other basic obligations that were increasingly honored in the breach was strict adherence to kosher laws. In many homes, householders lost interest in having separate meat and dairy dishes in their cupboards even if they did not have butter on the table when staples like brisket, tenderloin, and chopped liver were on the menu. But pork products of all sorts had no place in their kitchens. When they went out to eat at one of the many neighborhood Jewish delicatessens around the corner, they were comfortable ordering the "kosher-style" fare, including "delicious home cooked meals . . . like

mother used to make" that were tendered without any sort of rab-
binical supervision and were open seven days a week.[4]

The stock market crash of 1929 and the ensuing decade of the
Great Depression dampened the spirits of all Americans as they
attempted to cope with an economic calamity and an uncertain future. Although Jews in New York did not suffer as much as many
other groups, they too had to deal with the crises of failed businesses, unemployment, housing foreclosures, and a welter of family
pathologies that such difficult times had wrought. Women who had
left the workforce—a sure sign back in the 1920s that families were
on the rise—returned to daily jobs or took in boarders to cover rent.
The tensions of the day reignited on a scale greater than ever before
struggles among ethnic groups for their piece of Gotham's slippery
turf. The Germans, Jews, Italians, and Irish were frequently at each
other's throats. The Jews and the Irish did most of the fighting, with
troublemakers stoking the animosity between groups. This was the
New York Jewish world that the Glickman family lived through as
Marty grew up from birth in 1917 through his high school years.[5]

While the Glickman family's life closely fit that era's Jewish neighborhood experience, they progressed more quickly than the majority
of their fellow Jews in their early economic success and social adjustment within the new country. Both Marty's paternal and maternal
families (the Glickmans and the Schwartzs) began their exoduses
from Romania to America in 1910–11 because they had endured
enough of the cynical, long-standing anti-Semitic policies of the
Bucharest government. They were also awfully tired of avoiding the
spates of pogroms that endangered life and limb. For example, in
their hometown of Jassy (Isai in Romanian), the capital city of the
principality of Moldavia, the second largest city in the country, riot-
ers took to the streets in 1899 at the instigation of the local prefect.
Anti-Jewish students from Isai University joined enraged peasants
in the attacks. When the damage was done, officials "ordered the
Jewish storekeepers to clean up the debris of their wrecked stores
as if nothing had happened." Then a year later famine gripped the
country, affecting Jews and Christians alike. In 1907, troublemakers

were at it again, spurred on by a peasant revolt that began out of town. In 1909, alleged anti-Christian tropes in a Jewish-written play, which was performed at Jassy's National Theatre, stirred anti-Jewish revulsions in the city. To make matters worse, for those who were spared physical assault, there was no sign from the national government that the civic status of Jews as a minority group without most rights was soon going to improve.[6]

Indeed, Romanians had made every effort to deny the Jews the emancipation they had promised the great European powers in return for their national independence at the Berlin Treaty Conference of 1878. Soon after that gathering, the prince, later to become the king of Romania, Carol I, began working to undermine the agreement. This "cynical fraud" was common knowledge on the streets of Jassy. Compounding the troubles, state officials demanded that Jewish young people had to be exposed to secular education with a strong dose of Romanian language and culture. Elementary-age and secondary school youngsters had to be enrolled in the government's state schools, where they were burdened with teachings of disrespect for their ancestral past. If they chose to avoid such overt vexations, they could attend their own private Jewish schools, where the curriculum was closely monitored to ensure that Romanian values were taught. The strong and vibrant Hasidic groups in the country, including in Jassy, hewed to the old Jewish ways and resisted these efforts. However, modern Jewish schools, led by those who embraced the protocols of the Jewish Enlightenment, were established to satisfy the government while trying to inculcate a modern Jewish identity among their charges. Still, large numbers of families—perhaps the majority—sent their youngsters to Romanian schools. By the turn of the twentieth century, in some places close to 30 percent of enrolled students were Jews.[7]

It is not known how the Schwartz family educated its children. But the Glickmans were among those who entered their sons into Romanian schools with the hope that the acculturation of their next generation would be a conduit to integration into the larger society and ultimately to enable them to achieve their emancipation. They wanted to be modern Jews and to find a re-spected place in general society. A key indication of how Abraham and Sarah Glickman wanted themselves and, more importantly, their sons to be viewed was the non-Jewish first names, Moritz and Hermann, they had given to their youngsters. If they wanted their boys to fit in, Hebrew names like Moshe or Zvi would not play well in public elementary and secondary school classrooms and playgrounds.

The daily and grade-by-grade experiences of the two boys in this Christian environment have been lost to history. But there is one incident that indicates that for all of the family's efforts to blend in with the gentile majority, Hermann experienced, at least once, the sting of discrimination. Ironically it was a sporting event that Hermann never forgot and became part of Glickman family lore. As the story was told and retold, there was a "gymnasium field day" at school where the featured event was a 100-yard dash. Hermann Glickman won the race "but the medal . . . they gave it to the may-or's son. Me, they gave two pennies." Hermann never said that he was passed over as winner because the town did not want a Jew as champion. After all, "his classmates encouraged him to run because he was the fastest boy in the neighborhood." Nepotism may well have been in play here. Yet he was not rewarded for what he had achieved. When Marty Glickman would relate this tale, he would remark that his speed as a runner "stemmed from a wonderful gift I got from my father." But he would also say, thinking about what he would experience himself at a track meet in a far larger sports arena, "My father and I, we didn't get our medals." The hurtful family memory from a Jassy track meet would stick with Marty.[8]

By 1910, when Hermann was eighteen, he had had enough of the old country. He made his way to the port city of Hamburg, Germany, where he climbed aboard the steamer *Blucher* in December 1910, ar-riving at New York's Ellis Island on January 11, 1911. Abraham and Sarah Glickman would come to the United States some years later. Soon after settling on the Lower East Side, Hermann changed his first name to Harry, a more American-sounding forename. Once

again, a name choice represented a desire to be part of a larger society. But he retained his family name, the first indication that the
immigrant Glickman also wanted to maintain some connection to
his ancestral past. So disposed, from the moment he set foot in the
United States, Harry put his Romanian background behind him
as he made every effort to quickly acculturate. Growing up, Marty
would never hear a word of Romanian in his home, and his father
did not speak much Yiddish either, a statement of the relative powers of Harry's strong American identity as opposed to his enduring
Jewish affinity. An English speaker to his core, second-generation
American Jew Marty would nonetheless pick up many phrases of
the Jewish lingo that would remain part of his vocabulary. These
were words that he shared with fellow Jews and sometimes even
with gentile acquaintances and listeners.[9]

On the *Blucher*'s manifest Harry's occupation was listed as clerk.
Although these designations often were inexact, presumably the
secondary-school-educated young man had some training, making
it possible for him to hold an office job. This position placed him a
step above most fellow immigrants, who started out in America as
factory workers. A marriage license from five years later testifies to
his calling as a "salesman." He was moving up toward eventually
becoming a proprietor of a cotton goods business. It was at that
point, on June 24, 1916, that Harry married Molly Schwartz in a
small synagogue on Forsyth Street.[10]

The young couple were acquainted with one another back in
Jassy and most likely met up again in a social society from their
same hometown. By that time Harry had outgrown his childhood
reputation as "one of the wild kids who pulled girls' hair and ran
away." In New York, it was common practice for newcomers to seek
out fellow Jews who hailed from their hometown and shared local
customs and memories. Such ethnic connections provided comfort as individuals sought to find their way within the new country. Reestablished friendships among families led to intramarriages.
Soon after their nuptials, Harry and Molly, possessing the where-
withal to make a move out of the most crowded streets in the city,

set up housekeeping outside of the Lower East Side in the South Bronx, at 614 East 136th Street. It was there that Marty was born on August 14, 1917. Three years later, the family moved a mile or so farther north in the borough to 574 Tinton Street, where they still lived in a predominantly Jewish immigrant area, though fellow residents of their building were not only Jews born in Europe and in the United States but also a few Christians. A Russian-speaking immigrant boarder—perhaps a gentile—named Gussie Gurow, who was an "operator" in the garment trades, helped the family pay the rent. But the family was doing well enough for Molly to become a stay-at-home mom. Prior to her marriage, she had worked in "ladies waist" manufacturing. The Glickmans were an achieving family striving toward middle-class status. At the age of six, Marty was enrolled in Public School 25, conveniently located close to Tinton Street.[11]

In the mid-1920s, the family joined the tens of thousands of like-minded Jews of comparable economic means in the great migration to new outer-borough neighborhoods. Glickman memoirs have the family bouncing around several Brooklyn neighborhoods in Brownsville and Bensonhurst, before settling in a family enclave at 763 Coney Island Avenue within Flatbush, a half-mile walk or five-minute run from Ocean Parkway.

Marty Glickman would characterize his home as a tenement. Actually, it was a four-story apartment house within a row of similar residences, much like the many "four- and six-story apartment houses both walk-ups and elevator buildings" that then filled up Flatbush. More importantly, it was a Glickman and Schwartz family building composed almost exclusively of members of the two extended families. They lived under the same roof and watchful eye of Abraham Schwartz, who owned the house. No fewer than seventeen members of the coalescing families—adults, children, sons-in-law, and so on—resided in four of the six available apartments. An Irish American family, the McElroys, lived on the same floor as one of the Schwartz-Glickmans. Sadly, Morris Glickman was not among this large extended group. A private in the American army, he died on October 20, 1918, of bronchopneumonia, very likely a victim of the infamous Spanish Flu, while stationed at Fort Slocum on the tip of Long Island Sound near New Rochelle, New York.[12]

Like with many Jewish and Christian families of that era, it is entirely possible that pooled family incomes afforded the Schwartz-Glickman crowd the ability to cover the mortgage and other carrying charges on their real estate holding. As of 1930, grown-ups in the family worked as a glazer, a manager, and an insurance agent. The *paterfamilias*—the head of the tribe—sixty-year-old Abraham Schwartz, was enumerated as a tailor. That was his trade when he started out in the United States. Much like many other Jewish immigrants, when he did well enough to have cash on hand to invest, he looked toward owning real estate. His grandson-in-law, Harry Glickman, was noted as a jobber in cotton goods. Harry's office was located back in the old neighborhood of the Lower East Side at 467 Broadway, north of Canal Street. Molly continued to stay at home, taking care of Marty and his two younger siblings, Sydney and Irene. On the economic side of the street, Marty's immediate family was making enough money to own an automobile, a sure sign of wealth in the 1920s. As Marty grew up into his teenage years, he was enveloped in a warm, comfortable Jewish ethnic environment among parents, grandparents, aunts, uncles, and cousins.[13]

However, much like the other Jews of that generation and area, Harry and Molly's commitment to religious strictures and observances was of secondary importance. Harry and Molly were careful to not bring *treif* foods into their apartment, but they served both dairy and meat dishes on the same set of plates. If they wanted a fully kosher meal, they walked across the hall to Abraham and Sarah Schwartz's apartment. Those few steps constituted the gastronomical and generational divide. Indicative of the residue of Harry and Molly's religious feelings was their interest in enrolling Marty, when he turned ten, in the Hebrew School of the Ocean Parkway Jewish Center. The synagogue, with its commodious twelve-hundred-seat sanctuary, was situated across Ocean Parkway, a half-mile stroll from home. The family rarely attended services except on the High Holidays. Still, Harry and Molly believed that it was worthwhile for Marty to have a bar mitzvah, just like so many of that generation's boys. So they hired "individual Hebrew instructors" to complement what he learned or did not pay attention to at school. One such *melamed* (teacher) made a particularly bad impression on the young man. Marty remembered that he was an "old rabbi with a huge beard who smelled. He had a terrible body odor and he would sit alongside of me and go over my maftir and haftorah." That was the portion of the service that the boy performed by rote at his bar mitzvah, which for Marty took place in August 1930 in a small synagogue near Monticello, New York, where the summer camp that he attended was located. He got through that religious training trauma, though he would have much preferred to be outside "playing ball doing what everyone else was doing like running under the poplar trees on Brooklyn Streets." Marty long averred of his Jewish education that it was "ridiculous those lessons were and even Hebrew School was because I was taught to speak Hebrew without knowing what the words were." He was on the way to becoming, in his own words, "a cultural Jew," proud of his heritage and of his family's background but minimally concerned with its religious demands. Much later developments in his life would do far more than his bar mitzvah to define his Jewish identity.[14]

When he freed himself from his annoying, ill-smelling teacher, Marty usually found himself agreeably on the streets of his neighborhood, mostly among Jews but also among boys from Irish and Italian families who also called Flatbush home. The fellows on his block coalesced into a street club called Acme and proudly wore jackets with the group's name on the back. Kids on other streets also adopted names for their informal associations. Glickman memory has it that generally the white ethnic groups coexisted rather peacefully even though "many Italian kids hung out together, many Irish kids hung out together" and the Jewish youngsters did likewise. There was an Italian street gang to be avoided and "occasionally, an Irish kid would try to beat up a Jewish kid. But it was rare . . . nothing severe. In truth, I experienced no real feelings of anti-Semitism."[15]

When he came back up the steps of his walk-up, he often found his father waiting for him, happy to hear all about his athletic exploits. From an early age, even while the family was still in the Bronx, Marty was earning street credibility as "the fastest kid on the block." He later recalled that he and his friends "would run around the block, starting in opposite directions. I was so much faster that I could run around the block, get to the starting point and sit down on a stoop and wait for the other guys to finish." Marty was also the first pick when the guys chose teams to play the quintessential New York street game ringolevio. Quick on his feet, he was able to avoid being tagged and had sufficient speed and darting ability to free teammates from jail while being sure to avoid parked cars. He was also quite adept in playing salugi, another kid sport that was popular in his neighborhood. Decades later he would explain its quite informal rules: "You took any object, a rolled up sock, a bunch of crumpled paper, a ball and you played keep away from each other." Glickman possessed all the essential moves to succeed in these games, which ended only when parents called the boys back to their apartments for dinner. More formal sports, like baseball or football, took place on Prospect Park's fields, which come wintertime also offered elevations that were perfect for sledding.

Harry knew that the family had a sports prodigy in their home from age five or six because father and son would race against each other along Coney Island Avenue down to the beach along the Atlantic Ocean. This intergenerational friendly competition did not last too long. Marty became just too quick for his old man. But sports were a topic of conversation across their dinner table. In the 1920s, there was much to discuss, as that decade was a "Golden Age of American Sports." Harry was not only a former athlete but also quite the sports aficionado. He fit that era's profile of the inveterate fan and passed on this ardent interest to his son.[16]

In the 1920s, with "post war economic growth . . . workers had shortened work weeks." They had more time "for recreational activities" and "money to watch sporting events live in person." Movie theaters carried newsreels of the most recent exciting events. Fans also could stay at home and tune in on their now widely available radios to play-by-play and blow-by-blow accounts of their favorite athletic heroes. In New York, baseball's Babe Ruth and Lou Gehrig had their thousands of followers. Detroit Tigers fans cheered Ty Cobb's every move. The Chicago Bears' Red Grange was the first nationally acclaimed standout in the early years of the NFL. But Notre Dame's Fighting Irish, led by their legendary coach Knute Rockne, eclipsed him in popularity. Fight fans watched Jack Dempsey, and so many others, battle it out in the square ring at major indoor and outdoor arenas. In the segregationist America of the time, whites did not consider outstanding African American athletes worthy of admission to their pantheon of stars. Major League Baseball was off-limits to Blacks until 1947, when Jackie Robinson broke the color barrier. But whites surely took note of the abilities of Negro League stars like Satchel Paige. They also followed the continuing in- and out-of-ring exploits of former heavyweight champion Jack Johnson, even as Jess Willard, a "white hope," finally defeated a fighter who was a figure of great racial pride in the Black community. The many big-city newspapers covered the golfing triumphs of Bobby Jones and Walter Hagen and tennis's Big Bill Tilden. There was even a female champion for Harry and Marty to talk about. Babe Didrikson triumphed in a variety of competitions, including winning a gold medal in track and field at the 1932 Olympics.[17]

In September 1923 Harry was actually at New York's Polo Grounds, on the scene for one of the most famous boxing matches of that time as Jack Dempsey knocked out Luis Angel Firpo in the second round, but not before the Argentine contender had knocked the champion out of the ring in the opening round. The excitement of that first knockdown inspired artist George Bellows to paint *Dempsey and Firpo*, which became one of the most famous sports images of the twentieth century. The match also so thrilled Harry that when he returned home from the prizefight to Tinton Street, he regaled his friends with his own account of the fight, pretending that he was a radio announcer. Little Marty, then all of six, already knew about the outcome of the contest because he was allowed to listen to the broadcast via a crystal radio set. That late-night permission was a sure sign of how important sports were to the Glickmans. Little did father and son know that Harry's performance adumbrated Marty's future vocation.[18]

The 1920s was also a golden age of Jewish sports. During that decade, some seventeen Jewish boxers held world championship belts, and Jewish fight fans flocked to see their heroes defeat all comers. In Jewish neighborhoods, the popularity of the "sweet science" was so profound that, as a marketing device, some Italian American fighters adopted Hebrew noms de guerre. In response to readership interest, the *Forward* ran a weekly boxing column. On July 28, 1922, the morning after Benny Leonard—Harry Glickman's favorite fighter—outpointed fellow Jew Lou Tendler in a twelve-round contest in New Jersey, the results made the front page of the most popular Yiddish newspaper in New York. By 1925, two other Yiddish dailies, the *Jewish Daily Warheit* and the *Jewish Morning Journal*, carried the results of Leonard's fights and those of other Jewish pugilists. A Jewish newspaper columnist in Philadelphia would later opine, "The most famous Jewish person in America in the Roaring Twenties was a world champion boxer named Benny Leonard."[19]

During that same period, pundits were saying that basketball was a sport "at which Jews excel." As proof, scribes and fans could point to the success of the Philadelphia SPHAS, out of the South Philadelphia Hebrew Association, who beginning in 1918 barnstormed all over the East Coast and Midwest, competing in a series of semiprofessional leagues. Back in New York, City College of New York's squad, composed largely of Jewish players, was making its mark in round ball under the tutelage of Nat Holman, one of the greatest Jewish players of that era. Between 1929 and 1931 four Jews led the "Wonder Five," representing St. John's, to victory in sixty-eight of their seventy-two games. They were recruited to this Catholic school because of their athletic prowess, and when the Brooklyn school won, their classmates on campus were delighted. The team's success caused Dan Parker, sports editor of the New York *Daily Mirror*, to gush, "The Litvak [Lithuanian Jewish] is all powerful even in such originally Celtic institutions as St. John's of Brooklyn, which year after year turns out almost 100 percent Yiddisher quintets that are among the best in the land."[20]

The interest and prominence in these competitions of the second-generation children of immigrants, however, brought into high relief long-standing ambivalences about athletics and physicality among those who had come from the Old World. It was a source of tension in many Jewish households. Most of those of the older generation had come from a cultural and social environment where sports participation was often unknown and certainly was not hallowed. They could not—or would not—understand how important American games were to their children. Such was the attitude of the father who in 1903 turned to *Forward* editor Abraham Cahan for advice on how to deal with his son, who was devoted to baseball: "What is the point of this crazy game? It makes sense to teach a child to play dominoes or chess. . . . The children can get crippled. . . . I want my boy to grow up to be a *mensch* [an upstanding adult], not a wild American runner." The grandmother of future renowned comedian Eddie Cantor felt similarly. "Baseball player" was the worst name she could think of. For her, "a baseball player was the king of loafers."

Cahan understood the depth of such complaints but at the same time suggested that "the body needs to develop" and that "baseball is played in the fresh air." Youngsters, he counseled, might play the national pastime "as long as it does not interfere with their education . . . bring them up to be educated, ethical and decent, but also to be physically strong so they should not feel inferior." However, Cahan worried about what might befall Jewish boys who played football. He saw that violent sport as a "really wild . . . game. . . . Accidents and fights occur in football, but baseball is not dangerous." Doing more than just tendering guidance to a letter writer, in a thoughtful effort to bridge the generational gap on athletics for a wide audience, in August 1909 the *Forward* published a diagram of a baseball diamond that graphically explained the game's "fundamentals . . . for the non sports person." Still, tensions were unabated in many households for in the end, as downtown raconteur Irving Howe observed, "Suspicion of the physical, fear of hurt, anxiety over the pointlessness of play: all this went deep into the recesses of the Jewish psyche."[21]

If parents were worried about their children playing baseball, did not understand wide-spread interest even in the supposed noncontact sport of basketball, and were very concerned over what would happen to their boys when they hit the gridiron, many more mothers and fathers were downright horrified to see their sons bloody themselves as prizefighters. In response to constant criticism and to allay fears back home, many Jewish pugilists adopted non-Jewish names when they competed, in effect sneaking away from parental censure. For example, Beryl Rasofsky fought as Barney Ross, Moische Shneir as Mushy Callahan, and Arthur Lieberman as Artie O'Leary. It was said that Louis "Kid" Kaplan adopted the name Benny Miller "because mama wouldn't have a boxer in the family." The renowned Benny Leonard, Harry Glickman's favorite, was born Benjamin Leiner. Yet often left unsaid was the palpable sense of pride on Jewish streets when their tough guy beat up a gentile opponent in the ring. These moments of exaltation did not dispel the remembered traumas of pogroms in Eastern Europe, but they helped. Those feelings might well explain why Jews turned out in large numbers to watch prizefights. What is certain is that many families got over their misgivings when boxers' purses supplemented their meager incomes.[22]

Back in their apartment on Coney Island Avenue at what could be called the Glickman athletic training table, Harry and Molly had absolutely no reservations about Marty or their two other children recreating on a daily basis. They bought in totally to Cahan's view of the values of physical fitness. For them, the "concept of fresh air, good food" invigorating "healthy, strong" children made total sense. They differed with the famous editor on only one point. They had no apprehension about their talented multisport son playing rough-and-tumble football. Harry in particular, with his own athletic pedigree, was also sure to attend games and meets where from grade school on Marty often was victorious. As early as the fourth and fifth grades, the boy was awarded a silver pin from the Public

School Athletic League (PSAL) as the champion of field day. At those moments it might well have dawned upon Harry that unlike his youthful disappointment in Jassy, his son received the medal that he had earned. Such was part of living a good life in America. There was even more to cheer about when Marty attended the neighborhood's Montauk Junior High School. There he was outstanding in four sports—baseball, basketball, track, and swimming; the school's baseball and basketball clubs won city championships. His stardom on the gridiron would come a bit later in high school.[23]

Even as Marty Glickman basked in his family's approval of his athletic interests and achievements, there was an additional force in his life that contributed to both his approach to sports and his outlook on life. While still in grade school, the young man was captivated by the fictional exploits of Frank Merriwell, a star sportsman whom today we call the classic scholar-athlete. As author Burt L. Standish depicted this hero in a series of novels and short stories pitched to preteens, Merriwell showed how a player could be a success both on the field and in the classroom while displaying to admiring fans and friends alike intelligence, courage, resilience, and, when under attack, concern for others and emotional maturity. In one of his best-known sagas, *Merriwell at Yale*, Frank, who is never boastful and is magnanimous in victory, surrounds himself with a group of friends who learn from his sterling example. While willing to participate in college high jinks, Merriwell always keeps such activities in proper perspective. He does not drink or smoke and once convinces a classmate, who is struggling on the crew team, that he will be a "better man" if he "leaves his cigarettes behind." Putting his hand sincerely on his friend's shoulder, he tells him warmly, "I am interested in you, I want you to be a winner." For Standish through Merriwell, the measure of a Yale student lay in his ability to always display such "manly qualities." Marty Glickman saw Merriwell as "the perfect athlete and the perfect gentleman and modeled [himself] after him." Since Frank was a trackman among his many athletic pursuits, Glickman wanted most of all to be a runner. Critically because "the Olympic games were the goal of runners" from the tender age of twelve, he "wanted to be on the Olympic team." He might also have thought that on the road to Berlin, Yale might be a fine place to burnish his skills.[24]

Unfortunately for the Glickman family, while all continued to go well for Marty in school and on the field and court, the cheering at home was severely muted in 1931 when Harry was convicted and jailed for eighteen months in a bankruptcy fraud case. As his cotton goods business foundered, Harry had appealed to the courts for financial relief. But notwithstanding what he had told the magistrate about being on the verge of bankruptcy, he had in fact "concealed assets" in the neighborhood of some fifty thousand dollars in stocks. Harry sold the assets "at bargain prices and deposited the proceeds in a score of banks." White-collar crimes of this sort were common during the Great Depression. But the family must have been humiliated to have Harry's malfeasance reported in the *Brooklyn Daily Eagle*, the paper with an enormous circulation in their neighborhood, especially the report that when he was forced to surrender his assets to his creditors, "he returned nothing to his partners claiming he had lost all he had in craps games in Manhattan hotels."[25]

Harry Glickman left incarceration a broken man. He struggled to gain and maintain steady employment. To make matters more difficult, he continued to squander his family's income on gambling, even going so far as to seize Marty's bar mitzvah gifts to pay off his failed wagers. Molly stepped into the financial breach, returning to the workforce as a seamstress in the garment center. In time, she rose to become a foreperson in a factory. These were difficult times in the house on Coney Island Avenue. But presumably, pooled family incomes from uncles, cousins, and grandparents helped out. Family memories have it that to Marty's disappointment "the cupboards were bare and the refrigerator needed more food." Still, Molly was determined that Marty would "not be forced to work" as many other neighborhood youngsters were obliged to do. He could concentrate on his books and his athletics.[26]

While Marty Glickman enjoyed Jewish neighborhood life in Brooklyn during the 1920s and the early 1930s, elsewhere in the United States there was another American world in play that just a few years later would dramatically affect his life. Until Marty entered high school, he was blithely unaware of anti-Semitism. If he sometimes heard antagonistic remarks from opponents on the gridiron—like "get the Jew bastard"—he chalked up the insults to jealousy because he was almost always winning. Hatred of Jews had little impact on his consciousness. After all, he suited up with a mixed bunch of fellows of varying ethnicities, and opposing clubs also fielded athletes from Irish, Italian, German, and Jewish homes. Like his neighborhood chums, they basically got along. If he ever had to retreat toward his own group, he could feel very much at home within James Madison High School since most of his classmates were Jewish. But outside of his borough, Jews, and for that matter other ethnic groups, were increasingly deemed as unwanted in America.[27]

In the 1920s, a long-standing "Anglo-Saxon tradition of exclusiveness" asserted itself as nativists, racists, and unapologetic anti-Semites carried the day in many places and hearts in the United States. The restrictionists' greatest triumph was Congress's passage, first in 1921 and then again in 1924, of immigration quota laws that legislated their view that immigrants from Eastern Europe—read Jews—or Southern Europe—read Italians—were undesirable since they lacked "any conception of patriotism and national spirit" among a list of other perceived deleterious characteristics. Making matters worse, a fear of "Judeobolshevism" became a rallying cry for haters as it was contended that Jewish communists, who had just helped millions of Marxist-Leninists triumph in Russia, would soon attempt to transplant their 1917 revolution to American shores. At the same time, Henry Ford's publication of the notorious and spurious *Protocols of the Elders of Zion* codified an apprehension that there was an international Jewish conspiracy on the move to corrupt America. That a resurgent Ku Klux Klan, with its Klaverns in forty-three states, could proudly march en masse in masks and uniforms through the streets of the nation's capital also articulated the nastiness of canards against Jews, Catholics, and African Americans.

All was also not well for many Jews who had been in this country more than a generation and who had rapidly Americanized.

Increasingly young men and a few young women who hoped to ascend to elite institutions of higher education found that these schools' own implicit quotas blocked their way. They ran into a genteel wall of social exclusiveness and later faced problems in employment and barriers to desirable housing.

In the 1930s, the Jews' sense of living on the margins of America society increased as Depression frustrations caused many of their fellow citizens to lose hope in the future of their democratic country. Political anti-Semitic groups of all sorts—some financed out of Berlin, others homegrown—blamed Jews for all that was wrong with the country.[28]

The young Marty Glickman was spared any meaningful encounters with the high-profile political anti-Semites of the day, like Father Charles Coughlin, who preached hatred on the radio out of his suburban Detroit parish and who organized his Christian Front organization to spread his message nationwide, or Fritz Kuhn, leader of the German American Bund, who had his New York followers primarily in the Manhattan neighborhood of Yorkville. Kuhn and his group had their moment in the limelight when they rented Madison Square Garden in 1939 for their Hitler-like rally. For all of his rantings, he never showed his face in Brooklyn. Yet the Christian Front made its forays into Glickman's Flatbush neighborhood. They held a few rallies on the street corners, not far from the Glickman home. If the Glickmans even knew that these anti-Semites had invaded their turf, they had to have been pleased that in 1938 the rough and ready Jewish War Veterans drove the obnoxious orators out of the area. Genteel social anti-Semitism likewise did not trouble the family, content as they were in Flatbush. Besides which, they also did not have the money to try to break into the expensive Forest Hills Gardens, that off-limits New York WASP preserve. Yet eventually Marty Glickman would have to deal with exclusion when he sought to fulfill his most desired quest—to be crowned an Olympic champion. Until he left Brooklyn and James Madison High School, he focused solely on becoming a Jewish Frank Merriwell.[29]

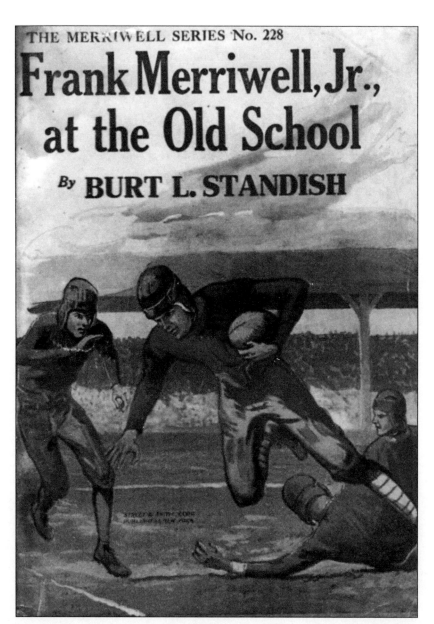

THE MERRIWELL SERIES No. 228

Frank Merriwell, Jr., at the Old School

By **BURT L. STANDISH**

Frank Merriwell, young Marty Glickman's role model. Credit: Public domain.

2

A JEWISH FRANK MERRIWELL AT A COLLEGE-BOUND HIGH SCHOOL

As Marty Glickman advanced in his athletic quests into his teen years and gained recognition for his excellence, the epithet he did not want to be hung on him was "tramp athlete." That derogatory term was used for someone who was totally caught up with athletic proficiencies and disdained intellectual activity. Today we might refer to such a weak-minded person as a jock. Glickman feared that negative appellation. He did not want to be an outlier within a student community where so many had their eyes glued to their books and fixed on earning high grades that would permit them to extend their formal schooling beyond twelfth grade. Within that educational environment, he endeavored to strike the proper balance as both a competent student and an outstanding athlete, even as he believed that ultimately his sports feats would carry him into college and most importantly to the Olympic stage. If all went well for him in classroom and on his varsity teams, he hoped to be esteemed, upon graduation, as nothing less than the Frank Merriwell of the James Madison class of 1935. His efforts were recognized and commended among his classmates. A profile of Glickman published at James Madison High School toward the end of his senior year projected how "Marty hopes to become a physician" and prognosticated, "If he is as successful in that undertaking as he is at track, he will become, without doubt, the leading man of the profession." The class yearbook prophesized similarly, in satirical style, that in 1950 a successful Glickman, still an athlete, would "be practicing his starts" at a reunion banquet. This prediction may have amused Marty. But he was gratified that same printed memento of his years on Bedford Avenue asserted, "Marty is modest and one of the best liked fellows in our graduating class. He is everybody's friend and snubs nobody," just like the fictional hero who was his role model.[1]

After graduating from Montauk Junior High School, he could have enrolled at two secondary schools, located almost equidistant from his home. Both Erasmus Hall and James Madison had fine academic programs and rivaled each other athletically. These institutions offered an agreeable combination of opportunities for a young man who wanted to fit in within the classroom and on the athletic field. It is not known why the family chose the Bedford Avenue school over its sister school on Flatbush Avenue. Perhaps they liked Madison's newer premises, including its modern playing field, as the school opened its doors in 1925. Erasmus Hall—the first public high school in Brooklyn—had begun serving its borough's youth at the turn of the twentieth century. What was certain was that if Glickman hoped to stand out in class while succeeding in sports, there was plenty of academic competition. In 1935, the year Glickman graduated, "students earned the highest scholastic average in the city and 36 were rewarded with college scholarships."[2]

Even staying on par with the close to nine hundred boys and girls who were in his grade constituted a challenge. The students of the class of 1935 were an uncommonly college-bound cohort and very different from those who attended many other schools. Amid the Great Depression, in New York and of course nationally, enormous pressure was placed on young people to work after completing secondary schooling to supplement sagging family incomes. Many youngsters even left high school without their diplomas. Others worked by day and attended evening college classes at schools that had minimal or free tuition. Still others, who were unable to find employment, enrolled in day sessions, figuring it was best to spend their time at college in search of their sheepskins. They prayed that when the economy eventually improved they would have university credentials to secure good jobs.

In New York, most students, Jewish and non-Jewish alike, did not attend college. A full-time occupation as a civil servant with an assured salary—like working in the post office—was the best future many could hope for. They did, however, have to pass competitive examinations that challenged even the most gifted students for a slot.

Jewish young men and women, however, were far more likely to aspire to attend college than their non-Jewish high school classmates. Jewish females pursued "higher education 2 to 3 times more often than their non-Jewish counterparts." However, when it came to sacrificing to help send their sons to college, Jewish families often required their daughters to help their brothers, often at the expense of their own educational futures. Part of the difference was cultural. There was historically a greater premium, or even pride, placed on sons rather than daughters advancing academically. And from a purely practical perspective, women could find employment as stenographers, bookkeepers, typists, and the like, drawing on skills that they acquired in high school that could be put to ready use.[3]

With a student population that was overwhelmingly Jewish,[4] James Madison High School graduates in the mid-1930s fit in many ways the citywide adolescent student population. Nonetheless, this cohort's educational goals and destinations deviated in some substantial ways from those who attended other secondary schools. Almost all Jewish young men desired to attend college, and the most popular choices were either City College of New York (CCNY) or its younger sister school, Brooklyn College, presuming in both cases that they had the grades to gain acceptance. They were part of a student body that in the 1930s was estimated at 80 to 90 percent Jewish. These colleges offered undergraduates a high-quality and tuition-free education. These students were comfortable studying among their own kind, even if some of their professors sought to break them from their ancestral backgrounds and ways of speech.[5]

These intrusive faculty efforts were lost on the many James Madison alumni who were not particularly interested in expressing their Jewishness at college. In high school too, most of them had shown little affinity for formal ethnic identification. There was a Young Menorah Club among the many extracurricular options like the chorus, debate society, and school newspaper. But the Jewish organization had few members. The group's 1935 attempt to introduce Hebrew into the curriculum through a petition campaign went nowhere. The students' Jewishness was primarily rooted in their informal street associations with their own kind. Marty Glickman shared that point of view, although he was friendly with the fellow who tried unsuccessfully to interest his classmates in Jewish history and contemporary Zionist ideas. His chum was a "field doctor," a student trainer who helped injured players off the football field. Marty appreciated his triage efforts.[6]

As Glickman contemplated his own college options, foremost in his mind was his desire to attend a school whose tuition his family could handle and where he could receive a quality education toward a professional career once his athletic activities concluded. Though his family was not impoverished due to the yeoman efforts of his mother, the Glickmans were nonetheless hard-pressed to cover college tuition. But settling for a post office–type job was out of the question for Marty and his family. Most important at that juncture in the life of the teenager was that he wanted to enroll where he could take additional and speedy steps toward fulfilling his ever-present dream of competing for America in the Olympics. Berlin—the site of the forthcoming 1936 Olympics—was his primary focus.

Glickman faced two fundamental problems, one athletic, the other academic, when he thought about possibly studying and playing at CCNY. In one arena, CCNY was well along in the mid-1930s in building its reputation as a national sports powerhouse. However, Glickman was earning athletic credentials in the wrong sport. During the years that Glickman was in high school, CCNY's basketball team won fifty-three of sixty-two games against top-flight competition from all over the country. At the time tickets were scarce not only for the college's on-campus gym but also for

Madison Square Garden, where "the capacity of 18,000 allowed for alumni, students and a general public lined up to witness exciting and well played basketball." But Glickman had decided to forgo roundball when as a Madison junior he focused on track and football. CCNY's unimpressive football program, on the other hand, rarely had a decent season. There was some excitement at the college the year Glickman graduated from Madison when Benny Friedman, former University of Michigan star and erstwhile New York Giant quarterback, was brought in to coach the team. But Glickman was not about to be a program builder. As far as the track team was concerned, it was a minor sport at the school, though its devotees could brag that an alumnus, Jeremiah T. Mahoney, had qualified for the 1906 Olympics. Mahoney's thirty-year-old legacy did not impress Glickman, though as we will later see Mahoney was destined to enter into Glickman's life before and during the 1936 Olympics. Finally, if Marty harbored thoughts about enrolling at CCNY, there was the disqualifying reality of his decent but unimpressive grades. He was not an Arista honor society member like some classmates who were admitted to an institution whose fans spoke of reverently as "Jewish Harvard." As a B student, positioned in the middle of the pack academically, Marty would never be called a tramp athlete, but he was not a celebrated scholar either. Although occasionally admissions accommodations were made at CCNY for outstanding basketball players with less than sterling classroom credentials, Marty was a star in the wrong sports. In the end, Glickman and his family could only hope that what he had going for him, more than anyone else in the class of 1935, was his uncommon sports abilities.[7]

When the young man arrived at James Madison in the fall of 1931, he was an accomplished four-letter athlete with two junior high school championships under his belt. If he used his talent wisely, he could potentially garner an athletic scholarship at some other school. In considering his options, it did not matter to him whether the campus of an interested university was in New York or elsewhere. Given the right opportunity, he would have no problem leaving Brooklyn behind. Moving out of the metropolitan area intrigued the young man: "College . . . out of the city was what I thought college should be." Though he would always love his family, this geographical break was a subtle statement of independence from his erstwhile community. Many of his classmates felt similarly, not to mention that they may not have had the grades for CCNY. They enrolled at institutions located far away from their Brooklyn bases—the College of William and Mary in Virginia, North Carolina College, Missouri, Michigan, Minnesota, Wisconsin, Northwestern in Illinois, Penn State, University of Southern California, and Ohio University. Others matriculated at schools situated closer to home, in Philadelphia, Boston, and Baltimore.

It did not trouble Glickman how he would be received in a very different social and educational environment. Often classmates of his from James Madison, as well as those who had attended other metropolitan-area secondary schools, found out when they arrived on campus that Jews from smaller Jewish communities and non-Jewish fellow undergraduates were not exactly thrilled to have "New York Jews" around. They were frequently stereotyped as obstreperous and ill-mannered and even as troublemakers. No matter, the well-behaved Glickman would mind his manners. And given his athletic pedigree, he could fantasize about becoming a "Big Man on Campus."[8]

Most crucial for him was to find a school that would award him a coveted athletic grant-in-aide. He could then train for the upcoming Olympics while preparing him for a professional career. The international games were already in play in his mind and heart, certainly from the time one of his teachers wrote in his junior high school yearbook, "See you in the 1936 Olympics." While pledging to himself that while on the athletic field he would do everything in his power to someday soon represent the United States, he also toiled in the classroom and labs toward someday earning that medical degree that his classmates had predicted.[9]

To maximize his attractiveness to a potential college recruiter, Glickman decided early on to focus his efforts on the track team's sprint events. He reasoned that if he did well, his individual achievements would be recognized widely regardless of how his teammates would perform. He did, however, find time in his freshman and sophomore seasons to play basketball as a shifty, expert ball handler. Most significantly for his future plans, in his junior year, implored by football coach Milton Torgan, who needed a "speed merchant" of Glickman's pedigree, he agreed to suit up for the gridiron team. Glickman quickly gained recognition far and wide, which only increased the ardor for his services in two sports among competing colleges. However, as a tailback and signal caller in the single wing offense he was careful to avoid an injury that could sideline his track career. He was praised in the local press that with "speed as his forte," Glickman did "not heedlessly plunge into a group of waiting tacklers in attempt to gain one or more extra steps." Rather, he intelligently stepped out of bounds to save himself for the next play. Commenting on this maneuver, one reporter suggested that Glickman was not exactly emulating "Merriwell," that generational hero to more people than just Marty. It is not known if Glickman read that piece in the *Brooklyn Daily Eagle*. But had he noticed that subtle, if annoying, takedown, Marty would not have agreed. Looking back on his days as a high school sports hero, Glickman would contend that he "achieved those things that I set out to do as a Frank Merriwell."[10]

Nonetheless, Glickman did not immediately dominate Madison's athletic scene. As a freshman, he stood way behind a squad of runners that was lauded for having "completed the most successful season of any track team ever produced in Madison." The star performer was Sid White, who had transferred from a school in Cleveland Heights, Ohio, where he had helped set a state record in the half mile relay and was deemed "a broad jumper of repute." White proved his mettle in New York when he leaped 21 feet, 7 inches to win the city broad jump championship. White would go on to become a star running back at Brooklyn College, once scoring four touchdowns in a game. Still, there was room for improvement in the track program, whose "performances, though highly commendable," garnered only sixth place in the citywide championships.[11]

Beginning his sophomore year, Glickman started to step forward, in the words of a classmate reporter, as potentially "the greatest runner ever to put on spiked shoes for Madison as well as the fastest schoolboy sprinter in America today." He was praised in his senior year as having "done more to put Madison on the sports map of the country than anyone in the ten-year history of the school." As a sophomore, he shined in dual meets against local Brooklyn opponents, won the citywide public school championship in his events, "breezing through his heat, semi-final and final." At the close of that campaign, he tied "the state record in winning the hundred in 10.5 seconds."[12]

Madison's track squad posted a "reputable," if mediocre, record during Glickman's junior year. But the now acknowledged star "eclipsed" the efforts of everyone in the locker room. Highlights of his campaign included "the City Championship meet where Glickman . . . conquered all-comers in a record tying sprint for the first-place medallion." Later, at the State Championship event, he "proved the star of the day" as he bettered his 100-yard dash record. Desiring broad commendation, Glickman was pleased how his "sensational feat brought him state-wide acclaim in numerous newspapers." At a contest at Princeton University, "Glickman outdid a national known Canadian Olympic star and attained for himself and Madison the prestige that accompanies the upper circles of track athletes."[13]

James Madison football coach Milton Torgan kept close tabs on Glickman's activities and believed that the runner could be essential to bringing a city football championship to Bedford Avenue. That would be its first grand triumph since 1927. If all went well, Glickman might join Tony Valentine, an erstwhile "crack first baseman" whom the coach recruited from Madison's baseball team, and "basketball and baseball star" Al Caruso in bolstering a squad that Torgan thought could defeat the school's arch neighborhood rival, Erasmus Hall. Optimism reigned at the school in the fall of 1933, especially when the team shut out the Brooklyn College freshman team in a "practice game" before taking on the Dutchmen and their star quarterback, Sid Luckman. It was "news" to one local reporter how the usually "gloomy" Torgan was now so upbeat. However, when Erasmus "routed" Madison 19–0 before a packed house of fifteen thousand onlookers at Erasmus Field, the coach was again his unhappy self. Having won Brooklyn "bragging rights," Erasmus moved toward another public school championship, while devoted "Black and Gold" fans could only hope that they were but a year away.[14]

A few months after the Erasmus defeat, Glickman reassured his fans that despite the disappointment of losing that key matchup, his football experience was worth his while. In his view, his gridiron efforts were a graphic contradiction to the idea that the rough-and-tumble sport impairs trackmen. He allowed that "playing football strengthened my muscles and hardened me physically" and elevated him "from a mediocre sprinter to a top-notcher and a champion." He claimed that when he was "in the open field or in running back punts," he "got the drive for the sprints and dash events." Glickman could hardly wait for a rematch against Erasmus and Sid Luckman.[15]

As the big rematch approached, a *Herald Tribune* columnist predicted that the outcome would come down to whether Glickman could outduel Luckman, who had "stood out for three successive years" as the city's top football star. In the prior matchup, Luckman had almost single-handedly determined the outcome of the battle, first with a 35-yard romp in the opening quarter and later with a "line plunge" after halftime. He also tallied an extra point with a skillful drop kick and would have been credited with yet another touchdown had a teammate not dropped a wide-open pass at the goal line. But now Glickman had "blossomed forth as a first-rate football player" who "while smaller and less powerful" than Luckman "has all the attributes which go to the making of a star player and in their meeting the all-scholastic post for the year might well be decided."[16]

As the teams prepared for their encounter at Ebbets Field, fans agreed that "on a 100-yard straightaway and in track wear Marty Glickman probably would beat Sid Luckman by ten yards or more." The question was, would "speed on cinders" be enough to win "on the scarred turf of a football field?" At that juncture, "the top topic of conversation in schoolboy circles was the comparison of Marty Glickman . . . with Sid Luckman, the Erasmus hero." Madison supporters believed that their star had the edge since the team's line had been bulked up since the last encounter. Now "Torgan's beef trust, a solid front add[ed]up to an astonishing 1,442 pounds" for the campaign. Glickman would be able to "snuggle behind that wall."[17]

A day before the game, "pessimistic" Erasmus coach Paul Sullivan worried out loud that his boys were "going to be bumped off" since he "rated Glickman as 100 percent better than last year." His players were fully aware of what they were up against since it was noted that "this tilt has a lure all its own—that of a fierce neighborhood rivalry. Not only do the majority of students in both schools come from the same residential sections but in many cases from the same homes. And the Madison-Erasmus engagement is an all-year topic." Once again the fight in the Flatbush environs was for street supremacy. One other "angle of interest" that might have amused spectators as they marched to the stadium was a newspaper man's quip that the two competitors both wore "number 42, both played the quarterback position and the Hebrew for Glickman is 'luck'—a prank of fate or what."[18]

The twenty thousand fans at the game witnessed a decisive defeat of Luckman as Madison beat Erasmus 25–0. Aided by a strong defensive line, Madison kept Luckman in tow. "Every time he got his hands on the ball, he was sure within a moment to feel the clutch of three or four tacklers. . . . His celebrated off-tackle slashes were out of the question . . . even Luckman's known ability as a passer came to naught." On the offensive side of the ball, the strength of the line proved unstoppable as the Erasmus team was "helpless from the start and becoming more so as the battle progressed." In other, almost poetic words, it was reported how "a grim faced, low charging line opened the avenue. A smiling kid in slick silken football pants took the wheel as the ponderous powerhouse that is Madison began to roll. So Marty Glickman and his team went to town." In a defining moment of what had been billed as a personal Luckman-Glickman confrontation, in the second quarter Glickman, the quick-footed Madison safety, picked off a pass and ran 75 yards for a touchdown. Back on offense, Glickman threw two touchdown passes, thus personally accounting for most of his club's points, much like his antagonist had done a year earlier. It was noted that "as a result of Glickman's bang-up ball playing, Coach Torgan was all smiles." For a reporter who chronicled Jewish sports celebrities, it was clear that while "Sid is playing great ball this year, Luckman has been eclipsed by a new star in the high school galaxy." Fifty years later, Luckman would recall ruefully how he "chased" his opponent "all over the field and couldn't catch" him. Glickman's supremacy, at least that day, was evident, and tens of thousands of moviegoers who subsequently viewed newsreel clips of the game saw the emergence of Glickman as a national high school sports hero. From that point on, this "Flatbush Flash" was confident that a college scholarship was very possible.[19]

While Glickman basked in his celebrity, the ever-worried Coach Torgan was concerned that "optimism" among his players might be their undoing. They still had "four hard battles" ahead against worthy Brooklyn opponents before they could compete for the city championship. Happily for the Black and Gold, they "swamped" Boys High by 32 points with Glickman tallying two touchdowns, and subsequently shut down Lincoln 20–0. However, a few days before the New Utrecht game, Glickman took ill with "a grave attack of grippe and flu" and was hospitalized, placing the championship quest in doubt. Ever the devoted teammate, in shades of Frank Merriwell, Glickman sent a telegram to Torgan that the coach read "soberly" to a "hushed" dressing room of "grim" teammates imploring them to win without him. Inspired, the Madison squad rolled over the "inferior" Utrecht team, winning 45–0. After the game "somebody rushed to phone the news to Glickman."

It remained for the game against Manual Training High School for the star player to take his legendary story more than one step further in the spirit of Merriwell. Still convalescing after his release from the hospital, Glickman was supposed to sit out that tilt and watch the game from the sidelines. But with Madison unable to score as of halftime, and with the "Glickman-less eleven" having "no spirit," as "visions of defeat or a tie stalked the . . . dressing room," a "fretting" star on the sidelines, fresh out of "sick bay . . . threw off his blankets for two minutes and realized a touchdown and victory by that move." For a *Brooklyn Daily Eagle* observer, that effort "fired the imagination of everyone who saw it . . . as this truly remarkable player . . . the backfield flash supplied the spark." A week later, now "fit and ready," Glickman led Madison to a city championship in front of twelve thousand fans at Ebbets Field. This "chief ground gainer's" personal highlight was a third-quarter 53-yard sprint to the end zone that sealed a 12–0 victory.[20]

In the days that followed, James Madison's football team became almost a national program when it was invited to travel down south to meet a champion club from Miami. It would have been "the first for a New York City public school" to represent the city and also was potentially a great additional showcase for Glickman, "a player generally considered a certain star in the collegiate ranks." Sadly for Marty and his teammates, the PSAL voted against the trip, feeling that the "idea was not in accord with the highest aims and purposes of school sports," concerned as they were that "high school athletes . . . not be overtaxed" with additional games. It is not known how Glickman reacted to this disappointment, except that he was busily preparing to compete in his next varsity sport of indoor track.[21]

In December 1934, Glickman was honored in several quarters for his football exploits. First Team All-City ballots revealed that "the Madison ace was the unanimous choice of every coach and everyone who saw him play." The Jewish Telegraphic Agency's

Bulletin designated him as "the outstanding football player in a stellar aggregation" of eleven great Jewish players in New York City, including Sid Luckman. It was also prognosticated that this "brilliant field general" was "destined for big things on collegiate gridirons." Feature writers for the *Brooklyn Daily Eagle* went even further when they listed Glickman in their year-end "headliners of the Year" column as among "ten youngsters," including a pianist, a Russian-born dancer, and a seven-year-old "genius," all of whose "merit in their particular fields are outstanding." Glickman was singled out for having "won football honors galore and promises to become an important asset to some future college team."[22]

During Glickman's last semester at James Madison, he returned to prominence at indoor and outdoor track meets, though it took a while for the sprinter to get into top form. By his own admission, "Football knocked a lot out of me. I'm just beginning to get into my proper track condition." It was reported how "it took him two months to get over a case of football legs which he picked up last fall, driving Madison to the city gridiron championship." While he did his utmost through strenuous "workouts every day," a new schoolboy rival named Ted Ellison of De Witt Clinton High School appeared on the scene, replacing Luckman in the minds of local sportswriters as a challenger for the title of New York City's greatest high school athlete.[23]

In January 1935, at a Brooklyn interscholastic meet, Ellison "turned in the feature individual triumph" in the 100-yard senior dash as he "handed Glickman a decisive set back—the latter's first defeat in over a year." The Bronx school champion "flashed to victory" by over two yards in front of two thousand fans, who rose out of their seats to cheer a new local schoolboy celebrity. The result was somewhat surprising and fueled further discussion since Ellison's best times were in the 200-yard race. For the next two months, track fans' attention pointed toward a rematch of the two stars at the public school indoor championship that was billed as "the outstanding duel of the season." As the meet drew near, Glickman "voiced the opinion that he 'would take' Ellison" before the season was over, while Ellison was "modestly defiant to the challenges of all schoolboys." However, Ellison ultimately decided to enter his favorite event, the 200-yard race, which he won handily. At that same meet Glickman, described as the "chunky James Madison football halfback, erased the meet record in the 100" after recovering from a slip at the start of race.[24]

As the outdoor track campaign opened in April 1935, the possibility of the two stars finally meeting recaptured attention. Ellison said that he was anxious to "settle the sprint dispute with Marty Glickman." Glickman reiterated that he was "confident he could take Ellison." There was even some talk of a two-athlete race. The showdown between Ellison and Glickman took place in early May at Princeton University, where the "Flatbush Flash" bested his opponent by "a few feet." In a sense both young men were winners that day since Ellison won "his specialty," the 200-yard dash, finished second in the broad jump, and walked away as the meet's individual high scorer.[25]

In the weeks that followed Glickman focused on a personal quest to break ten seconds in the 100-yard dash. He achieved that goal at a meet at RPI, where "spanked by a blustering breeze" the "low slung speed merchant shattered" the mark, coming in at 9.75 seconds. He would finish under ten seconds four times in his final high school season.[26]

Marty Glickman graduated from James Madison in June 1935. Despite "Depression [economic] problems," he would later recall how, all told, he had a "happy life as a popular school athlete." His only significant disappointment was his defeat in a run for school president. Previously he had won election as seventh-term president "with a plurality of 566" votes and was put in charge of an upcoming "grade dance" complete with an orchestra. Glickman and his friend and campaign manager Marty Abramson, who chronicled school football triumphs for the *Madison Highway* school newspaper, hoped to parlay attention over his sports achievements into an electoral victory. But Norb Salpeter, who was designated in a grade poll as "class orator," bested him in that contest.[27]

Yet undoubtedly like most high school graduates of that and most eras, he would leave high school with no small degree of apprehension about what lay ahead in his future. He chose a cryptic epigram for his yearbook profile, which read in part, "Life lies before me but shut is the door and careless happy as I used to be. Never again shall I in all my years be free." Whatever his worries about the future were by the time he was finished at Madison, his athletic accomplishments had brought recruiters of various types from several schools to his Flatbush doorstep. Due to the recruitment efforts of a group of Jewish alumni of Syracuse University, he chose that institution. He could then look forward to being a college man. There this Brooklyn boy would enter a very different American world and be part of a very complex and challenging interwar American Jewish saga.[28]

Left
AL HANDLER
Guard

Right
MARTY GLICKMAN
Halfback

Marty Glickman and his teammate Al Handler in a 1937 Syracuse University football game program. Credit: Fargenblue via eBay.

3

RECRUITED TO FIGHT QUOTAS AT SYRACUSE UNIVERSITY

IMAGINE the following sports scenario at Baker Field in northern Manhattan, home of the Columbia University Lions football team, any given fall Saturday between 1935 and 1938. Star quarterback Sid Luckman lines up behind a hefty group of blockers that includes center Jerry Stein and tackle Al Handler, alumni of that great James Madison '35 championship team that had caused him such great grief. But now they are invaluable teammates. After calling signals, Luckman hands off the ball to Marty Glickman—his former nemesis—who sweeps around the line of scrimmage for an impressive gain. Soon thereafter, Luckman drops back to throw as Glickman sprints downfield, receives the forward pass, and charges well past midfield toward the end zone. The two great players embrace after the fleet halfback scores a decisive touchdown. Coach Lou Little smiles proud that his concerted recruitment efforts had succeeded in bringing some of the PSAL's best graduates to his school as Columbia garners national sports recognition.

At least that was the story line sportswriter Lew Zeidler of the *Brooklyn Daily Eagle* dreamed up for his readers when he circulated the rumor that Little was "very much interested in the backfield flash" who "will probably enter Columbia" in the fall 1935 along with those two named teammates of the erstwhile Madison "wrecking crew." In the winter or early spring of 1934–35, speculation abounded all over town about Glickman's college plans. Observers also wondered whether he would compete in football or just concentrate on track. Just a week before Zeidler's piece appeared the *Jewish Telegraphic Agency Daily Bulletin* let it be known

that "the sprint champion and top-notch football player has received scholarship offers from seven universities . . . to play football." A month later, Arthur Patterson of the *Herald Tribune* reported
that Glickman's enrollment at Columbia was a sure bet and suggested that the young man's "decision . . . should be the cause of
a few happy moments not only for Lou Little . . . but also for Carl
Merner, the track mentor." Ten days later, Zeidler indicated that
Glickman's choice was still pending when he wrote that "Al Clark,
Erasmus Hall's all-scholastic tackle has decided to trail along with
Sid Luckman and matriculate at Columbia" while "Glickman . . . is
still mulling Syracuse and Columbia offers." Little was in aggressive
pursuit of Brooklyn's stars, while other sports suitors were also dog-
gedly in the neighborhood. Five weeks later, at the end of February
1935, Zeidler wrote with certainty that "it's always news when a local
athletic luminary makes up his mind as to the college he will enter.
Marty Glickman . . . has decided that he will visit the campus of
Columbia University for the next four years and, of course continue
his football playing under Lou Little." However, a month later, an
unnamed correspondent for the *Brooklyn Daily Eagle* scooped other
writers when he announced not only that Glickman was certain
to enroll at Syracuse but that "he may give up football to concentrate upon track. Tom Keane, Orange coach may see to that even if
Marty wants to continue his football activity."[1]

In pitching their institutions, the college representatives stayed
clear of speaking about the quotas that stymied other Jews who
had superior high school grades from gaining admission. Little,
for instance, did not mention that at Columbia University, of the
five hundred freshmen on campus in 1929, only ninety-two were
Jews. What the coach did say, as he drummed his fingers, sitting
anxiously at Harry and Molly's kitchen table, was that their star
athlete son was a desired candidate. Little assured the Glickmans
that Marty would fit very well within a student body that would
love him as he brought glory to their school.[2]

A recruiter from Yale University trekked his way from New
Haven to Flatbush ready to boast of his school's sterling academic

and athletic prominence while saying nothing about its restrictions on Jews. For a generation, Jewish attendance on his campus had been capped at roughly 10 percent. Rather, he was keen to emphasize how Yale's athletic reputation was as great as its scholastic fame and how Glickman would be happy and respected on campus. He was sure to point out how on the gridiron, as early as the mid-1880s, Walter Camp had designed the "basic structure of American football." As a coach, his players complied a 67–2 record across five seasons from 1887 to 1892. In the decades that followed, the Bulldogs produced All-Americans almost every year and competed against the top teams in the nation. The recruiter also was proud to point out that as of 1914 its home games were played in the gigantic Yale Bowl, which seated some seventy thousand spectators. This stadium was then the largest such sports venue in America. In 1934, when high school senior Glickman was thinking seriously about college, Yale defeated Princeton, shattering its rival's thirty-game winning streak. If Glickman played at Yale, said the recruiter, he would be called upon to add luster to its already storied history in front of adoring fans. Yale's track program was also nationally noted, with seven Olympic berths in events that were called "athletics." Glickman could contribute to Yale's standing in that sport too. He could continue to be, as the young man saw himself, a Jewish Frank Merriwell.[3]

However, as much as the college's sports department wanted Glickman on their teams, there was apprehension within the Yale Quad about the quality of his academic training for this top-flight academic university. To help him mature and ultimately be ready to make the grade, Glickman was directed to attend Mercersburg Academy, a college-preparatory boarding school in south-central Pennsylvania, for a year prior to formally applying to Yale. This solution ran counter to the young man's life plan. He wanted to enter college in 1935, win in the Olympics in midsummer 1936 after his freshman year, return to school for three more years, upon graduation secure a good job, and then marry his high school sweetheart, Marjorie (Marge) Dorman.

The two Madison students became an item during his senior year, while Dorman was a junior. They met on a city bus on Kings Highway and took in shows at the Loew's Kings Highway movie theater, and the relationship blossomed into "a commuter court-ship." Marge would recall how "we used to say, a quarter past eight, I'll meet you on the bus." Marty was so happy when early in their relationship this girl, whom he described as having "magnificent eyes and a great pair of legs," attended his game versus Boys High School with his parents, even if her presence got in the way of his performance. Amid the game, while Marty became preoccupied "looking and smiling" at her, he allowed an opponent to catch a pass for a touchdown. As Marty was deeply in love, the prospect of wait-ing an additional year to be married, as the Yale people prescribed, was not for him. Romantic impulses had to have made Marty and Marge wonder if any out-of-town school would satisfy them.

Columbia made much more sense. If their scenario worked out, Marty would play and study in New York while Marge would pur-sue her dream of becoming a dancer in Broadway musicals. Marge actually had early success. Soon after graduation, she earned a spot in George White's "Scandals," a long-running Broadway revue much like the even better known Ziegfeld Follies. One of the "George White Girls," she danced with such famous perform-ers as Bert Lahr and Rudy Vallee.[4] Later in life she taught dance.[5]

Lou Little was well known to Glickman and the entire Madison athletic community. In the spring of 1935, he had just published a tribute in commemoration of the school's ten years of excel-lence in sports. There he emphasized how "college football al-ways has and always will depend to a vast extent on the kind of football played in high school." The recruiter was clearly on the prowl. In further promoting the Lions of New York City, he was sure to point out that he had already corralled Luckman and that the deal he offered to his former rival was also available to Marty. The Erasmus star had nine schools after him, including Princeton, the University of Pennsylvania, NYU—where a former camp counselor of his had played ball—and the U.S. Naval Academy.

Syracuse University was also a possibility since Luckman's brother had attended there. But upon meeting the coach after attending a Columbia-Annapolis game at Baker Field, Luckman chose Columbia. Ironically, he was there to check out the Midshipmen's team. In his memoirs, Luckman asserted that Little's sell did not emphasize football. In a "loud but courteous" voice, the coach asserted "Columbia didn't have any soft touch to offer . . . there would be a chance to work hard, football on the side; a grind of studies to beat all grinds." During this era at colleges, a "grind" was a student who focused exclusively on studies, the exact opposite of a "tramp athlete." Luckman was told he would have to do as well as those with wire-rimmed glasses when he was not exploding out of the backfield. Little "expected[ed] football players to be model students . . . equally adept at blocking and social science."[6]

What Luckman's recollections did not indicate was that he would be able to do it all in the friendly environment of the university's New College and not Columbia College. Unlike the flagship undergraduate college, this auxiliary branch of the university welcomed Jews. He was enrolled in that progressive program until it closed in 1939 and only finished up at Columbia College. At the New College, Luckman—who was at best an average high school pupil—did not have to worry about maintaining the minimum GPA required for athletic eligibility since no grades were given within this experimental regimen. During his senior year, the star quarterback was occasionally given a valuable assist from "certain profs. [who] actually took an interest in football." For Luckman, it was a "fair exchange for the efforts our players had put into botany and physics classes."

Little, his assistant coach Albert Spurlock, who headed the New College's Physical Education Department, and his supportive dean, Thomas Alexander, pulled off this coup with university higher-ups. Not only was Little able to secure a place at "Columbia" for seven other varsity football players who were key to the Lions' successes on the gridiron, but the deal at the New College was also tendered to, and accepted by, young men who ran track, wrestled, and fenced for Columbia. The most attractive emolument that had to have impressed the Glickmans was that Marty could attend the New College on an academic scholarship. There also were opportunities from alumni fans to provide him with part-time work during the school year and over the summer. Columbia did not offer athletic grants-in-aid.[7]

As Little moved to close the negotiations, his remaining issue might well have been whether the two Brooklyn superstars could share the limelight that would be theirs in New York and beyond. Luckman was all set to suit up with Glickman. Years later, he would recall that the "feud" that newspaper scribes loved to "gush over" came to a friendly end when the Luckmans invited the Glickmans over to their Brooklyn apartment for dinner, where they "patched" up any residual hard feelings between these two competitors who had "fought each other tooth and nail in every game [they] played." The day after that sit-down, the boys took in a pro game at the Polo Grounds and watched some others fight it out for a change. Subsequently, he said, they became "chums . . . almost inseparable each summer." Marty remembered Sid as a great player, a much better passer than he, though Glickman believed that he was the better runner. In his opinion, they were never fast friends.[8]

Lou Little's well-conceived recruitment strategy went awry, however, when a group of five alumni brothers from the Sigma Alpha Mu (SAM) Jewish fraternity at Syracuse reached out to Marty and his family and spirited him away with a quite different set of arguments. From a purely sports perspective, Glickman already knew that the Orangemen had "a very good football team," but it was their track team with "a fine coach" and "a great reputation for Olympic champions" that stood out for him. Syracuse's first Olympic champion, Myer Prinstein, who just happened to be Jewish, won gold medals in three Olympics, 1900, 1904, and 1906. More recently, Ray Barbuti had won the 400 meters at the 1928 Amsterdam Games. Glickman knew that if he came to campus in the fall of 1935, he could team up with two-time All-American Ed O'Brien—outstanding in middle-distance races and a prime candidate to compete in Berlin. As an Olympic hopeful too, Glickman recognized that track "was the individual sport regardless of how the team did." He would be judged solely on his personal achieve-ments. However, as much as these "well-to-do" former students, as Glickman called them, "loved" their alma mater and looked forward to this recruit eventually bringing more sports honors to the school, they were out for much bigger game. When they discussed his future, first over lunch at the St. George, a fancy restaurant in Brooklyn, and later on a long drive up to northwest-ern New York, it became clear that "they wanted to get a Jewish athlete" of his great quality "into Syracuse to help make it easier for other Jewish students to be admitted." These men were willing and able to cover his tuition during his first year at school. Other expenses that came with college life would be left up to the young man. Funding was always a most critical issue for the athlete and his family. If he accepted, this offer would be the first time Marty Glickman would be drawn into involvement with the problems Jews of his time faced from collegiate anti-Semitism.[9]

Mordecai (Mort) Starobin, one of the alums who would fund the scholarship and a scholar-athlete of significant note at the school, explained the predicaments Jews faced at Syracuse in much the following way: There had been a time just a couple of decades earlier when Jews were very accepted on campus. In 1916, chancel-lor James Roscoe Day had told financier John D. Rockefeller that Syracuse would "welcome Jew, Gentile, Protestant and Catholic" at the university. Day's comprehensive agenda was to expand the reach of his institution, which previously had been a small Methodist college, into a large nonsectarian school. Under that mandate, between 1918 and 1923, precisely at a time when other schools were talking about and ultimately moving to restrict Jewish enrollment, the percentage of Jewish students at Syracuse increased from 6 to 15 percent. Many of these Jewish students hailed from New York City, and some lacked the funds to attend. Tolerant and accommodating, the school went so far as to use monies "raised by collections in the Methodist Churches" to help out these potential enrollees. Day also turned to Syracuse native Louis Marshall, head of the American Jewish Committee and the only Jewish member of the university's board of trustees, to seek funds for indigent Jewish students from well-to-do members of the Jewish community in his hometown and in New York City. As Starobin told his story, he indicated that there was a tradition of outside sources helping Syracuse Jewish students in need. More importantly, Day and his vice chancellor, Frank Peck, told Marshall, a renowned defender of his people and a local political power broker, that they were "glad to have Jews come" and "saw no reason why we should discriminate against Jews . . . or any other race seeking an education." The chancellor contended, "We are more democratic" than other schools, including many in New York.[10]

Starobin might also have mentioned to Glickman that early in Day's tenure Myer Prinstein had brought honor to Syracuse by winning gold medals and, as importantly, by doing so with sensitivity to Syracuse's religious values. This Jewish athlete was a model member of the university family. The story was that during the qualifying rounds in the long jump at the 1900 Paris Olympics, Prinstein led by a few inches. But then a religious calendar issue embroiled the athlete. The finals were slated for Sunday, and Syracuse—then still a denominational institution—forbade its athletes from competing on the Christian Sabbath. When French officials would not change the date, Prinstein followed his school's policy and did not suit up. Meanwhile, he was told that, ostensibly in the spirit of true sportsmanship, his archrival, Alvin Kraenzlein of the University of Pennsylvania, also agreed to sideline himself, only to change his mind and win the gold medal. Prinstein challenged Kraenzlein to a run-off to determine who was the superior athlete. When his now nemesis refused, Prinstein punched his rival. Soon thereafter, Prinstein won gold in the hop, step, and jump and four years later won two gold medals at the St. Louis games.[11]

This Jewish student's achievements, and loyalty toward his alma mater, which had to have warmed Day and Peck, were totally lost upon the Christian undergraduates and alumni who began to make opposition to Jews well known when Day left his office in 1922. Early in the administration of Charles W. Flint, a Ku Klux Klan Klavern was created on campus, with some two hundred students and faculty signing on to its racist, anti-Semitic, and anti-Catholic protocols. They rallied in full white sheet regalia, burned crosses near campus, and demanded that strict quotas be placed on unwanted Jewish students. On one occasion, the haters were particularly upset that the word was out, apparently fostered by Jewish students, that Syracuse was a "university that treated the Jewish boy right."

The attack against Jews so similar to what was being said elsewhere in academe was that while they might do well in the classroom, they constituted a foreign cultural element deleterious to campus life. Many Christian students did not want to socialize or share the same dormitory space. Jews simply did not fit in. The fear among restrictionists was that if nothing was done, the school faced a "disproportionate invasion of Jewish students." One allegation had to have struck Starobin in the craw. In February 1923, during his junior year, several members of the Senior Council, including the editor of the university newspaper, appealed to Chancellor Flint to impose restrictions on Jewish enrollment. Their criticism focused on the allegation that Jews were not participating in athletics. It was a canard not rooted in reality.[12]

Forget about Prinstein; the fact was that Starobin was an outstanding, nationally recognized "veteran left tackle." By the time he was a senior, opposing coaches like Hap Frank of Penn State had remarked how Starobin was the "'hardest hitting player,' he ever played against." He was also a first-class shot-putter and was praised as "Coach Keane's trump card" in all track and field meets. Starobin's athletic profile was a point of emphasis that had to have impressed Glickman as the alumnus detailed sports and Jewish life at Syracuse. Glickman also had to have respected the fact that Starobin, a prelaw major, had been an honor student at Syracuse for three years; no "tramp athlete" he. Moreover, Starobin was far from a unique Jewish sports figure on campus. In 1924, it was reported that he was one of "nine Jews [who] constituted an important cog in the Orange football squad." That same year another Jewish two-sport athlete, Sid Mendelson, was projected as a leader on the basketball team while winning the All-University Tennis Championship. Jewish players also found their way onto varsity teams in lacrosse, wrestling, hockey, cross-country, and soccer. For the New York Jewish newspaper that proudly chronicled these athletes "it was easily perceptible that the Jew, where given an equal opportunity has shown himself to advantage." But anti-Semites on campus did not recognize that truth and were not interested in Jews occupying a position on an equal playing field.[13]

Flint's public disavowal of the students' request, which mollified Marshall, was small consolation for Syracuse's increasingly marginalized Jews, who noticed that the protesters were not censured by the administration. Jewish women on campus during the years 1928 to 1935, the period exactly prior to the efforts to recruit Glickman, were keenly aware that the school often segregated them into separate dormitories. Young Jewish men and women alike were kept out of their respective Christian fraternities and sororities. For Flint and his lieutenant and future successor William P. Graham, the outspoken council members' attitudes "represented the majority sentiment" of undergraduates and possibly alumni contributors too. Sympathetic to these sentiments, the admissions officers shifted their recruitment efforts away from large Jewish population areas. Due to these strategic moves, in 1932 the percentage of Jews on campus was down to 12 percent and the leadership's unannounced but planned goal was to ensure a Jewish presence of under 10 percent so that Syracuse educated "the type of student we desire."

The fantasy that Marty Glickman could succeed where Starobin and the other top-flight Jewish athletes on campus previously had failed in turning around opinion toward and policies about Jews through winning games and meets for Syracuse proved to be a quixotic quest. The hope that a Jewish journalist once expressed that "if Jewish students at the University of Syracuse were known to be good athletes, no one would dare hound them and demand restrictions upon their educational opportunities" did not pan out. Glickman's eventual achievements as a track man and backfield football star for the Orange did not rally those alumni, benefactors, and students who were not enamored of the Klan or the restrictive policies to support Syracuse's Jews. As far as recruitment was concerned, during Glickman's years at the school, 1935–39, "the percentage of Jews admitted to Syracuse ranged from seven percent to nine and a half percent." The situation would not change for the better until 1942, when William P. Tolley began his tenure as chancellor. Despite some enduring unhappiness among Christian alumni and students to his door-opening polices between 1939 and 1945, the Jewish percentage rose from 7.5 to 18 percent. Nonetheless in the spring of 1935, the quintet of SAM alumni advocates was hopeful that they had made a compelling case to Glickman as an athlete, and maybe also as a Jew, to enroll at their alma mater.[14]

It is not known how deeply the young man was moved by Starobin's and his fellow fraternity brothers' worrisome discussion about exclusionary anti-Semitism at Syracuse. But as they spoke, he did wonder why these friendly fellows had to step up for him "while others," perhaps he was thinking of Christians, who were players with sports pedigrees inferior to him "received scholarships." What Glickman did not recognize was that during this era in intercollegiate sports, almost all athletes around the country, from freshmen through upperclassmen, did not receive their grants directly from college officials. That was the province of "boosters" of all sorts who funneled monies to awaiting coffers while university leaders spoke glowingly, if disingenuously, about the pristine amateurism at their institutions. Under-the-table arrangements were quite common. The $175 per month stipend that the people of "West Virginia"—truly an "out of town school"—reportedly tendered to Glickman, which he did not follow up on as he thought about Yale, Columbia, and Syracuse, most likely emanated from such an unofficial source. Starobin and his compatriots were offering to support their favorite son much like other alumni were reaching out to other top-flight players, although the SAM brothers approached Glickman with the best of intentions that went beyond athletic achievements. The narrative that was relayed to him did, however, make him explicitly aware for the first time in his life of the problematics of being a Jewish college student in 1930s America. It also projected him as a key participant in the honorable quest to ameliorate the dilemma of restriction and prejudices at their school. It was quite a burden to shoulder for a young man who until then had never seen his religion and ancestral culture as a problem. Glickman did not rise to the challenge of personally addressing the anti-Semitism at Syracuse, but he was grateful about the SAM brothers' offer of substantial financial aid to attend college. He would recall decades later, about the series of meetings, only that he "liked the Syracuse people and alumni who seemed so interested in me personally" and was "impressed" by "their seriousness." At the end of the recruitment season, Marty Glickman signed on with Syracuse University.[15]

Like all freshmen, Glickman faced the challenges of adjustment to college life. On the academic side, he initially planned on preparing for the career as a physician that he had contemplated at James Madison. But after a tough go during his first semester, when he struggled in physics and chemistry classes, he realized that the premedical curriculum was not for him. The requisite laboratory work that would occupy many hours during the week would also take him away from the athletic fields. As always, foremost in his mind was his quest to become an Olympian, but without being tagged as a "tramp athlete." He quickly changed his major to political science. That discipline required much less extensive study time. Thinking far ahead, he pondered eventually becoming "a city administrator or work[ing] for the national government." He would graduate with a bachelor's degree in June 1939.[16]

His out-of-class existence during his first year was quite spartan. He called it "thin-line living." His scholarship from the SAM group did not include room and board or cash for out-of-pocket expenses. With no money to afford residence in the dormitory and not yet a brother who could live in their fraternity house, during the first two semesters Glickman and four other students, athletes all, lived in the gymnasium wrestling room. One of his roommates was Al Handler. He was one of the other fellows Lou Little had been after months earlier. Little probably pitched the New College idea to him too as the Columbia coach was widely recruiting the city's best players. The SAM brothers were again one or more steps ahead of Little as they offered the same deal they presented to Glickman to this stout if underpublicized lineman. His yeoman efforts would not be easily recognized or lionized by the public, but Starobin and other knowledgeable alumni also knew that Glickman needed someone tough to block for him. Handler, who shared the rumble seat with Glickman on that crucial long ride up to Syracuse when the issues of what their enrollment might mean to other Jews were discussed, also heard the SAM guys' worries loud and clear. But like Marty, Al did not embrace the fraternity brothers' larger concerns as his own. He, too, was only in search of his sheepskin while succeeding on the gridiron.

Among Glickman's other confreres in the wrestling room was Bob Stewart of Rochester, New York, who had "never met a Jew before." The friendship that developed and endured between the two young men would have pleased Day, the integrationist former chancellor. Outside that immediate circle of penurious athletic freshmen, there were nine other James Madison alumni, six women and three men, with whom Glickman could well have interacted. Most of these students had been Arista members who had made the cut as admissions had become increasingly restrictive when it came to Brooklyn Jews. Marty recognized Morton Handler when he bumped into him on campus. He was a fellow who had written about Marty's football achievements in the school's yearbook.[17]

To have some spending money at school and bus or train fare to visit his folks, and, more importantly, to see Marge in Brooklyn, Glickman worked some odd jobs. He served as a waiter in the frat house six nights a week. On Sundays he worked at a Greek diner called Cosmos and helped himself to leftover rolls, unless an affluent, Syracuse-native SAM brother invited him home for dinner. Glickman also found a position as an usher at a local movie theater, sold shoes at the school, and, with Handler, cleaned the swimming pool, getting down on their hands and knees to remove the scum. After bribing the janitor with a bottle of whiskey at Christmastime, the older man worked while the athletes just showed up and swam. This was a 1930s version of a common practice today where privileged college sports stars are "hired" to "water" the artificial grass on the football field. It is a sly "legal" way of slipping them additional funds. Glickman took advantage of the offer of free admission to any movie theater courtesy of owners who were also football boosters. This bonus too was a mini adumbration of how today's fans fete star athletes with whom they like to be linked. These emoluments made for a "very pleasant time, a happy time despite the fact that [he] had a thin dime in [his] pocket."

Glickman did very well in his athletic pursuits. His most impressive track performances were first achieved indoors, at the Millrose games in February at Madison Square Garden, where he came in second in the 60-yard dash against a world-class field of runners. He did even better outdoors, when he twice beat Olympic hopeful Ben Johnson at the Metropolitan Championships and then at the Olympic Eastern Regional Trials. As a freshman, his best moments in football took place *after* he was instrumental in an upset of Cornell University. With the clock winding down and the Big Red ahead by a touchdown, Glickman intercepted a pass and ran almost the length of the field for the winning touchdown. Later on that day, when he was selling programs in the stands for extra cash, he was thrilled to hear the public address announcer tell the crowd that he had won the game against an archrival. He was also gratified when a student sportswriter for the college newspaper wrote a ditty in praise of his exploit:

> The field was awful wet, the track was awful slow.
> The kid was on the bench, the coach didn't think he'd go.
> But then the lead changed hands, and Orange turned to blue.
> "Ribs," he looked around, and Marty came to view.
> "It's a muddy field kid, and the going's kinda tough,"
> "Don't you worry coach, pit me in, I'll make 'em cry enough."
> So on the field he went and stole a pass away,
> Ninety yards to a touchdown, and Marty saved the day.

Glickman was on his way to becoming a Syracuse gridiron standout.[18]

As a freshman Marty did not line up against Luckman, to the disappointment of those who wished to witness a replay of the great Glickman-Luckman 1935 Ebbets Field confrontation. Luckman took the year off to concentrate on his academics. Little was clearly serious about his players doing well in their classes and labs. When they did meet again on the college gridiron, the matches were anticlimactic. Glickman reported that he had "no outstanding games against Columbia." Luckman's recollections of his most important matchups as a collegian did not include his tilts against Syracuse. During the fellows' first year on their varsity teams, Columbia won; the second year they tied, and Syracuse triumphed in their senior years.[19]

Glickman got along well with his teammates off the field. Once he earned a scholarship, he had a place at the training table, where he regularly ate and there chatted amicably as an equal with his fellow athletes, who could not care less about his religious origins as they all gobbled up what was served. Observance of kosher laws was of no concern to Marty when being one of the guys. One night he thought the main course was lamb chops but turned out to be pork chops. There is no indication that anyone tricked or forced him into eating this most Jewish religiously and culturally taboo food. When he asked for the entrée, "a guy looked at [him] with a big grin" and let him know what was on the menu. It was the first time he had ever tasted pork. He dug right in, "did not think twice about it," had no second thoughts about dining on that tasty dish "except [he] did think about [his] grandmother and grand-father" who were scrupulous kosher eaters and what they would have thought about his choice—if he ever told them.[20]

Both during his freshman year and as an upperclassman, Marty Glickman also moved blithely among athletes and generally within the Syracuse student body. He walked, ran, or strutted around campus quite happy both before and after he became an Olympic celebrity, notwithstanding the anti-Semitism that troubled so many other Jews at the school. When asked many decades later what it was like "coming from Brooklyn . . . and from a high school which was . . . significantly Jewish" and what "kind of atmosphere did he encounter" in a predominantly gentile world, Glickman admitted that "as a whole, there was a standoffishness, there was little doubt that there was a distinction between a Jew and a non-Jew." However, "nothing was done about it, nothing was said about it." As far as being singled out in the classroom for mistreatment was concerned, "there may have been just an awareness" of his religious background among faculty members, but "it was not in any derogatory sense, in any segregating sense. It was just that it was there in those days." Glickman also allowed that perhaps his feeling most comfortable among his own kind was of his "own making." He would recount that when he visited "gentile friends in a gentile fraternity," most of these social venues were off-limits to Jews, and "I was aware of my Jewishness." He believed that his sense that he was not totally wanted "could well have been self-imposed." While he "felt a distinction . . . it was not an inimical distinction." Most significantly, when he succeeded on the track or football field, he was known as a worthy Syracuse athlete, not as Marty Glickman the Jewish football player or Marty Glickman the Jewish sprinter.[21]

In accepting Glickman, and for that matter Handler, Starobin and other Jewish ballplayers as one of their own, Syracuse's athletic department and the university's leadership made a crucial statement on the weighty question, pungent at that time, about whether Jews, through sports achievements, could be positioned or even extolled as standard-bearers for their institutions. At other schools, including programs that the Orangemen played against, limits were placed on the number of Jews stationed in starring or leadership positions. Although a Jewish journalist of that era believed that "no coach who has regard for the university he serves and for his own reputation will discriminate against a candidate for a team on any ground other than inability to make good for his alma mater," sports quotas did exist. In the late 1920s at the University of Pennsylvania, "one of the best football players the university ever had, a Jew . . . warmed the bench almost all of three years." At an unnamed "eastern university," again in the late 1920s, the Christian rowers on the crew team made it clear to the Jewish senior where he fit in the rows. Rather than elect him as captain, they decided to forgo naming a student leader for that year. The following season, "they went back to having a captain and an eligible Gentile boy was elected." Then there was the case at a "state university" where a Jewish basketball player earned a spot on the team but wallowed on the bench while "players of much less ability . . . [were] sent into games." For a different Jewish newspaper writer who was not as upbeat as his colleague, these abusers were people "who have not yet freed themselves from shackles of prejudice with which they have been bound from youth."[22]

Such prejudice was akin to discrimination against Jews as editors in chief of student newspapers or as designees "in honorary fraternities, glee clubs, managership of social organizations" and dramatic groups. These all were coveted spots in extracurricular activities. One of the articulated fears of those who practiced discrimination was that if one Jew was put in charge, he would push for many others of his "type" to be included, thus altering the desired social balances of their elite societies.[23]

Bigoted college sports officials faced, however, a compelling problem that did not trouble an intolerant glee club maestro or dramatic society director. Unlike those who led the performing arts who were judged solely on the basis of often subjective critics' estimations, athletic mentors' successes or failures were always evaluated based on wins and losses. A club had to not only play but win. There always were students and well-heeled alumni with monies to contribute to their favored university who watched closely how their teams performed. They made their opinions known to coaches, athletic administrators, and ultimately university presidents. Those boosters who supported individual athletes had much to say. For better or worse, Jewish athletes were often considered a superior breed whose presence on a team would go a long way to ensuring victory for the school. In the most often quoted statement of the time about Jewish superiority in basketball,

Paul Gallico, sports editor of the *New York Daily News*, argued—with more than a little racism in his words—that that sport "appeals to the Hebrew with his Oriental background [because] the game places a premium on an alert, scheming mind and flashy trickiness, artful dodging and general smartalecness." That was the key to their alleged superiority. Gallico did not like Jews, but he was certain that they could play. The same might be said about the deep-down sentiments of University of Pittsburgh fans who applauded Marshall Goldberg and Benny Friedman's devotees at the University of Michigan, not to mention those who turned out to publicly embrace Sid Luckman. All of these Jewish stars posted win after win for their "home" team.[24]

Back at Syracuse, Glickman integrated well within a school tolerant for what he could contribute on the field. He was valued in what was a sports meritocracy. In his four years in the athletic program, he experienced but two minor kerfuffles over his Jewishness that temporarily annoyed him. Even if Glickman was hardly a deeply observant Jew, he decided, beginning when he was a freshman, to skip football practice on Rosh Hashanah and Yom Kippur. For his first two years on the squad, nothing was said or done about his absence. But during his junior and senior years, an unnamed coach dropped him for a while from the first team to the third when he did not suit up on those days. The coach did not indicate why this star performer was demoted, but Glickman felt "it was apparent" that the coach was unhappy that he had taken off for the Jewish holidays. The coach did not articulate his objection, and the player went about his business with the scrub team. At most, what had transpired was a very subtle form of anti-Semitism or perhaps just a Christian's lack of mindfulness of the significance of these special Jewish days. Both years his ability won out as Glickman was soon restored to the starting lineup as he "earned his spot back."

When he decided not to practice and then when the demotion took place, Glickman may well have thought of the greater problems one of his boyhood heroes, Hank Greenberg, had faced just a year before Marty entered Syracuse. In 1934, the ownership and manager of the Detroit Tigers pressured Greenberg, the foremost Jewish Major League Baseball player of that era, to play on the Jewish holidays. After much public discussion, Greenberg played on the Jewish New Year but took off on Yom Kippur.[25]

Glickman's attitude to such problems was to let his actions do his talking. If a bigoted opponent let loose with an epithet, he did not physically confront him. Almost all football players were bigger than he was. Rather than take up an unequal fight, the swift backfield runner "shrugged off" the nasty remark and "used his speed to get even." Even these moments were rare as "no one sought [him] out to pummel" him.[26]

As a respected and valued athlete, Marty Glickman enjoyed a privileged life at Syracuse often insulated from the prejudice that troubled so many Jewish students. On the Jewish holiday question, Marty was temporarily penalized, though with no serious consequences to his status. But rank-and-file Jewish students who were absent for a test on Rosh Hashanah or Yom Kippur were penalized. In 1926, the school's administration determined that it was not right for "a non-Christian sect with a rather small representation in the student body to regulate our form of educational practice." For Flint and Graham, it was "inevitable that a Jewish student at Syracuse who insists on observing the orthodox traditions of his race will be at some disadvantage." Despite some objections from a local rabbi and a few board people, that discriminatory policy that many Christian students supported remained in effect during Glickman's tenure on campus. In the end, while Marty Glickman was able and welcomed to wear the Orange's color in his athletic triumphs, his presence did not alter the status of Jews who had gained admission to Syracuse University in the mid-1930s. Little did he know as he completed his freshman year that the question of his standing as a victorious Jew on a very different and rarefied podium at the upcoming Berlin games would expose him directly to anti-Semitism through sports in a way that would undermine his long-held quest to become an American Olympic champion.[27]

A happy Marty Glickman with his U.S. track teammates at the Olympic Village celebrating Jesse Owens's victory. Glickman is in the back row, first person on the left. Credit: AP Images.

4

WELCOMED IN GERMANY

WHILE Marty Glickman lounged in a deck chair on the ocean liner S.S. *Manhattan* in July 1936 as the ship sped through "calm seas" across the Atlantic toward the port of Hamburg, he rested assured that the winds of controversy that had swirled around American participation in the Berlin Olympic games had died down. He smiled contentedly when he recalled the grand send-off he and his teammates had received as "thousands of relatives and well-wishers lined the pier, waving farewell" as the boat left New York Harbor. After much contentious debate, a decision had been made to accept the Third Reich's guarantees that its anti-Semitic policies in place since Hitler rose to power would not be allowed to infect what was projected as a pristine athletic festival. Glickman did not trust the Nazis; no American Jews did. Still, he hoped for the best and was driven to do his best toward fulfilling his lifelong goal of victory at the games. Interested in maximizing his first experience out of the United States, he might have dipped into *An Intelligent Traveler's Guide to Germany*, which was distributed to the athletes and noted "the usual sights in Germany but also called attention to various persecutions of the Nazi regime." However, he could not have cared less about the goings on at the Heidelberg Fete, taking place while the team was on its way from New York. This propaganda feast was designed to link the 550th anniversary of the founding of the city of Heidelberg, one of the iconic locales where revered medieval German nationalism was born, to the present-day resurgence of Teutonic pride under Hitler. While the Nazis memorialized the past, Glickman was off to the modern German capital of Berlin.

During the bull sessions with his teammates in his second-class cabin, which he shared with his Syracuse teammate Ed O'Brien, the prime topic of discussion was their shared hope for glory on the field or in the arena and the mutually held dream of standing tall on the podium, with gold medals around their necks, while the "Star-Spangled Banner" played and the U.S. flag was unfurled.

When Glickman was given his chance—like everyone else—to attend the Captain's Dinner amid officials from the American Olympic Committee, he pledged to them to do his best and promised that he would behave himself as a representative of his country. According to an on-the-scene reporter, as the boat progressed toward Europe, the much older leaders of the contingent, the so-called badge wearers, were mostly concerned that "all 234 athletes aboard obey the training regulations" including a strict curfew of ten o'clock. Early on in the journey, there were "breaches of discipline"—although the exact natures of the infractions were then not specified—among the sometimes rambunctious youth that had to be curtailed. These "non-conformists," it was said, "had cast a stigma upon the 98 percent of the athletes who had followed the rules." Glickman, one of the two youngest athletes to now proudly wear American colors and personally of fine deportment, was not one of the troublemakers. He was just happy to be among his fellow competitors. Avery Brundage, president of the delegation, who was pleased to report that "he is confident that the trouble is now over," very likely would not have recognized Glickman if they had passed each other on deck. A news photographer on board did, however, notice Glickman and Sam Stoller jogging around the boat and snapped an image of two smiling athletes committed to get their workout in. This pleasant photo appeared in many U.S. newspapers.

The only other time that Glickman stood out during the trip was when he agreed to participate in a variety show that Mrs. Ada Taylor Sackett, assistant chaperone of the women swimmers, helped organize. Marty was a cast member of "a lively skit" that was the grand finale of a "gay evening." It is unlikely that the next day he attended the "interdenominational [Christian] services and mass" that "a majority of the team attended." No one would have thought of conducting a parallel Jewish service for the handful of Jewish athletes in the Olympic contingent, including fencer Norman Armitage, equestrian Harold Isaacson, gymnast and rope climber Joseph Goldenberg, basketball player Sam Balter, and Brooklyn's Herman Goldberg, a catcher. But then again, back home Glickman rarely attended Jewish Sabbath prayers. He might have been a tad annoyed that on Sunday workouts had been "slightly curtailed" but would not have made a fuss. Instead, he would do his best to stay in tip-top shape on his own on the promenade deck. In the vernacular of sports, he was simply gratified that he had been "chosen in." He was part of his nation's most rarefied sports community. Three weeks later, his status and perspective would be changed when he was sidelined from participating in a featured track event in the Olympic stadium. At that turning point, Brundage surely knew who Glickman was and Marty would begin to hate Brundage. The abruptly marginalized athlete would despise the head of the American Olympic Committee (AOC) for the rest of his life.[1]

Germany was designated as a host country two years before the Nazi takeover. In April 1931, the International Olympic Committee (IOC) had awarded the games to Berlin. It was the sports world's version of the admission of the democratic Weimar Republic into the League of Nations some five years earlier. It was a statement that Germany was no longer an outlaw nation and additional proof that the Great War was truly finished for good. The international athletic governing body had every optimistic expectation that Germany would adhere to Olympic protocols. When Le Baron Pierre de Coubertin revived the ancient Olympic games in 1896, this quadrennial gathering of the world's top sports performers was supposed to "bring together the athletes of the world . . . thereby creating international respect and goodwill and thus helping to construct a better and more peaceful world." But when Hitler rose to power in the winter of 1933 and the government started to implement its first anti-Jewish policies, the IOC began to harbor serious reservations about its decision. At issue was their worry that the Third Reich would not adhere to "all the laws regarding the Olympic games." The international organization specifically demanded that the Nazi regime "admit to the German Olympic team German Sportsmen of Non-Aryan origin provided they have the necessary capability." Collaterally, Germany also had to pledge to provide athletic facilities to the Jews of their nation to prepare them properly to compete on par with all other athletes.[2]

Hitler, who inherited the IOC's invitation to the Weimer government, was no great fan of these international games. He added his belief in Jewish influence over athletics to his perverted list of Jewish conspiracies that he said undermined modern civilization. In keeping with his adherence to the canard against Jews in *The Protocols of the Elders of Zion*, which portrayed his enemy as corruptors of sports, just as they corrupted every aspect of human endeavor, the führer declared, "What Jews praise is poison to us." But his propaganda minister, Joseph Goebbels, immediately saw the games as a way of demonstrating the racial superiority of Aryan youth through their achievements on the field of play. The Nazis would also put on display the organizational and technological genius of Hitler's government in constructing venues that would impress visitors from around the world. To ease IOC reservations, at a meeting of international organizations in Vienna in June 1933, the Nazis assured officials that they would not prohibit German Jewish athletes from working out in their sports clubs and participating in the upcoming games.[3]

In so doing, Hitler's government officially countermanded a declarative statement that the head of the Reich's Ministry for Sports had made just a few weeks earlier. Captain Hans von Tschammer und Osten had said, "German sports are for Aryans. German Youth leadership is only for Aryans not for Jews. Athletes will not be judged by ability alone, but also by their general and moral fitness to represent Germany." When pressed, Tschammer und Osten would attribute the change in his government's policy to pressure from the international community. It was a common Nazi rejoinder to complaints against their racist behavior lodged against them early in their tenure.

In the two years that followed their pledge to follow the rules, it became apparent that the Nazis were indeed intent on reneging on their agreement. In November 1933 that same ministry ruled that Jews could not be on athletic governing boards. In August 1935 Jews were officially thrown out of Nazi sports clubs and prevented from competing outside of the Reich. That decree effectively determined that they could not represent the fatherland. But then again, as of mid-September 1935, with the promulgation of the Nuremberg Laws, Jews were deemed as no longer citizens of Germany. Observers of the scene in Germany, who may have had no interest in sports, understood that the regime had concretized its attack on Jews, which now went well beyond the April 1, 1933, one-day boycott of Jewish stores and businesses, the elimination of Jews from the country's civil service and other top-notch professions, and the uncoordinated street violence that had marked the first years of the Hitler regime. In early Nazi legislation against Jews, there were vague allusions to Aryan "athletes and sportsmen . . . serv[ing] the state and contribut[ing] to the production of a standard National Socialist human body." With the edicts that came down from Nuremberg, Jews were set apart from Germany's national, cultural, and athletic scenes.

In October 1935, an international swim meet that included American athletes took place before an all-Aryan crowd. A sign on the box office that read "Jews are not wanted" said it all. Members of the IOC board wondered what other highly offensive contradictions of its fair-play rules would mar the upcoming Berlin games.[4]

American Jewish advocacy groups were never taken in by Berlin's promises. They also harbored little faith that the IOC would ever effectively punish the Reich for its noncompliance by moving the games. They likewise were unmoved when some

American Olympic officials assured the public early on that they would guarantee that German Jewish athletes would be allowed to participate. Avery Brundage's statement to a Baltimore Jewish newspaper in April 1933 noting that "the games will not be held in any country where there will be interference with the fundamental Olympic theory of equality of all races" left them cold. This president of the AOC couched his views with a reminder that his stance was only "personal" and "unofficial."

In October 1933, the American Jewish Congress (AJCong), the nation's most aggressive Jewish defense organization, turned "to heads of various teams in every college throughout the country, requesting that Americans refuse to play in the Olympics if held in Germany under present conditions." Less than a month later, AJCong attempted to enlist "former American Olympic champions, asking them to associate themselves with their organization" and its cause. In mid-November 1933 AJCong solicited the heads of district branches of the Amateur Athletic Union (AAU), requesting that a potential American withdrawal from the games be placed front and center before the national meeting, to be held just a few days later. Their lobbying with this powerful and long-standing athletic body bore fruit because delegates from all over the United States passed an anti-Olympics resolution almost unanimously.[5]

AJCong officials' chances for success in their protest were chilled when General Charles Sherrill rose at the subsequent AOC conference to challenge the AAU resolution. While disingenuously asserting that he was deeply troubled about how "Jewish athletes are not getting a square deal in Germany" and that he was "an out-and-out enemy of anti-Semitism, just as I have always been of anti-Catholicism," he warned that such a tough-minded AAU resolution would "do no good for the Jews in Germany," but what was worse, he prophesized, "if an American team is prevented from taking part in the 1936 Olympic Games . . . then I predict that American youths throughout the nation will be disgruntled that they cannot because of the Jews." He prognosticated ominously that these unhappy Christian athletes, along with their friends and supporters, will "surely start an unreasoning move of anti-Semitism among all of those young people that will be hard to overcome."

Two years later, Sherrill elaborated further on his purported "fears" for the future of his "Jewish friends" even as he let it be known how he felt about the proficiency of Jewish athletes and his admiration for the Nazi regime. He told the *Washington Post*, "It was not easy to get a Jewish athlete and there has never been a prominent Jewish athlete in history." After two personal meetings with Hitler, he told Nazi officials, for publication in their newspapers, that the Reich's dictator was "an undeniable great leader" and applauded how he had brought back his nation from the calamity of defeat in World War I. The AOC dutifully followed Sherrill's lead and passed a flaccid resolution only calling upon Germany to remove existing stumbling blocks to Jewish participation.[6]

In January 1934, America received its formal invitation to join fifty-three other nations at the Olympiad. To determine what course to take and ostensibly to give the issue a fair hearing, amid growing criticism from the AJCong, other American Jewish anti-Nazi organizations, and Brooklyn congressman Emanuel Celler, in the late summer of 1934 the AOC sent Brundage on a fact-finding mission to Berlin, which his hospitable guides had planned out carefully. Upon his return Brundage reported that the Reich was fulfilling its pledge to the world sports community. The Nazis prepared well for this putative investigation. They officially designated more than twenty-five athletes from Jewish sports clubs as candidates for their Olympic team. Brundage's guides did not belabor the fact that as non-Aryans they were not allowed to train in the national facilities, but he did not meet with leaders of Jewish sports clubs to hear their potentially different side of the story. Upon his return, the AOC approved the report of its president and on September 26, 1934, voted unanimously to "accept the invitation of the German Olympic Committee."[7]

In light of that troubling decision, the AJCong had hoped that the AAU would reiterate its 1933 stance and vote at its subsequent meeting in December 1934 to boycott the games. However, to the Jewish groups' dismay, the national athletic organization instead voted unanimously to follow the AOC's lead, with the caveat that if conditions against Jews would deteriorate further, the AAU would reconsider its stance. They gave effective credence to Brundage's report. The voters included thirteen Jewish delegates who may well have not trusted Brundage's advocacy but apparently felt that they did not have the votes to override the AOC's position. At that point, Judge Jeremiah T. Mahoney, the newly elected AAU president who succeeded Brundage, did not dissent. But when there was an intensification of physical attacks against Jews, most notably the Berlin Riot of July 1935, Mahoney resigned the presidency. He then became the most outspoken Christian opponent of the AOC and a profound critic of Brundage and was fullhearted in support of an appeal to American athletes to personally avoid participating in these tarnished games. In a 1935 pamphlet titled "Germany Has Violated the Olympic Code," he detailed, in what reads as a quasi-legal brief, all of the violations of Jewish rights that the Nazis had perpetrated to date. It was a written rebuttal to Brundage's earlier pamphlet called "Fair Play for American Athletes." There Brundage had asserted how this country's athletes should not be "martyrs" to a cause that was not their own. Through 1935–36, Brundage and Mahoney, former colleagues within the AAU leadership and now avowed enemies, exchanged verbal broadsides in the press and on the stump.[8]

The boycott movement gained the support of a variety of Christian religious groups, but most Americans, including American Jews, remained blithely unaware of or were unconcerned about the controversy. Still, American Jewish athletes who harbored Olympic aspirations had a difficult decision to make. As early as August 1934, a month before the AOC voted affirmatively to Brundage's report, Samuel Untermyer, head of the Non-Sectarian Anti-Nazi League to Champion Human Rights, implored "athletes and others of World Jewry . . . not only to [not] compete but to keep away as far as possible from any form of participation in the Olympic Athletic Games." He made it clear how "it is unthinkable that any self-respecting Jew would accept the hospitality of a country that persists in insulting, degrading and persecuting our people." He might have added, subsequently, that within Austria and Czechoslovakia, countries that were leaning strongly toward the Nazis, Jewish athletes and their sports clubs were either fined or suspended for supporting the boycott.[9]

After their defeat at the AOC conference table and when stymied by the AAU's reluctance to battle Brundage further, Mahoney and Charles Ornstein, a Jewish member of the AOC and the representative of the Jewish Welfare Board within the AAU, hit on the idea of an alternative, competing athletic event in New York City. After some deliberations, they forged a partnership with the Jewish Labor Committee and together sponsored a World Labor Carnival that took place on August 15 and 16, 1936, at New York's Randalls Island. Approximately 450 U.S. and Canadian athletes competed in this anti-Nazi sports festival. Some were boycotting the Berlin games, others had failed to make the American team and were anxious to showcase their abilities, and a few were Jewish Olympians who had run in the 1932 Los Angeles Olympiad. But this alternative did not inspire much interest among the most elite performers. The field at Randalls Island was not the great stadium in Berlin. When they received their postcard notifications from the AOC months before the carnival was to take place requiring them to confirm their participation in the Olympics, if they were fortunate enough to make the team, they readily signed on and did not change their minds.[10]

Herman Neugass, who ran track for Tulane University out of New Orleans, received that coveted invitation. His athletic bona fides included his tying of the world record in the 100-yard dash in 1935, and a few months before the Olympics he was the Southeastern Conference sprint champion. But he was fundamentally opposed to participating in Berlin and quietly declined the offer to suit up for the upcoming trials. His demurral to the AOC became public when a gentile teammate of his announced that he

77

would try to qualify for the games since Neugass, a Jew, apparently had no qualms about competing. In response, Neugass explained his decision in no uncertain terms in a letter that was published in the *New Orleans Times-Picayune*: "I will not participate," he wrote, "in games in any country in which the fundamental principle of religious liberty is violated as flagrantly and as inhumanely as it has been in Germany." He argued further that it was his firm conviction "as an American citizen who believes sincerely in the cardinal tenet of freedom of religions," no American athletes should take part in these tarnished events.[11]

Jewish teammates on Harvard's track team, Norman Cahners and Milton Green, were all set to try out for the squad until Green's rabbi raised his consciousness. Before Rabbi Harry Levi of Boston's Temple Israel met with the two aspiring Olympians, neither of them had much of a notion of "the terrible things that were going on in Germany and the Nazi regime." Levi convinced them that they would never regret boycotting the games. Unlike Neugass, neither athlete publicly announced their decision, but when Green told his coach that he had declined, the mentor tried to persuade him, arguing that a refusal "would not do any good." Norman Cahners remained quite the popular fellow on campus. He was elected, in a highly competitive election, as one of two student representatives to speak at the university's Tercentenary Celebration to a crowd of some ten thousand alumni and a worldwide radio broadcast. He chose athletics as his topic, but there is no evidence that he referenced the Olympic controversy in his oration.[12]

Amid the 1935–36 basketball season, the Long Island University (LIU) basketball team, boasting a 25–0 record, was arguably the best college club in America. In those days, there was no official national championship tournament. The team's eight top performers, some Jews, some Christians, were prime candidates to represent their country in Berlin. Leo Merson, a Jewish player from Brownsville, Brooklyn, felt great pressure from his family, and from those in his neighborhood, to refuse the call to try out for the team. It is not known how his teammates felt initially about the chance to play on an international stage. However, at a players-only meeting, they agreed that if only one fellow demurred the whole group would stay away. When it became public that the Blackbirds voted to not show up at Madison Square Garden for the qualifying games, they endured some newspaper criticism for creating "ill feelings" and for giving "the wrong answer from a sports angle." The players did not announce why they had turned down the offer. Still, these athletes were warmed when their university president stood by them, asserting that "our conviction [is] that the United States should not participate" notwithstanding "the fact that our basketball team is now recognized generally as a possible Olympic representative."[13]

Over at CCNY, the renowned "Jewish college" of America and Mahoney's alma mater, there was, from the outset of the protest movement, widespread support for boycotting the games. Those who wanted to go to Berlin from their school were occasionally criticized within that campus community. In the fall of 1935, the City College Athletic Association (CCAA), with its all-Jewish seven-man board, positioned itself at the forefront of a schoolwide campaign to deny Hitler a major propaganda coup through the use of sports. The rank-and-file students needed little convincing of the correctness of this cause because it intersected with two fundamental values that they held dear. They were worried about the fate of their coreligionists under the heel of the Third Reich. And politically speaking, many of them, who harbored left-leaning feelings to begin with, were opposed to fascism of any sort worldwide. The same Great Hall, CCNY's major auditorium, that was the site of a "Boycott Olympics" rally in October 1935 was only three weeks later the venue for a "Mobilize for Peace Assembly."[14]

The college's student newspaper, *The Campus*, was full-throated in support of Mahoney's position as it asserted, "We will refuse to add America's 'Heil' to the Hitler madness." It also upbraided the editors of the *Yale News* for characterizing the boycott as "patently absurd." The view from St. Nicholas Heights was that their Ivy

League counterparts had "forsake[n] every ideal of the further-ance of humanity which is, in the final analysis, the end of all edu-cation." Student activists—CCAA leaders and others—proactively solicited thousands of signatures on petitions at CCNY, attempted to take the cause to other campuses, and garnered statements of support from most of the school's coaches, who decried "race dis-crimination." Nat Holman hoped that in "fairness to other ath-letes and athletes of all other countries" a more fitting location had to be found for the games. But if "the games are held in Berlin, we certainly should not participate." Lacrosse coach Leon "Chief" Miller, a Native American who had played at the Carlisle School with the legendary Jim Thorpe and who faced much discrimina-tion in his own life, empathized with "the restrictions and inhibi-tions" placed "on so-called non-Aryans athletes" in the Reich. He asserted that Germany was no place for American sportsmen.

The CCAA understood the sacrifice their elite performers were making in being part of an academic and social community that bore "the distinction of being one of the few institutions of higher learning which officially subordinated its selfish desires for a pos-sible Olympic winner to the moral principle of what it believes right and wrong." It was recognized that some of CCNY's out-standing basketball players, much like the fellows at LIU, deemed on campus to be "athletes of Olympic caliber," might have been selected to play on the team. For what it was worth, President Frederick B. Robinson, unlike his counterpart at LIU, did not di-rectly address the dilemma his Jewish athletes faced. From where he stood, "it would be better for America to send a powerful team to the Olympics including its best Jewish athletes and gain greater glory for our own country and for the Jewish people world-wide." But the student body, which was often at loggerheads with the administration on a variety of social and political issues, really did not care about his feelings.[15]

Elite CCNY trackman Benny Zlatnick was among the athletes whom the boycott campaign convinced to forgo the chance to try out for the Berlin games. This "erstwhile 200 meters sprint star," *The Campus* reported proudly, "has turned the other way." However, not everyone on campus fell into line. An outstanding fencer, S. Thompson Stewart, perhaps a Christian student, was totally unmoved by the protests. This tenth-ranked national saber man let the school paper know that for him "politics should [not] be permitted to interfere with athletics." The paper, known to pull no punches, did not criticize Stewart's position. But a student reporter went after the athlete's coach, Joseph Vince, taking him to task for his "non-compliance" with all journalistic requests to "clarify his views on American participation in the Olympics." First, Vince refused to comment on his disciple's decision, and when asked whether as a coach he would "go to Berlin . . . if you happen to be chosen [to coach]," he would only "smile" and say to a jaundiced correspondent, who lampooned the coach's foreign accented English, "that I cannot answer."[16]

However, other Jews hoped to receive that long-awaited postcard invitation from the AOC and then were thrilled when they qualified. And when they made the team and benefitted from the largesse of erstwhile boycott leader Charles Ornstein, who "helped pay the hotel bills of several members of the team while they were in New York" and "bought shoes for a couple of trackmen," these athletes were reassured that they were not traitors to a cause that had run its course.[17]

At the basketball tryouts at Madison Square Garden, a reporter asked UCLA's Sam Balter whether he was "going to go to the Olympics" given that "they're being held in Hitler's Germany." Prior to that question, Balter "had never given it a moment's thought." For three months thereafter, Balter considered the ramifications of his projected participation and felt pressure from Jewish groups to decline. But others told him "that it was absolutely imperative that [he] play." This reasoning was "what kind of propaganda team would it be if . . . there were no Jews on the team." Brundage's assurances convinced him to board the S.S. *Manhattan* to fulfill his "lifetime . . . dream to be an Olympian." Once in Germany, Balter had some second thoughts about his decision, first when upon arrival in Hamburg Hermann Göring greeted the team and went overboard in "praising the German government"; he was also taken aback when he set foot in the Olympic Village and was handed propaganda brochures "with caricatures of hooked-nosed people." Still, he stayed on the team and won his gold medal. It was a triumph that he deemed as "the greatest achievement of his life." Balter believed that the publicity from his playing in Berlin "helped launch his career as a successful Los Angeles radio, and later TV, sportscaster."[18]

As a sixteen- or seventeen-year-old youngster still in high school when the Olympic participation imbroglio began, and then as an eighteen-year-old freshman at Syracuse when crucial personal decisions had to be made, Marty Glickman did not articulate a position about the controversy that was engulfing those who fought the AOC or those who backed away from the games and the others who decided to play. Glickman would recall that as a political science major he was well aware of the Nuremberg Laws and for a brief moment while at school even considered dropping out and joining the opponents of fascism who were fighting in the Spanish Civil War. That war, which has been characterized as a "dress rehearsal for World War II," began a month or so before he enrolled at Syracuse. But he kept that radical thought to himself. In a dark moment, Glickman may well have thought that those Jewish athletes who supported the boycott might well be among those who could not make the team. Fellow high-class runner Herman Neugass would not have agreed. Nor would those LIU fellows who played just a few neighborhoods away from where he grew up.[19]

If he had picked up the *Syracuse Daily Orange* when he arrived on campus in September 1935, Glickman would have noticed Ed O'Brien's column on his travels to Germany the prior summer and his views about the upcoming Olympics. O'Brien, the athlete who eventually shared a cabin with Glickman on the S.S. *Manhattan*, was a big man on campus. His track exploits were chronicled regularly in the newspaper. What this Olympic hopeful had to say undeniably carried weight both among fellow athletes and within the larger university community. In his article, after reporting that he and his fellow Americans "were treated very well by all Germans," he submitted that "I see no reason why we should not send a team." He was "convinced that the racial and religious question is purely a domestic affair" and that "all the athletes with whom I have talked believed" as he did. To do otherwise, according to O'Brien, would "impugn the good sportsmanship of the United States."[20]

Not everyone at the school concurred. A few days after O'Brien's opinion piece appeared, an unnamed writer to the editor—identified only as H. B.—argued that "America with its several Jewish athletic stars should not allow a team to be sent to Germany" to enjoy the "companionship of a people that commits atrocities." Athletic administrator Dr. Leslie Bryan felt similarly. In November 1936 he told the *Syracuse Daily Orange* that the Olympics should be transferred from Berlin. He did not, however, call for his athletes to boycott the game, if the Olympics remained where they were planned. The student body president backed Bryan asserting that the upcoming event was "not good for sports and it would not disgrace America if she stayed out." But the prior year's captain of the track team, Eldon Stutzman, not only echoed O'Brien's views but even questioned the accuracy of reporting about German behavior. For him, "the U.S. is making a big mistake, if it does not participate. . . . There is so much ballyhoo concerning Germany that you can't believe half of the stuff that is written." This opinion sat well with O'Brien, who in a subsequent article submitted how "most of the opinions offered are from people who have no interest in sports."[21]

In the spring of 1936, the *Syracuse Daily Orange* dutifully reported on the mostly successful attempts of Syracuse athletes to qualify for the games. There would be no organized boycott at that school. When the campus radio station interviewed track coach Tom Keane in May 1936, the focus was solely on how well Syracuse runners might do in Germany. If there was any pressure on freshman Glickman as the intensity of the debate subsided, it would be if he decided not to try out.[22]

Notwithstanding all that was said within and without Marty Glickman's earshot, in retrospect he would assert that the boycott movement "didn't make much of an impression on me or most of the athletes striving to make our Olympic team." As he remembered his feelings as the games approached, "There never was any question . . . about going to Germany. Ever since I realized that I could run fast, I aspired above all to be an Olympian." Though clearly the protesters had their say in some quarters, they made no impact upon Glickman, who did not hear a "hue and cry not to go," not from a rabbi, not from his Jewish friends, "not one member of any organization . . . *nobody* [emphasis his] said, 'Marty don't go.' including [his] folks." The World Labor Carnival was certainly not for him. He was aware of the Nazi policies toward Jews. But for him this treatment did not differ much from "persecutions Jews had suffered from time to time in all parts of the world" including the United States, where there was "bigotry and exclusion right here at home." What he did know—and what his family had impressed upon him from an early age—was that a "Jewish youngster was never inferior to anyone else." If he thought at all about making a statement about Nazism, he would do it on the cinder track of the Berlin Olympic stadium. His private position was that he would show that "if a Jew could win, it would disprove this myth of Aryan superiority." Although it may have dawned upon him that there had not been many great American Jewish athletes competing in prior Olympics, he did not "carry a burden of Jewishness" to the track. He would not be competing for the Jewish people—as he focused in 1936 on qualifying for the track team.[23]

Though some sports wags had predicted that Glickman had only "a 50 to 1 shot for the Olympic team" back in February, after he raced to a "surprising" second-place finish in the 60-yard dash at the prestigious Millrose Games in Madison Square Garden, a confident Glickman had already told his friends that he would "be

in Berlin in August." But to get there he had to outrun a group
of outstanding, world-class athletes who also coveted a spot. The
competitors included Marquette University's Ralph Metcalfe,
Jackie Robinson's brother Mack, who ran for the University of
Oregon, Frank Wykoff and Foy Draper of the University of
Southern California, Sam Stoller of Michigan, and Jesse Owens
of Ohio State University. Owens was the odds-on-favorite in the
sprint events. To have a ticket punched to line up in the games'
individual 100-meter event, a sprinter had to come in first, second,
or third. The fourth through seven finishers would be designated
as teammates in the 4 × 100 meters relay. The 100-meter dash
ended in what we would call a "photo finish," with Glickman, at
first glance, in third place, besting Wykoff and Draper in a very
close call. However, Dean Cromwell, the University of Southern
California coach and soon to be the U.S. track coach at the
Olympics, protested the original decision, arguing that his men
crossed the line ahead of Glickman. When the judges ultimately
concurred, Glickman was pushed down to fifth. Still, though disappointed and confused that the officials' reversal had pushed him
away from the individual 100-meter competition, he had nonetheless achieved his Olympic goal.[24]

Having first made what would turn out to be a momentous
decision to run in the forthcoming games, and then having succeeded in his quest at that qualifying meet on Randalls Island,
Glickman packed his bags and proudly included in his luggage
every piece of the American Olympic outfit, which consisted of
a "white straw hat, blue blazer with the Olympic shield and white
pants." He might have had a new pair of running shoes, courtesy
of Charles Ornstein. He did not stand out in the crowd when the
S.S. *Manhattan* dropped the team off in Hamburg, on the way by
train to the German capital. However, when his teammates and he
arrived at the city's main train station, amid a crush of reporters,
an American Jewish medical student expatriate recognized him
and sought Glickman out to explain what he was doing in Hitler's
Reich. This young man was studying to be a physician in the heart

of Nazi territory because he "could not get into an American medical school because of quotas" that limited the number of Jews admitted in his home country. It is not known how this interlocutor gained a seat in a German medical college given its own severe restrictions against Jews. No matter; this brief encounter did not upset Glickman, though he long remembered that meeting. If anything, that brief conversation confirmed for him the correctness of his decision to be among his fellow champions from America at the athletic carnival over which Hitler would preside. At this point, he still believed "anti-Semitism was anti-Semitism no matter how you sliced it." There was anti-Semitism at his home university too, even if it did not really affect his life as a student, and now he was on his way to fulfill his Olympic dream. In addition, he and the other U.S. competitors were warmly received at the train station and on the route to the Olympic Village. Glickman wrote to his parents, "Thousands of people lined the streets . . . it was like a Broadway parade. . . . Men who had been with former Olympic teams said this was by far the greatest reception ever given to an Olympic team." An American sports reporter at the dock heartily agreed: "All the worry about how the Jewish members of our Olympic team would be greeted on their arrival has been dissipated." They were unnoticed. After all, the writer mused, while counting incorrectly the ethnic backgrounds of the athletes, "Only Marty Glickman and Sam Stoller are Jewish."[25]

Once ensconced in the Olympic Village, Glickman and Stoller went about their business almost anonymously as they prepared for their event. As the games proceeded, the talk of the American team, and just about everywhere else in Berlin, was the victories of Jesse Owens in three individual track events, the 100- and 200-meter dashes and the long jump. Each triumph gave the lie on the biggest stage to Hitler's dream of using German victories in these international games to project the image of Aryan supremacy to the world. As far as "the two Jewish members of the American team" were concerned, the *New York World Telegram* stated that "Marty Glickman and Sam Stoller are going about training without either attention or annoyance, neither of which was anticipated." According to the on-the-scene report the only time the two young men "were conspicuous subjects was when Mr. Bill Bingham, manager of the American track and field team came across" them chowing down a breakfast that included many slices of bacon. It was not noted what Bingham thought about these Jews' culinary choices. Glickman did not care. Most likely, the AOC track and field chairman, who had backed Brundage's reportage about alleging favorable Jewish conditions in Germany during the boycott controversy, was pleased about how well these boys were fitting in among his other charges at the training table. Back home, if the Glickman family checked out the *New York Evening Journal*'s roving photographer shots of happy American Olympians enjoying their camaraderie at a team meal, they would have noted that Marty Glickman, "one of the two Jews on the squad," was a pictured athlete "quaffing his thirst while Roland Romero, best of our hop, step and jump looks on." At the next table sat Glen Cunningham, "ace in the 1,500 meters," shown accommodating an autograph seeker. The Glickmans had to have been proud that while their boy was identified as "one of the two Jews on the squad," he was fitting in comfortably with his fellow "stars who will represent Uncle Sam at the international games in Berlin."[26]

A few days before Glickman and Stoller were set to run the *New Yorker* ran a cartoon that predicted victories for the two Jewish runners and embarrassment for the Nazis. Rabbi Louis I. Newman of New York described the image as depicting a "race in which handsome Nordics are taking part only to meet defeat at the hands of a little hairy-legged Semite." The stereotyping of his fellow Jews did not offend the good rabbi, and he too prognosticated that Glickman and Stoller would triumph. Newman also happily applauded a report that "the Nazi Storm-troopers" stationed to guard the athletes in the village "are saluting negroes [*sic*] and Jews in defiance of Nazi ideology and preachment." A Chicago Jewish sportswriter gleefully announced that "Glickman and

Stoller are getting a big kick out of having stalwart Nazi storm-troopers greet them a dozen times a day with 'Heil Hitler.' What Stoller and Glickman said in reply we leave to your imagination." But we do know, based on a Glickman letter to his folks, that he wrote, "I get along with my German pretty well. I understand it very well." His facility was based on his rudimentary knowledge of Yiddish that he picked up from his basically English-speaking home. Dealing with the foreign language barrier, Glickman "often helped the other fellows." No one cared how he had acquired that linguistic proficiency. As far as those storm troopers were concerned, Marty reassured his parents, "there are lots of uniforms here. Every time a uniformed man passes any of us they always salute. We have lots of fun with them." Had anyone asked what they then thought of Hitler, he most probably would have said, like most American Olympians, in a decidedly disrespectful manner, "he looks like Charley Chaplin."[27]

For Glickman and his baseball teammate Herman Goldberg, the only potentially troublesome occurrence with Germans took place when they ventured out of the village and hitchhiked to the Olympic stadium to watch some of the proceedings. A driver and sports fan who just happened to be a Wehrmacht lieutenant picked them up and asked for their autographs. Concerned about the reaction of this military man to their readily identifiable Jewish surname, Glickman and Goldberg waited for the moment when they were dropped off and then quickly scribbled their signatures. The officer remained all smiles.

The friendliness of those stationed patrolmen and the lieutenant may have had much to do with instructions passed down to the general population in *Der Angriff*, an official Nazi publication. In an effort to project the most positive image of their country to visitors, every citizen was called upon "to be a host" as these games were nothing less than "a historic opportunity to do away with all the prejudice against the German nation that was mounting in many quarters." Nazi chief Goebbels viewed the games as "the propaganda possibility of a lifetime." For him, every "shop owner, taxi driver, train conductor, waiter or policeman" could be trained to be "politically-oriented propaganda men." The home crowd was told to be "more charming than Parisians, more easygoing than the Viennese, more vivacious than the Romans [Italians] more cosmopolitan than London" and even "more practical than New Yorkers." Including Gotham's denizens as possessing positive qualities for Berliners to emulate ran totally counter to what Nazi anti-Semites spewed daily about those who lived in the largest Jewish city in the world. But at this moment, in front of a world at play, the Reich wanted to be liked.[28]

Nazi officials at the Berlin Olympic Stadium. Credit: Courtesy of the United States Holocaust Memorial Museum, Wendie Theus.

5

SIDELINED IN BERLIN

In the days leading up to the 4 × 100 meters relay race in the Berlin Olympic Stadium, ticketed as a signature event within the games and scheduled for the final day of competition, Marty Glickman strolled confidently among competitors from more than fifty nations from all over the world and made friends easily. Thinking back to the opening ceremonies, a week or so earlier, he was gratified to wear his country's colors and proud that he, like all American athletes, did not raise their arms to Hitler in the Olympic salute that awfully resembled how the Germans paid tribute to their leader. The most the U.S. contingent would do was to turn "eyes right" as they passed the führer's box in the grandstands. Perhaps it was then, when they spied Hitler, that the joking about him looking like Charlie Chaplin began in their midst. As an American patriot, Glickman was also pleased how his team's flag carrier did not dip Old Glory to a foreign potentate as other countries did. Right then and there, his only concerns were athletic and he was sure he could handle them. As his teammates and he prepared assiduously for their moment on the track, they worked hard to master the crucial baton-passing technique to ensure a smooth handoff at the end of every stage of the race. If Glickman had any nightmares, they would be the frightening vision of dropping the cylinder, which would have disqualified his foursome. He had no prescience of the real-life horror that awaited him a day before the race in a small room within the Olympic Village. There he and Sam Stoller would be set apart from all other U.S. athletes. They were sidelined while fellow trackmen competed.[1]

All had thus gone blissfully well for Glickman until what he would call "the meeting" took place on August 8, 1936. As Glickman repeatedly told the story of his and Sam Stoller's exclusion from the competition, the trouble began when the track coaches, Dean Cromwell and his assistant Lawson Robertson, spoke about a worrisome but unconfirmed report that "the Germans were hiding their best sprinters saving them for the 400-meter relay to upset the heavily favored American team." To stop the Germans in their tracks, they determined that Stoller and Glickman were to be replaced by Jesse Owens and Ralph Metcalfe, who would join Foy Draper and Frank Wykoff, two of Cromwell's protégés from the University of Southern California, on the squad. At that point Glickman had to have sadly recalled that if Cromwell had not interceded in favor of his guys back at the Randalls Island Olympic qualifying meet—and through effective force of influence had not pushed him out of the individual 100-meter competition in Berlin—Cromwell's fears and his argument would have been moot. In his darkest moments, Glickman might have wondered what the coaches would have done in Berlin if he had just run a few steps faster in New York and whether that early intercession had been preplanned for the moment at hand.[2]

Reacting to this unexpected challenge, Glickman broke the "stunned silence in the room" and brashly rebutted the coach: "There'd be no reason to believe the Germans are any kind of threat." It was clear to Glickman, and probably to all his teammates, that their opponents had no such hidden world-class runners. In addition, the previously designated foursome had been practicing as a team for ten days. Putting in last-minute substitutes who might fumble the stick was just bad strategy. And if indeed there was a real threat in the offing, while nobody could outrun Owens, the fact was that in practices Glickman and Stoller outpaced Draper and Wykoff. So much for sending the best four men to the track. Rising to support his teammates, Owens told the coaches, "Let Marty and Sam run, they deserve it. I've already won three gold medals. I'm tired. They haven't had the chance to run. Let them run." Cromwell shut down Owens's position immediately and curtly. Pointing a finger at Owens, he declared, "You will do as you are told." Owens would say no more, nor would his fellow teammates, Black or white, step up to support the Jewish runners. Still unwilling to accept this decision, Glickman almost had the last word. "Coach, you know," he said, "Sam and I are the only two Jews on the track team, there's bound to be a lot of criticism back home." It remained for Cromwell to end the unequal conversation between coaches and performers with "we'll take our chances." Cromwell's intuition that the incident would blow over proved to be largely correct.

"Angry and confused, not able to digest it all" and deeply frustrated, Glickman, when the substitute racers were called to the starting line without him and Stoller, sat alone in the athletes' reserve section of the grandstands, located only a hundred feet away from the chancellor's box, where Hitler sat with his entourage. As Glickman witnessed the American team win the race in world-record pace—a time that would last for twenty years—"frustration" and "a desire for revenge welled up within" him.

In the days and weeks that followed, Glickman felt even more alone as almost no one came to his side. Cromwell unabashedly defended his decision. Robertson privately articulated just the meagerest of regrets. The general media's reactions ranged from backers of Cromwell's, Robertson's, and their boss Brundage's actions to those who hoped that the whole unhappy incident would not cloud the glory of American victories at the games, especially how Owens destroyed Aryan myths, to those who thought that the big controversy out of the American camp was Brundage's out-of-line involvement, not in the Glickman and Stoller case but in his sidelining of a female athlete who had violated the AOC's training rules. Looking ahead, they wished that the heavy-handed Brundage would not oversee future teams. Some writers even had some uncharitable words about

Glickman's and Stoller's reactions. Friendlier scribes acknowledged the runners' immediate sadness but were pleased with
how upbeat they appeared to be.

If Marty Glickman had been sent copies of the *Brooklyn Daily
Eagle*'s coverage of the "meeting" and its aftermath, he had to have
been very annoyed that the paper, which his family and friends
read, also did not focus on the problems he and Stoller faced. It
preferred to headline the treatment of the woman who offended
Brundage. Most disconcerting was the approach of some major
Jewish newspapers, which stopped very short of seeing the ouster
as an act of anti-Semitism. Rather they praised the boys for not
dwelling on discrimination as the root cause of their exclusion
and advised them to move on with their careers. In Glickman's
case that meant preparing for the upcoming fall football season at
Syracuse University. These reactions from all sources chilled whatever hopes Glickman could have had that anyone, Jew or non-Jew,
would rally to protest his exclusion.

Within this atmosphere, wherever he turned, the most Glickman
would say about why he was out of the race was "politics." Then,
and for decades thereafter, Glickman would use vague terms to
publicly depict what had transpired during those days in Berlin
that turned ugly. When queried, Glickman kept to himself his own
certain belief that anti-Semitism—and not nepotism or favoritism
on the part of Cromwell toward his protégés—was the reason he
was not permitted to run and triumph.

When he returned to campus in the fall of 1936, all he would
remark about the sidelining was that he was "greatly disappointed."
Otherwise, he tendered a positive report about the games even as
he pledged to those around him that come the next Olympiad in
1940, he would "win it all." He consoled himself that with three
years to go at Syracuse running track and playing football, he
would refine his skills, and look forward to subsequent triumphs
on the international stage. Yet the 1940 Olympiad, slated first for
Tokyo and then for Helsinki, Finland, never took place as the
world was by then entrenched in the Second World War.[3]

After the most traumatic moment in his life, Sam Stoller might have been consoled for a brief time when on the boat back home to the United States Lawson Robertson came up to him "and very apologetically admitted that he had made a mistake in not letting me run." The coach revealed that he "stayed awake nights thinking of it and his entire trip was spoiled on that account." The coach did not make clear precisely what were the origins of the mistake for which he was seeking forgiveness. By the time he landed in New York, Robertson had gotten over his discomfit. He told reporters, "The fact that Stoller and Glickman are Jewish had absolutely nothing to do with their removal. I hope no one misconstrues the move." Stoller never recovered from the sidelining, announcing that he would "never run again." When he returned to the University of Michigan for his senior year, he competed but was never again the same as an athlete, and in many respects his life was ruined.[4]

Dean Cromwell slept very well as he crossed the Atlantic, satisfied with his actions and feelings about what he might have called the "Jewish question." He gave voice to his prejudicial views two months after the Olympics in a speech in Los Angeles to three thousand cheering followers of the German American Alliance: "If you read any of the reports of the unpleasantness in Germany or of the reception of the American Olympic team, don't believe them. The reports were written by boys of the wrong nationality." He more than implied that the critical writers were Jewish scribes from New York when he asserted that "only one-seventh of the population" in that city were American-born. He vowed never again to set foot where the ocean liner had dropped him off in that un-American locale. Three weeks later, Brundage seconded his close colleague's opinion, though he offered his strong remarks in New York. Speaking at a German Day rally in Madison Square Garden, he asserted that he stood foursquare against "aliens who seek to undermine our American institutions. . . . We can learn much from Germany." Back in Los Angeles, Cromwell backed off from his statement when his university president, under criticism from alumni, called for an "immediate investigation." In defense, he called his remarks "jocular." Still, Cromwell survived the school's inquiries into his opinions. When all was said and then not done, he remained in his post for another twelve years. The word on the street among Jewish athletes in Los Angeles was that they would not be welcomed on his squad.[5]

In his lengthy report to the AOC composed soon after the games, Brundage, to offset criticism, asserted how "an erroneous report was circulated that two athletes had been dropped from the American Olympic relay team because of their religion." These unnamed athletes, of course, were Glickman and Stoller and "had been taken only as substitutes." For Brundage, the best men had been picked to represent the country, and their world-record performance had "proved the wisdom of adhering to the rules." The nationally renowned sportswriter and broadcaster Grantland Rice weighed in, similarly stating, "Lawson Robertson . . . picked the best U.S. team regardless of race and color thereby using wise judgment despite any criticism." His colleague, *New York Times* reporter John Kiernan, agreed that "Robbie added speed to his . . . relay team by the change and easily could justify himself on that score." A far as Glickman and Stoller were concerned, Kiernan asserted that while "when the news was flashed back to the United States there was a cry that Hitlerian influence had been at work," there was no kowtowing to the Nazis in this strategic move. The "two Negroes"—Owens and Metcalfe, who replaced the two Jews—"wouldn't have sent Herr Hitler into raptures . . . even if he had paid attention to it." What Kiernan chose to ignore was the different attitudes of the Reich toward Black as opposed to Jewish athletes. In their telling of what transpired in their games, the Nazis submitted that Owens and his teammates were "auxiliaries" brought over by their American masters to perform for the United States. Jewish athletes were a very different breed among the country's minorities. In response, Jeremiah T. Mahoney, who was still uniquely vigorous on the offensive against the coaches and ultimately against Brundage, his nemesis of long standing, was quick to riposte, "Denials to the contrary, it was pure anti-Semitism that kept Sam Stoller and Marty Glickman from competing." But it was a rare commentator who would speak even obliquely about anti-Semitism in Berlin.[6]

On-the-scene reporter Jesse Abramson, correspondent for the *Herald Tribune*, was not nearly as explicit as Mahoney was in suggesting that religious prejudice was in play at the "meeting." In his coverage of the sidelining, Abramson took note that "Lawson . . . taking full responsibility" for the switch in runners was "severely censured in American quarters for his selections." The coach "seems to have gone out of his way to break the hearts of the two sprinters" as they "became the only athletes who did not compete in the Olympics." As to why this decision was made, Abramson allowed only facetiously, in the very last line of his article, "It is only a coincidence that they also are the only Jewish boys on the track team."[7]

Famous sports cartoonist Phil Berube, on the other hand, described Glickman as far from heartbroken. Rather, his drawing depicted the runner as "disappointed but happy." Next to his image of a smiling athlete in U.S. team garb, he wrote, "Lightning speed of Owens, Metcalfe prevented Glickman from competing in the U.S. Olympic 400 meter relay team. . . . Disappointed, he cheered the rest when the time record was broken!" Shown sitting on a trainer's stool, thinking ahead, Glickman, this "slick man on the gridiron," was musing, "Ah well, football season will be on soon."[8]

In Abramson's follow-up observation, two days later, as part of a long piece on Olympic track results, he calmly noted that the relay "was the romp everyone except Lawson Robertson . . . expected it to be" as the foursome cruised to a world record triumph. The writer repeated that the two excluded sprinters had "every right to be on the team," even if "the team might not have broken the record." The Jewish issue was not mentioned.[9]

The *New York Times* picked up the story of Glickman and Stoller and the 400-meter race three days before the "meeting." It then reported that Robertson felt that Owens, "the Ohio State Negro has done just about enough in one Olympics," and that despite the runner's protestations would not participate in the relay. Though the coach had not "yet decided who will make up the 400 meter team," Glickman and Stoller were "considered certainties on the basis of trials the last two days." The day of the event that took place without the Jews, the paper noted only that criticism might be forthcoming from "those Americans who feel that as many of the boys as possible should get a chance to compete." There might be some criticism afoot because the AOC had violated a fair play canon. However, the much bigger story that garnered far more attention in the newspaper was the ongoing battle between Brundage and Eleanor Holm Jarrett.

Jarrett was one of the key "non-conformists" on the ship bearing the Olympic athletes during its passage across the Atlantic. Because of "drinking and parties" in violation of training rules, Jarrett, the reigning 1932 Olympic 100-meter backstroke champion, was dismissed from the American team when the boat reached Hamburg. The AOC head had alluded to her in speaking to a *Times* reporter on the boat, noting that she had been identified and severely punished. Yet beyond punishment for that onboard transgression, Brundage now was intent on disqualifying Jarrett from future competitions, alleging that she had forfeited her amateur status through "cover[ing] the Olympics for a newspaper syndicate." Showing which contretemps intrigued the newspaper more, it was said on the day of the relay race, "American Olympic officials [had] spent a worrisome day as a result of *some adverse comment* over the dropping of two Jewish sprinters . . . as well as the reverberations in the *celebrated* case involving Mrs. Eleanor Holm Jarrett." One source of aggravation for Brundage was a letter sent to the AOC from a *Times* reader who identified herself as a "teetotaler." Her complaint was that Holm Jarrett "did what thousands of our so-called best people are doing every day" since repeal of Prohibition. "Why pick on her? Public opinion demands that you reinstate Mrs. Jarrett. Justice and fair play demand it." No letters appeared about Glickman and Stoller. As far as the report on the American victory in the race was concerned, it was simply pitched as part of a large article on Olympic results, as but another American victory and "in record time."[10]

An article within the tabloid *New York Daily News* implied that Brundage had a special affinity for the Nazis and was a stick-in-the-mud to boot. It referred to the head of the American athletic group as *"Herr Doktor* Avery Brundage, the chief *wowser* of the AOC on temperance, morals and prohibition of everything." This killjoy, it was said, was continuing his unnecessary campaign against Jarrett and it predicted facetiously that "immediately upon his return to the United States, *Doktor* Brundage will storm the country demanding the death penalty for Mrs. Jarrett."[11]

Columnist Jack Micey had enough of both battlers: "I am sick and tired to hear what Avery [Blue Nose] Brundage has to say about Eleanor Holm and vice versa. . . . I do wish the two hair-pullers would please pipe down." Articles in his paper that detailed Brundage's ongoing moves against the athlete and Holm's efforts to benefit financially from the imbroglio's publicity bored him. He believed that the bigger story was the triumphs of athletes like Owens and "some of those other Yankees who are defending the good old Star Spangled Banner over in Berlin."[12]

Fellow columnist Jimmy Powers wanted his readers to know that notwithstanding Hitler's reported snubbing of Black athletes "the conduct of the German fans in Deutschland" was exemplary in sports venues that were "spotless" and that the "United States team was given the best quarters in the Olympic Village." There they were happily off souvenir hunting among their fellow competitors. For Powers, the most important news was that "this year . . . we are tops" as America was on the road to garner the most medals. The Glickman-Stoller controversy was only briefly referenced in a report from an Associated Press dispatch that noted how Glickman allowed that the "influential" Cromwell was "looking out for Southern Californians." He did not cite Jew hatred as the reason for Cromwell's decision.[13]

During the Berlin Olympiad, the *World Telegram* covered the games more extensively than any other New York newspaper. Every day, results and features appeared on page one. In the sports section, columnist Joe Williams contributed on-the-scene pieces on major developments and interesting human interest stories. Famous sports cartoonist Willard Mullin chipped in his own creations. Both Williams and Mullin had much to say, or to depict, about how Owens's victories struck at the heart of Hitler's myths about race. Newspaper editorialists decisively rebutted Nazi allegations that these Black athletes were essentially hired hands, if not slaves, brought to Berlin by their white overseers to perform for America. For these writers, "Owens's triumphs—and America's—is in no way diminished by the silly attitude of Nazi propagandists who are saying that our commanding place in the international contest is due to what they call our 'black auxiliary force.'"

When the Jarrett and Glickman-Stoller stories broke the day after the "meeting," the newspaper focused its headline attention on the barring of the woman athlete. Much like other papers, the runners' problems were neither emphasized nor editorialized, although it was noted that "Marty Glickman, the New York Jewish boy," did "hurl" an accusation that "politics influenced the revisions of the American sprint relay team."

Two days later, the editorialists went after Brundage, in no uncertain terms, over the Jarrett incident. For them, the AOC leader "has gone as far as he needs to, we believe, in competing for the blunderers title." These writers had nothing to say about Glickman and Stoller. Subsequently, Williams offered a comparable final word about AOC leadership over what they did to the woman swimmer. "In view of the strange conduct of the Olympic brass hats on this trip, I am beginning to believe an entirely independent set of examinations should be introduced to apply to officials. Some of these possess a positive genius for behaving like old women."

However, as far as the coaches' decision was concerned, Williams believed "as a result of the meeting the four *originally* picked by Robertson took the field and not only won the race but broke the world record." Glickman and Stoller were not really replaced; the right runners had toed the cinder marks.[14]

As far as Glickman's "hometown" newspaper, the *Brooklyn Daily Eagle*, the very organ that had dutifully followed his athletic exploits from grammar school through his first year in college, was concerned, the treatment of the Jewish athletes also did not grab the top billing. Like the papers back in Manhattan, whose words were read nationally, there was no editorial comment about the exclusion offered out of Brooklyn. On the day of the controversial race, the paper's boldfaced page one headline read, "Mrs. Jarrett Defiant under Permanent Ban; U.S. Takes Decathlon." "Marty Glickman Says Politics was Reason for His Ouster" appeared at the bottom of four subheadings. The Jarrett story continued on page 28, headlined as "Permanent Ban on Mrs. Jarrett Raises Her Ire." Below that statement, the paper reported, "Glickman joins in attack on actions of Olympic Officials," and in the very last paragraph of the long article it was noted that "Glickman bitterly assailed the coaches for *favoring* the Californian [runners] under circumstances which seemed likely to develop further repercussions before the 1936 Olympics books are closed." Once again, when in this case a conceivably sympathetic Brooklyn reporter wrote about Glickman, he made no reference to anti-Semitism. No further discussion of the incident took place while the team was overseas.

A day later, on August 10, a short article appeared praising how well the U.S. team was doing in the games, as it earned the "highest honors since '12 games." At the bottom of the piece, it was again indicated that Stoller and Glickman had "lost their place on the sprint team" and that Stoller had announced he had decided to "give up running" because "he had not been treated fairly in being dropped from the team." But the newspaper offered no details about why that athlete had been excluded.[15]

On September 2, 1936, the *Brooklyn Daily Eagle* revealed that trouble was brewing between Olympic athletes and Brundage's officials. The leaders were "scurrying for cover in the face of a law suit for damages" filed by the Jarrett family. On another front, the young people were complaining that the AOC was "ordering them to barnstorm" throughout the country "as though they were hired hands" to enable the American committee to recoup expenses. One additional publicized complaint was that on the ship back from Germany, AOC officials provided themselves with first-class cabins while the sportsmen and women were relegated to second-class accommodations. To the players' minds they were the stars of the games, not the badge wearers. For correspondent George Currie, the "one *cheerful* note," as squabbles were clearly afoot in various quarters, was that Stoller told him that the runner "unqualifiedly refused to believe that Lawson Robertson . . . left him and Marty Glickman off the 400 meter team because they were Jewish."[16]

In the weeks that followed, with Glickman back at Syracuse and with the 1936 football season on the horizon, the *Brooklyn Daily Eagle*'s sports staff did not revisit the events that had transpired in Berlin. These writers' and columnists' attention, and very likely the interest of the general public, turned to wondering how this star running back would do in the approaching campaign. One columnist for the *Brooklyn Daily Eagle* sensed that "Bensonhurst fans are wondering how Marty Glickman, their native son will do on the gridiron." The big question in the neighborhood was now whether he would risk injury in that most violent sport or "save his legs since they are so valuable in track" since "a splendid future is expected of Glickman who won a berth on the United States team that competed in the Olympic games in Berlin." What had happened to this local youngster at the Summer Games was no longer in play.[17]

Glickman's fans did not have to wait long for an answer about his sports choices. Early in November, a game approached between Syracuse and Columbia that once again pitted Glickman against Luckman. It was a highly anticipated rematch of the two stars who had met in that memorable 1934 tilt that James Madison had won, securing for the team the city championship. As previously noted, this college game and subsequent matchups between the Syracuse and Columbia stars did not live up to expectations. For another *Brooklyn Daily Eagle* columnist, and like the 1934 showdown game, the etymologies of the two Jewish stars' names were intriguing, as the only Jewish sidelight to the 1936 game was the "curious analogy—Glick in Jewish means luck . . . a very literal translation of Glickman would be Luck-man." Just like before the 1934 showdown game, their names intrigued a reporter. But as far as what had transpired in August 1936 was concerned, it was simply noted in passing: "Glickman went overseas with the United States Olympic team as a sprinter and though he did not see action, he is recognized as one of the nation's foremost speed merchants."[18]

Among three of American Jewry's most important weeklies that followed closely the athletic developments in Berlin, there also was no discernible outrage about the sidelining. In the days that led up to the "meeting," they noted with pride the activities of Glickman and the other Jewish athletes as they prepared to compete and were especially pleased with the exploits of Jesse Owens in forcefully rebutting Hitler's racism on the track. The takes of those Jewish journalists resembled those of the non-Jewish American news outlets. More often than not in the reporting of what had befallen Glickman and Stoller, their barring was linked to the mistreatment of Mrs. Jarrett and Brundage was attacked more for his mistreatment of the female athlete. None of these newspapers did much more than to "hint" or "wonder" about the veracity of the rumor that anti-Semitism was at the root of the exclusion. No editorials appeared discussing the specifically Jewish angle of the controversy, though one paper suggested that a "satisfactory" answer must be found as to the origins of the incident. In one opinion piece the two athletes were praised for not making a big fuss over being forced to step away from the event.

The *American Jewish World,* published out of Minneapolis, was known to Jewish sports fans nationally for its interest in chronicling the achievements of Jewish athletes. The designations of their annual "Jewish All-American" teams were widely followed. So positioned before the games, it heartedly wished "good luck" to those off to Berlin. It sensed "a feeling of genuine satisfaction that among the American athletes are ten Negroes and half a dozen Jewish athletes who are sure to teach Mr. Hitler a lesson about the Nazi theory of Aryan superiority."

When Jesse Owens won his gold medals, one columnist rejoiced that the African American's victory will "result in the complete collapse of Nazi propaganda." The weekly further predicted that their heroes "will romp home with an impressive array of first place" finishes. While the paper was concerned about the fate of German Jews who were readying to flee the Third Reich out of fear of "perils" after the games, there was no apprehension about how the American stars would be treated amid the Olympiad. Writing about Glickman and Stoller, the paper asserted that they will "run with all get out."[19]

A week after their optimistic expectations when the runners' experiences turned sour, the paper informed its readers through a "special report" from Berlin that while "it may have been nothing more than American Olympic Committee 'politics' . . . there are some observers . . . who are wondering whether it wasn't the fine hand of Hitlerism which caused the elimination of the two Jewish runners." The *American Jewish World* was not sure and offered no editorial comment, on the action. However, it did tell its readers that the athletes "were quick to declare the action of the track coach was not motivated by anti-Jewish feeling." Glickman was quoted as allowing—just as he had said to the general press—how Stoller and he "were eliminated by a coach who wished to show favors to University of Southern California trackmen."

The *American Jewish World*'s final prognostication was that the "Glickman-Stoller and Eleanor Holm Jarrett cases are expected to furnish the American Olympic officials with more than a few headaches." Looking ahead, a columnist hoped out loud that Avery Brundage will "get the ax over the *Jarrett* affair," not the Glickman-Stoller story.[20]

In its September 4, 1936, edition, appearing less than a month after the Berlin games ended, the *American Jewish World* published a picture of Glickman and reported that he "had returned from Berlin where he was scheduled to take part in the Olympics under Nazi supervision . . . but at the last minute was taken off the squad." But the big "scoop" in that edition was "an exclusive interview" that a "reluctant" Sam Stoller had granted to journalist Bernard Postal where the athlete reiterated that "prejudice or discrimination had nothing to do with" the sidelining. Rather, Stoller contended, "it was only politics, favoritism and the intricacies of the coaches" that prevailed. From that point on, no further discussions or explanations were published about why that exclusion had occurred. However, through the end of 1936 and into the years that immediately followed, the paper closely covered Glickman's football and track achievements. At the start of the 1936 football campaign, it was reported, "Marty Glickman, a schoolboy rival of Luckman, seems to be going places with an ordinary Syracuse team." In 1937 and then in 1938, the paper announced that the fleet-footed running back had been elected to the second team of its vaunted Jewish All-American squad.[21]

In 1948, twelve years after the Olympic games, the newspaper noted "an interesting sidelight" to a visit by Owens to Yankee Stadium, where Glickman was broadcasting a ballgame. The announcer stated, the paper said, for the *first time* what Cromwell who was "recently under fire for his anti-Negro and anti-Semitic expressions had done to this Jewish athlete." But Glickman's fullhearted public articulation of what he fully believed had happened to him as a Jew, with explicit accusations of anti-Semitism on the part of Olympic officials, would await to close to five more decades.[22]

The *Sentinel* of Chicago had picked up the story of the two Jewish runners once they were ensconced in the Olympic Village and wrote about how amused they were to have Nazi guards greet them with the odious "Heil Hitler" salute. In the paper's first number after the sidelining, editor A. A. Freedlander offered a two-tiered response to goings-on in Berlin. First, writing in an up-beat vein, he declared that "the hand of God was plainly manifest in the fact that the arch denier of the worth, physically and other-wise of any but the pure Aryan stock had to witness the decisive triumph of Negroes." Owens's achievements, which thousands of fans cheered in the grandstands, were "nothing less than a debacle to the Nazis." Turning to the mistreatment of the Jewish trackmen, he called for a "satisfactory answer . . . to why were Stoller and Glickman not allowed to run." In his description and analysis of the Brundage groups' malfeasances, the sidelining ran second to the "*persecution* of Mrs Jarrett."

For this Jewish newspaper too the treatment of Jewish athletes was not front and center, nor were the prejudicial roots of the dis-crimination clearly delineated. Only "hints" of "prejudice" were suggested. Not only that, but by that time the *Sentinel* had already told its subscribers that "Marty Glickman has made peace with American Olympic officials but Sam Stoller is still going around with a longer nose than usual and feels sorry that he ever went to Berlin." Readers were informed that Glickman in a post-Olympic meet was showing how wrong the coaches were who "believed he was not fast enough." That was as far as the *Sentinel* went in criti-cizing Cromwell and Robertson.[23]

In line with its sister Jewish weekly, New York's *American Hebrew* asserted right before the games that "whatever victories American athletes may win will be at the expense of everything-politically, religiously and socially subversive to America." The paper rejoiced when the competition began and "the real heroes of the Olympics were non-Aryan, Negroes to boot," while taking to task the fans in the stands who did not acknowledge Owens's victory. "Only the Nazi newspaper *Der Angriff* has spoken of them disparagingly." To bolster their depiction of how the unsportsmanlike Reich leaders handled their defeat, the *American Hebrew* republished "a timely parody" that had appeared in the *Daily News* under the headline of columnist Ed Sullivan. Sullivan wrote, "A Blackbird"—meaning Owens—"traveled 4,000 miles to Berlin and sang his song three time better than it ever had been sung before. . . . And they gave him gold medals and here little oak trees on which to perch but the blackbird was coldly and cruelly snubbed." The writer-poet continued, "Adolf Hitler snubbed him because there is a new and strange philosophy that a man who kills Jews is better than a colored man."[24]

A week later, a newspaper editorial contrasted the absence of good judgment and sportsmanship of Cromwell and Robertson "lacking the imagination to behold two American Jews carrying American colors in the presence of Hitler and 100,000 Nazis with the gallant behavior of the Jewish lads" who "could or did not object to being displaced by Owens." While certain that the youngsters "will carry the unfair treatment they received as a wound to their last days," the piece explicitly pointed out that to their credit "the Jewish lads never cried prejudice and anti-Semitism. They took the breaks in the spirit of true American sportsmanship." The *American Hebrew* would have no further comment on the Berlin events, save to note in passing, as the football season began, that Glickman, whose "speed makes him a threat every time he touches the ball," is "best remembered as the American sprinter that was not allowed to compete when the Olympic team reached Berlin."[25]

Upon Glickman's return to campus in September 1936, the *Daily Orange* asked O'Brien and him to "relate first-hand stories of their time at the games." Glickman's report gave every indication that he was quickly on the road toward making peace with his exclusion. In an upbeat report, he began by saying, "My trip to Berlin this summer was by far the outstanding thrill of my young life." He happily recollected that "from the moment I qualified for the team, I had one thrilling experience after another. We were treated royally aboard ship and all during our stay aboard." He did not complain about being relegated with his teammates to second-class berths on the way home, but he did note his battle with seasickness.

For him, Jesse Owens was "the ace thrill producer of the entire aggregation," but the most "outstanding race at the meet . . . was the mile race" in which another of his American teammates "ran away from the field." As to the widely alleged snubbing of the Black champion by the German chancellor, Glickman would only say quite calmly that "in [his] opinion, Hitler certainly did not go out of his way to congratulate Owens, Metcalfe and Corny Johnson." He simply related how the Nazi dictator "left his box immediately after Owens's event making it impossible for him to extend the greeting he did to white victors."

Turning to the Holm Jarrett affair, he testified how "we all felt that her case should not have been treated so severely." He quipped, "Gee she's sorta, kinda smooth and did indulge in a glass or three of champagne." For Glickman, unfortunately Brundage chose to make a federal case out of this minor malfeasance.

In the last lines of the column, Glickman admitted that he was "greatly disappointed when informed that Stoller and myself were not going to run in the relay race." He was "certain" that "we could have won with as little difficulty as the quartet that did." Glickman was "somewhat consoled however, when [he] had the opportunity of defeating the German sprint champion at Hamburg" after the Olympics. In his recounting, Glickman did not mention politics, favoritism, or religion as a factor in his exclusion from the relay race.

It remained for Ed O'Brien, in his piece that appeared next to Glickman's in the same edition of the daily, to mildly critique AOC officials: "I thought Marty Glickman got a raw deal. I think Coach Lawson Robertson made a blunder." The basic problem, as O'Brien saw it, was how "a lot of [coaches] were there because of politics and not through any special merit on their part." There was no further discussion of Berlin in the *Daily Orange*. Just two days after Glickman and O'Brien's memoirs were published, a student sports columnist announced excitedly—as the football season approached—that Glickman would wear 77: "The number made famous by Galloping Ghost ['Red'] Grange was given to [Syracuse's] speed merchant for the coming year." It was said, "Marty Glickman the fastest man ever to perform for Syracuse" was "the fastest man in captivity." The Jewish halfback was then preparing to take on Clarkson in the opening game of the 1936 season.[26]

Marty Glickman's behavior, except for his private fullthroated comeback at Cromwell at the closed-door team "meeting," must be seen within the context of his time and status as a young athlete and Jew. The media was not informed, or perhaps chose not to report that he had told off his coach. Even Jesse Owens, who had initially risked speaking up until his coach silenced him, did not rise to say anything more after the lockerroom confrontation. When he arrived back in America, Owens stated only that he was "sorry" that Glickman and Stoller were left out. But in the end he felt that "the coach named the fastest team he thought he had for the day," and although he believed "the other boys ought to have their chance . . . they took it like good sportsmen despite what was reported."[27]

Glickman's not speaking publicly about anti-Semitism that he believed motivated his exclusion, preferring to state that "politics" was in play within the AOC, underscores how players back then were subservient to athletic authority figures. The words of coaches and administrators were the final say. That is very likely why the Olympic contingent's complaints, upon their return to New York, about their accommodations on board and their refusal to go on tour for the AOC were deemed worthy of media attention.

More important, Glickman's own reticence to call out prejudice and to create an uproar over anti-Semitism was in line with the way many Jews—perhaps most Jews—of that era dealt with Jew hatred. They were nonconfrontational, concerned about what aggressive responses might ultimately mean for their status as members of a minority group.

By analogy, this noncombative approach may be seen in attitudes toward the much larger and enduring anti-Nazi boycott that AJCong and the Non-Sectarian Anti-Nazi League inaugurated, beginning in March 1933, with the help of a number of other Jewish, labor, and Christian humanitarian groups. For Samuel Untermyer, head of the Non-Sectarian League, and fellow Jewish leaders of similar dispositions, championing the Olympic boycott initiative fit totally as a logical subset of a multifaceted agenda. These activists organized public protests in Madison Square Garden demanding an end to Nazi persecutions and then promoted a boycott of German-produced goods and services. While the league had its supporters, only a minority of American Jews backed Untermyer's aggressive stances, just as most Jews of that time were not interested in the Olympic boycott. If anything, there were voices among American Jews who were very concerned that such activities not only would rebound against German Jews, who were under Hitler's heel, but also would undermine the position of American Jews.[28]

For example, in February 1935, with the overall American boycott ongoing and the sports boycott movement well in play, journalist Louis Minsky worried out loud about the problems a "policy of aggressiveness" might mean for American Jews. He wrote, in response to an opinion that a spokesman for "Brooklyn Jewish Democracy" argued, that "if it [anti-Semitism] is brought into the open and the subject of public opinion focused upon it, it could not live." Writing in the prestigious *Menorah Journal*, Minsky argued that the outspoken "overlook the sad reality that the Christians are apt to get sick and tired of Jewish denunciations of . . . evil." It was not helpful that strongly worded complaints appeared in general New York newspapers, like the *World Telegram*, which picked up the story.

For him, Jews could not go it alone against hatred. The "policy of fighting anti-Semitism by public agitation, parades, mass meetings, oratorical invective, persistent moralizing, boycott without regard for the consequences" would serve no positive purpose. What was needed ultimately was the help of "sincere Christians" who would embrace the cause as their own. If Minsky had been asked to evaluate the value of the sports boycott, he would have asserted that Jewish protesters needed more friends like Jeremiah T. Mahoney in their corner. But the reality was that there were not enough such committed non-Jewish allies around. Most Americans shared the view of Ed O'Brien, who was convinced that America should be in the games, or even the opinion of fellow Syracuse student athlete Eldon Stutzman, who thought the news about anti-Jewish behavior in the Reich was just plain overstated. It was even suggested in some quarters that Jews were "overplaying the Jewish hand in America as it was overplayed in Germany before the present persecution." The writers and editors of the Jewish media that covered Marty's exploits accorded with Minsky's quietist view. They reacted prudently to the offenses against Glickman and Stoller in Berlin and told them to move on with their lives. The Jewish community of prewar America approached risk taking very warily.[29]

Back home in Brooklyn, Marty's often "hot-headed" father, who once knocked out an anti-Semite on his block who had cursed a Jewish neighbor, seethed with "anger and disappointment." This inveterate sports fan, who was so proud of his son, must have listened to the radio broadcasts of the games live from Berlin and had to have been outraged by what he did not hear from the announcers for CBS and NBC. The sidelining was barely alluded to on the airwaves. Famous sportscaster Bill Henry remarked that the "American team . . . had a rather surprising personality which had not been expected." Much like Bill Henry, his counterpart in the radio booth, Ted Husing did not even mention Glickman and Stoller when he called the final race.[30]

When interviewed at his Brooklyn home, Harry Glickman told a reporter how "bitter" he was "over the treatment accorded his son." When he heard about the replacement, Harry "was on the point of sending Marty a cable to come home, but Mrs. Glickman told [him], it would be better not to stir up any trouble." The discrimination visited on his son was, to his mind, without doubt anti-Semitism, as he told his interviewer: "We are Jews, to be sure, but we are good Americans. There must be something wrong somewhere . . . it certainly does not look like American sportsmanship to me." While Harry Glickman had his angry say in August 1936 about his son being ill-treated, decades would pass before Marty Glickman would say, in no uncertain terms, "Brundage and Cromwell did not want to embarrass their Nazi friends by having two Jewish athletes stand on the winner's podium."[31]

Upon Glickman's return from Berlin, two other incidences of prejudice deeply troubled the young man. One occurrence involved the sidelining of a Black teammate at Syracuse. The other manifestation of discrimination was directed at him due to the exclusionary policies of the New York Athletic Club. In both cases, he stewed with anger but kept his anger to himself.

The first instance involved Wilmeth Sidat-Singh, a classmate of mixed East Indian and African American ancestry, who was Glickman's teammate on the Orange's football club. Before a game against the University of Maryland, a Baltimore newspaper "revealed" that the brown-skinned Sidat-Singh was in fact a Black man as it defined racial identity. The local authorities told the coaches that "it would be dangerous" if Sidat-Singh suited up for the game. To avoid controversy, Syracuse officials acceded to this segregationist demand. This decision sat well with Chancellor Graham, who if he had his druthers would have preferred that a Black man not represent his university to begin with. But he held his fire when it came to Sidat-Singh playing home games so as not to antagonize tolerant elements within his college community.[32]

Glickman, the team leader, did not rise to protest the decision. He would recall that he reasoned, "It's that kid Glickman again. You were the kid who didn't run in the Olympics because you're Jewish. You caused a ruckus then and now you'll be causing trouble by walking out of this football game and causing the whole team not to play." His prudent mindset at that time told him to not "stir up trouble as a Jew." Ironically, this cautious sensitivity was akin to the attitude of so many Jews who worried what a boycott of the Olympic games might mean to their tenuous place in their country in the 1930s. General Sherrill had warned that if non-Jewish American boys and girls did not play, they would blame the Jews, with potentially fearful consequences. This endemic reticent mentality also told those Jews who talked about the evils of racism among their own kind to say nothing out loud about the prejudices that undergirded Black life in their segregationist country. For Marty Glickman, the exclusion of his teammate had to have brought to the surface a recognition of the hypocrisy in an America that for a moment had honored Jesse Owens and themselves for his victories against Hitler's racism and now was back to enabling racism in sports.

The public humiliation of his friend brought into real-life focus the message of an article that he had read a year earlier, in January 1937, amid the indoor track season the year after Berlin. This correspondent praised Glickman for moving on without complaint about what happened at the Olympics. The writer asserted that rather than "beef," the Olympic runner "embarked upon a campaign" over a six-week period "to establish himself as America's No 1. *'white hope.'*" This journalist—and perhaps many more—who looked at him as a Jew, a member of a minority who had been sidelined but did not protest, now depicted him as nothing less than a champion of the white race, able to beat Black men like Jesse Owens. This was proof that as much as he had been marginalized and his childhood dream was shattered, the fates of Jews and Blacks in the restrictionist United States were so very different. His memory that Jesse Owens, just a few months earlier, had risked talking back to Cromwell on Stoller's and his behalf in the Olympic Village while he stayed silent when Sidat-Singh was excluded stayed with Glickman for the rest of his life.[33]

The second case of bigotry was the anti-Semitism of an elite New York sports institution that barred Glickman from working out before his return to Syracuse, just a few weeks after he was sidelined in Berlin. This experience reminded him once again that Jew hatred was alive and powerful not only in Germany but also back home in the United States. The New York Athletic Club (NYAC) was a renowned and high-profile bastion of WASP exclusiveness. From its founding in 1868, its membership was for "Christians Only," and for white, male Christians at that. It harbored the type of genteel social discrimination that Jews faced in many social, educational, and business situations in the pre–World War II period. Whether or not Glickman was highly attuned to the NYAC's standard policies, when he approached its gates on Central Park South, he assumed there would be no problem with him practicing with a gentile teammate. Notwithstanding events in Berlin, he was an American Olympian and a world-class sprinter. But his superior sports status meant nothing to the NYAC official who curtly turned him away. Glickman would recall how it was only on the subway on his way back to Brooklyn that he fully realized that he had been victimized, in no uncertain terms, because he was a Jew. Again, he kept the pain mostly to himself. Decades thereafter, after he became a famous New York sportscaster, Christian friends who were members of the NYAC implored him to join the club, asserting that times and attitudes had changed. But he would not set foot in that building, always referred to the club "in derogatory terms," and was awfully pleased when the NYAC track meet was removed from Madison Square Garden's calendar because of a boycott over its refusal to admit women. It was not until 1986, in the beginning of an era when he became increasingly forthright about his experiences with anti-Semitism, that he agreed to be honored at the NYAC's annual banquet along with Fred Lebow, the Jewish founder of the New York City Marathon. At that moment, he carefully, yet definitively, told his audience what had happened to him while congratulating the NYAC for its changed membership policies. He would consider that speech the "most heartfelt address" he had "ever given." But membership was still not for him.[34]

Madison Square Garden in the 1940s when Glickman began broadcasting.
Credit: Courtesy of CSU Archives / Everett Collection.

6

NEW YORK'S BROADCASTER

WITH his dream still very much alive of standing on the podium at the projected 1940 Tokyo Olympics, Syracuse University track star Marty Glickman continued over the remainder of his intercollegiate career to build his national reputation as one of the country's foremost sprinters. Proud of his efforts to be considered among elite American runners, he was pleased that the *Syracuse Herald Journal* sent a photographer to the IC4A track meet to "catch . . . the Olympic sprint star" prepare for that major meet with a series of front-page pictures of his running style.[1]

While he racked up additional victories in track, his loyalty to the Orange's football program undermined his sprinting prospects. As a star running back on a mediocre football team that won fewer than half of its games, he coped with the constant crash of bodies on the tundra that eventually slowed him down. He would later admit that he "was never again as fast as [he] had been in 1936." Nonetheless, he performed well enough that as a senior the *American Jewish World* selected him along with Luckman as members of the backfield on a "Jewish All-American team."[2]

Glickman's most impressive football performances took place in his junior and senior years against Cornell, then a national power. In 1937, in an upset of the heavily favored Big Red, Glickman scored two touchdowns and made a saving tackle at the end of the game that secured a 14–6 victory for the home team. One delirious report on the game, rendered most likely by a fan from the old neighborhood as the word of the triumph got around, described the heroics of the "Baby Face Marty Glickman, the quiet

Brooklyn boy from James Madison High School" whose "flashing speed furnished the fire and inspiration which lifted the coldly determined and fighting boys in Orange above a fine Cornell team." When Glickman, "the Olympic sprinter in football togs dashed on a serpentine blaze forty-four yards for the first touchdown," it gave "the crowd of more than 20,000 a bump which resembled an earthquake shock." No less remarkable for this observer was the effort of "little Glickman who, after other backs had failed, hurdled over the Big Red line for a second touchdown." In the final minute of the game, the "stocky compact" but diminutive star who weighed in at only 165 pounds stopped a 200-pound Cornell All-American at the three yard line, as during that era of football players were on the field for both offense and defense. In 1938, again as an underdog to Cornell, Glickman was pleased to assist his friend, Sidat-Singh, who threw the winning touchdown in the closing seconds of another Syracuse upset. At that moment when the Orange triumphed, Sidat-Singh was a hero on campus.[3]

Glickman's exploits moved Sidney Hyman, a local haberdasher in Syracuse who saw the possibilities of capitalizing on the player's growing popularity. He hit on the idea of having Glickman host a weekly sports show on a radio program that he sponsored. Glickman initially was intimidated about the prospect of being on the air. As a child, he had coped with stuttering and had taken a speech class to remedy the problem. He feared that residual issues with pronunciations would humiliate him during broadcasts on WSYR. He always had trouble enunciating the letter "s," which came across as a hissing sound. While "scared to death," the offer of fifteen dollars a week for his work, more lucrative than waiting on tables, was an enticement too good to turn down. In preparation for the Thursday night summary of the week's sports event, he "read poetry out loud rapidly to help develop clearer pronunciation" and reread the scripts time and again to get his facts straight. Even though he flubbed at the opening of his first show—Glickman started his evening report with a cheerful "good afternoon"—the novice developed a following among his college mates and Syracuse natives who tuned in to his "eastern accented voice." Although at that point in his life, while still in school, he was still telling people that he was preparing for a profession as a "civic administrator," the seeds had been planted for his broadcast career, which would be marked by fine preparation, accurate reportage, and clear articulation, albeit delivered in a dialect that was often seen as possessed of a "New York" accent.[4]

Upon graduation in June 1939, Marty Glickman returned to New York City into the waiting arms of Marge Dorman. Although occasionally, during his college years, he went out with Christian sisters from sororities that were off-limits to young Jewish women undergraduates—he could get into those buildings only when picking up dates—his heart always belonged to Marge. They frequently kept in touch during the school year through telegrams back and forth when either had exciting news to relate or to inquire when Marge was scheduled to arrive at the upstate campus for a weekend visit. Marty made it down to New York City several times during the track season, with the college paying his travel expenses. They were inseparable during summer vacation. Their relationship deepened when Marty returned home upon graduation. Often after the twosome attended a Broadway musical, Marty, quite the romantic, would scribble on the show program his feeling that the production would have been even better if Marge had been onstage. Marty Glickman and Marjorie Dorman were married on December 25, 1940, and set up housekeeping in the old Flatbush neighborhood at 100 Avenue P. A year later they were blessed with the birth of their first child, Elizabeth. John followed in 1945, David in 1949, and Nancy in 1953.[5]

In the first years of their marriage, Marty and Marge, like so many other young couples struggling during the still-lingering Great Depression, sought to balance his long-range goal of being a broadcaster with the immediacy of just earning a living. Indeed, even before their nuptials, Marty worked as a salesman at Gimbels Department Store while he sought a job—any employment—in the radio industry. On the weekends, he supplemented his income through playing semipro football for the New Jersey Giants until Marge, fearful that football players were ripe to be injured, convinced him to end his formal athletic career.

His first semi-break occurred in the winter of 1940 when WHN radio hired him on an event-by-event basis to cover track meets at Madison Square Garden. His experience as a featured athlete at that arena convinced the station that this neophyte announcer was qualified for that post. He caught on at WHN in 1941 with a more permanent but hardly lucrative post as a "go-fer." Here, his college connection with a Syracuse football alum helped secure his appointment. He worked well in his multiple assignments that included running errands for the station manager and the on-air personalities, tearing texts off the news wires, and preparing scripts for *Today's Baseball*, which re-created the highlights from the afternoon's Yankee, Dodger, and Giant games. A year later, in 1942, when his station acquired the rights to broadcast Dodger games, he joined his more experienced colleagues on pre- and postgame shows where they argued about the outcomes of ballgames. In November 1942, a radio columnist for the *Brooklyn Daily Eagle* praised Glickman as a "local boy etc. (and how!)" who was making good at WHN while helping present the "station's exclusive see- and tells of the Ranger's [hockey] games on Garden ice . . . [and] still lives in the old hometown" of Brooklyn. He was commended as a devoted father who "is just as reticent covering the charms of their year-old Elizabeth as we are about the Pussy Kitten," a very loveable and huggable cat.[6]

In 1943, the patriotic Glickman left the neighborhood and Marge and Elizabeth behind and joined the Marines. As a college graduate, he secured a commission as a lieutenant and was stationed on the Pacific island of Kwajalein. There he integrated well with his fellow soldiers and experienced no anti-Semitism from men in the ranks or from fellow officers. After being on the outside in Berlin, it was nice for him to be counted in the chow line within the military community. Like so many Jewish men in the military at that time, he became associated with fellows who had never seen a Jew before and earned some barracks cachet through his ability to play ball so well during downtimes. The only sad moment for Glickman during wartime occurred when he found out that his friend Sidat-Singh—a member of the all-Black Tuskegee Airmen in the segregated U.S. Army Airforce—was killed in a training flight. Knowing of their comradeship, his grieving mother sent Glickman a picture of her son in the cockpit of his airplane. That photo, which Glickman held on to, reminded him of his failure to speak up in that Baltimore locker room. It was another indication of the differing statuses and fates of Jews and Blacks as minorities in America. Glickman would muse decades later that Sidat-Singh was "qualified to die for his country, but he wasn't good enough to play football against Maryland."

Glickman was fortunate enough not to see the island-hopping action that victimized so many of his fellow soldiers. Aware of his background as a sports announcer, the military designated him as a "night fighter controller," where he was tasked to "speak rapidly and crisply" in guiding airmen away from the enemy and ultimately to the safety of their home base. To set the scene for his pilots he used a radarscope, a device that he later utilized in broadcasting back home. His one informal contribution to the war effort, which likewise helped him refine his professional skills, was his organizing of "a sports broadcast for enlisted men" that featured a weekly football contest that "attracted responses from all over the island." The "inducement [was] a keg of beer for the enlisted man who hits the most winners."[7]

Upon military discharge in December 1945, he picked up where he had left off at WHN, continuing his nightly stints at the microphone of *Today's Baseball* complete with simulated crowd noises and the sound of bats hitting balls. He stayed around for Dodger postgame shows and gave late night sports updates reports. He turned out at the Garden to broadcast track meets, covered outdoor boxing matches, and, given his star football pedigree, was a good fit to do local college football games.[8]

During the winter of 1945–46, fresh out of the Marines and ambitious to find his niche in the broadcasting business, Glickman prevailed upon his bosses at WHN to have him begin to cover college basketball from Madison Square Garden. There were renowned announcers of major sports in New York and all over the country. In Gotham, Don Dunphy handled boxing. Mel Allen was the play-by-play man for the New York Yankees. Red Barber, who became one of Glickman's mentors, was best known for handling Brooklyn Dodger games. Clem McCarthy and Bryan Field followed horse racing. Nationally, Ted Husing and Bill Stern were long associated with college football and a myriad of other sports and entertainments. But no one had yet become the voice of basketball, and Glickman seized upon that opportunity.[9]

Through letters back to WHN while he was still in the service, he began campaigning to call basketball games and overcame his boss's predisposition that "the only people who are interested in basketball go to the Garden and watch the games." Glickman had already attempted, in December 1942, a dry run at seeing whether a basketball broadcast was viable when he covered an unmemorable matchup between the North Carolina Pre-Flight School and LIU. This tilt was arranged to raise money for the Red Cross, but almost no one tuned in to hear his account.[10]

Glickman's argument now was that basketball was the quintessential New York sport that youngsters played in the schoolyards and gyms of the city, with literally millions of devoted fans in the neighborhoods who cheered on the legendary college squads from CCNY, NYU, LIU, and St. John's. Thousands flocked to the Garden almost every week for college doubleheaders as their loyal favorites took on many of the best college teams from all around the country. A half century later Glickman reminisced that the New York–accented call "'Meetcha under the Marquee at the Garden' was the signal for a night of sports excitement." Writing as a native who understood his city's sports population so well—for he was one of them—Glickman recalled that "the basketball-wise New York fans would come directly from their jobs, many walking over from the garment center on Seventh Avenue. It was a young crowd, second generation Americans mostly" and many of them were precisely like him, American Jewish children of immigrants "whose folks had emigrated from Central and Eastern Europe before and after World War I." They all got together under "the graceful marquee on the west side of Eighth Avenue between 49th and 50th streets." They all believed that they knew the game: everyone "was a basketball expert—at least in his own mind." Before venturing into the multi-tiered arena, fans often stopped at Nedicks, the downscale food shop next door to the Garden's rotunda where they ate hot dogs and drank orange sodas. Many who hoped to make a killing those nights checked out the lines and then placed bets with their bookies. The better-heeled attendees sat in their office clothes downstairs while many of the real cognoscenti "hurried up five flights of stairs" to get the best seats in the balcony. Upstairs, the sightlines, except for the first few rows, were not great. The disgruntled in the cheapest seats often called out "down in the front." For any announcer, interpreting the on-court goings-on for the knowledgeable who could not get a ticket would be an extraordinary challenge. But it was an opportunity that Glickman was ready to assume for those who personally were not part of the Garden scene on any night. Fans were anxious, almost obsessed, to immediately know how their squads were making out. Glickman argued that broadcasts would help, rather than hurt, attendance. He was heard first on the radio and soon thereafter would be seen and heard by television's growing audience.[11]

Glickman would be privileged to perch himself next to his Garden microphone and among his friends during the last great era of New York supremacy in college basketball. He believed, and so many others concurred, that he "literally invented basketball broadcasting," even if his prime mentor as a broadcaster was baseball eminence Red Barber, whom he revered. Glickman asserted that Barber was nothing less than the "best sports announcer who ever lived." In describing a baseball game, Barber was sure to paint "a perfect word picture" allowing his fans to "see the game" with "descriptive words" delivered with the "right inflection always with the good voice . . . always in control." For the "Old Red-Head"—his moniker—it was not useful to say just that the "shortstop made a catch." It was imperative to depict in sparse but correct words how the fielder corralled the batted ball. The trick for Glickman was to apply many of Barber's professional principles that worked so well during slow-moving baseball games with their "few moments of action" to the "bang-bang" pace of basketball. There would be no time in the Garden for Glickman to slowly spin entertaining yarns or to tell jokes as Barber often did, offering reflections between pitches as "rapid-fire" basketball action unfolded before him with players rushing up and down the court. The only possible respite for Glickman, during which he could tell an anecdote, was during a time-out or at halftime. Amid the fifteen-minute break between halves, he would invite top local college coaches, like Nat Holman or St. John's Joe Lapchick, into the booth for their sage impressions on the action. But he did follow his mentor's lead in avoiding just saying that a "great play" was completed. Instead, he would help listeners "visualize" how "a driving left handed lay-up banked in off the boards" or "spinning away from the basket" was accomplished. He would also try, though not always succeed, in "taking his time" in presenting the action that flowed so quickly on the basketball court.

Very often, however, the excitement of the moment got the best of him. Then he broke a few of Barber's cardinal rules, namely, "Don't hurt your vocal chords. Never raise your voice. Never yell. When you are broadcasting, talk in a natural range, well under your full strength, when the crowd yells shut up . . . let the roar of the crowd go into the microphone . . . and when it subsides, then and only then resume speaking." One of Glickman's fans recalled that "he could speak as quickly as he could run," albeit in an intelligible voice that was "smooth and assured." He broadcasted at a pace once estimated at "hundreds of words a minute." Glickman once admitted that for an hour after a radio broadcast he would "feel bad in the throat—it takes that much out of him." Had Red Barber heard that aside, he would have smiled knowingly.[12]

Glickman had also benefitted from tuning in to the radio broadcasts of Foster Hewitt, who painted word pictures of an even faster game, ice hockey. Listening to his accounts from Toronto, where Hewitt followed the Maple Leafs, Glickman learned to develop "basketball equivalents" to hockey descriptions like "crosses the blue line" in creating the on-the-court "geography" for his hoops work.[13]

Early on, as Glickman worked both on the radio and soon in television, his distinctive approach toward reaching his audience garnered the applause of a columnist from *Variety*. This media critic saw his way of broadcasting as an answer to the general "swelling chorus of criticism of basketball as a sports spectacle and, by extension, a TV spectacle . . . based on the static nature of the game due to fouling and tactic of freezing the ball." But with Marty Glickman at the mic, "cage game emerged as a virtuoso spectacle. . . . The show has ingredients of click with athletic aficionados, one of the main ones being rapid-fire authoritative deliveries of Glickman." A wife of a ballplayer who played many games that Glickman broadcasted tendered an even more meaningful evaluation of his performance when she informed her husband, who was anxious to tell her all about what she had missed at the arena, "I *listened* to Marty and *saw* him on the radio." Along those same lines, and around that same time, Glickman received what he considered his "greatest compliment" when Holy Cross coach Buster Sheary told reporters that he had great success against NYU in the Garden because he scouted his opponent through "listen[ing] to a couple of Marty Glickman's broadcasts."[14]

Glickman was on hand as the city's top teams hosted nationally ranked clubs and players like backcourt ace Bob Cousy of Holy Cross and centers Oklahoma A&M's Bob Kurland and DePaul's George Mikan, two of the first outstanding big men, not to mention Syracuse's Jim Brown, better known for his exploits on the gridiron. Glickman would recall that the most exciting single moment he experienced as a basketball broadcaster took place in 1946 at the National Invitational Tournament (NIT) when a long-forgotten player for Rhode Island State named Ernie Calverley made a 55-foot desperation shot at the buzzer to tie heavily favored Bowling Green. Rhode Island went on to win that game in overtime. But for his listeners and for the entire city of New York, the most exciting games took place in 1950 when the CCNY Beavers won both the NCAA and NIT championships on the Garden's "home court." Glickman broadcasted those games and basked in the excitement that enveloped Gotham, especially when their team, led by Jews and African Americans, soundly defeated the all-white University of Kentucky team from that segregated southern state. For Glickman, it was reminiscent of what Owens had done to Hitler fourteen years earlier as CCNY thrashed the club whose coach, Adolph Rupp—note his first name—vowed to never recruit a Black player. Sadly for New York fans, just a year later a basketball scandal rocked the city as it was found that some CCNY players, in cahoots with gamblers, had shaved points in their contests to please gamblers. When the truth became known, Glickman was especially grieved about that enduring blot on a sport and a city that he loved. He felt that he should have known better since the offenders were neighborhood guys. He lamented how "you saw them on the street. You saw them drinking malteds at the corner candy store. It was a big family." Glickman was well aware that gambling was part of the scene on game night, and he was attuned to the "booing and catcalling that had little to do with the winning and losing but a lot to do with the point spread of the game" when an otherwise skilled player somehow missed an easy shot. Often bettors descended back down from their hard-backed seats between games and during halftime to the lobby to see if the odds had changed. Intermission was a busy time to double down or change wagers. The tragedy of the 1951 point shaving scandal also brought Glickman back to the saddest part of his youth when his father was caught up in the culture of gambling, to the detriment of his family. While Glickman continued to cover college basketball for decades thereafter within and without the Garden, from that point on his major interest in the game was broadcasting for the city's professional team, the New York Knickerbockers. It was a position that he garnered in 1946, with the start of the NBA. Still quite an athlete, Glickman often worked out with the players.[15]

In 1948, Glickman's career received an additional boost when he was selected to be the radio voice of the New York Giants. He replaced his mentor Barber, who had covered the team during the war years and throughout the 1946 and 1947 seasons. Since his home station WHN, later to be renamed WMGM, owned the rights to the broadcast, this former football star who already had done some local college games was a natural fit, even though at the outset of his career as the voice of Big Blue, professional football in New York lagged far behind baseball and basketball in fan popularity. His Sunday afternoon broadcasts were then supplementary to his work at the Garden. When a Giants' home game ended first at the Polo Grounds at the uppermost point in Manhattan and then, starting in 1956 at Yankee Stadium over the Harlem River to the Bronx at 161st Street and River Avenue, he had to use some of his sprinting skills to hustle on to the IRT subway to get back down to Forty-Ninth Street and Eighth Avenue to prepare properly for the evening's college or Knicks game. One of the ways Glickman, the professional who once stammered, prepared his voice and diction for a game was to "recite from the poet Chaucer." On many occasions, much like "a pianist stretching his fingers or a singer clearing his throat," he would "limber up" through speaking out lines from Edgar Allan Poe's famous poem "The Raven," as in "Once upon a midnight dreary. . . ." He was, as one newspaper media columnist called him, "possibly the busiest of our local radio-television broadcasters."[16]

During the second year of his work for the Giants, he shared the booth with another broadcast luminary, Ted Husing. Although Glickman was duly impressed with the "beautiful" voice quality of his partner and his "melodious" delivery, which he tried to emulate, Glickman, keen to give listeners an accurate account of what they could not see, chafed when Husing would say "things that did not make sense." In his opinion, the senior broadcaster "didn't know the game" the way he, the former high school and college star, did. Husing ended up "describing things that were not happening." After one year with the Giants, Husing departed from the New York sports scene. Marty Glickman remained with the Giants for most of the next quarter century as pro football's popularity spiked in town and elsewhere and became America's foremost spectator sport.[17]

Glickman contributed mightily to the game's eventual acclaim in New York. Hours and days after a Giants win, fans could be heard on the streets of New York imitating his excited signature field goal call: "It's high enough, it's deep enough, it's through there, it's through there." Or when they played in sandlots in their neighborhoods and a fellow ran for a short gain, they might say he "gained a couple or three yards," using the same terminology that Glickman used to describe what a Giant running back like Alex Webster, a star in the 1950s and 1960s, might have done the prior day in the big ballpark in the Bronx. Yankee Stadium held close to sixty thousand spectators, but millions felt they were watching the games from their homes or tuning in from their cars. At one point, a survey of local television viewers determined that 65 percent of them were listening to his radio accounts with the sound of their television sets turned off. His passionate devotees also appreciated that although a home team rooter, he was honest enough to focus on the opponent's impressive showing when the Giants did not play well. He would "talk about what made [the opposition's] play strong." For five years, between 1960 and 1965, color commentator Al DeRogatis ably assisted Glickman in bringing a wealth of expertise about the arcane intricacies of football to Giant games, win or lose. "DeRo," as Glickman affectionately called him, was so proficient in predicting forthcoming plays that listeners felt that they were close to overhearing the goings-on in the huddle. DeRogatis had a heads-up in making his "anticipatory calls" because Giant coach Allie Sherman let him see the team's playbook prior to games. The broadcast twosome adhered to Glickman's cardinal rule that "even if you are bored during a blow out [noncompetitive game] you had to find something to get excited about at least for the sake of your advertisers who put you on the air." The duo's fans appreciated these efforts.

Educators were also pleased if the day after a game students consulted with dictionaries for definitions of words like "torpid," "desultory," and "phlegmatic," terms they had heard from the teacher in the stadium broadcast booth. But in 1951 teachers and parents were unhappy if their children repeated the blue words that once crossed Marty Glickman's lips when a kickoff receiver ran the entire length of the field for a touchdown. Overenthused, he cried out, "There's Buddy Young tear-assing down the sideline." Though he immediately realized what he had done, Glickman did not apologize on the air for his mistake. But his listeners surely noted his error and for a time thereafter called him out.

Jewish listeners were gratified when Glickman interspersed Yiddish words in his accounts. He had "no hesitancy about it" and even said "I particularly like to use it with gentile people." It was a subtle indication of his comfort with his Jewish background among his fellow New Yorkers, even as he was fluent with Chaucer and Poe and wanted to be an American broadcaster. It was a nice linguistic synthesis of ethnic and American identities. He once explained that although he "didn't think in Yiddish . . . very often in making a point the Yiddish phrase will come up" and he "would utilize it." In his view, "some of those phrases [were] more expressive than anything I can say in English." In fairness to most fans who did not understand Yiddish as they intently followed the action, he offered up a translation. Some of his color commentators who were real out-of-towners appreciated his explanation.[18]

In 1973, a contract dispute and miscommunication between club and star sportscaster led him to leave the Giants and become the announcer for the rival Jets, to the chagrin of his legion of fans. Six years later, when the rights to the Jets were sold by WOR radio to WCBS, this outlet wanted their own man on the air and Glickman was sidelined. This second front office management decision again did not sit well with his fans. One letter writer to the *New York Times* expressed best the ire of so many New York sports fans when he upbraided this "crass refutation of quality." He and all the other listeners were "now deprived of hearing a voice of excellence, integrity, skill and professionalism." The decision to take "a living legend . . . the finest play-by-play broadcaster in radio sports" off the air "puts shame to all the childhood dreams that reward greatness." In 1988, at the age of seventy-one, Glickman was returned to his booth at Shea Stadium. When he was back every Sunday afternoon during football season, another journalist who also was outraged when his hero had been removed rejoiced that "the master . . . with that crisp sidewalk-flavored cadence that always put you alongside the 50-yard line" was back. For him and so many others, "the game of football was never as perfect in person as when Glickman was describing it for our ears." Glickman stayed at the Jets microphone for five more years. His last Jets broadcast was on December 27, 1992.[19]

While basketball and football were this foremost New York sportscaster's most remembered prime-time events, over the close to half century of his preeminence, there was almost no athletic competition in Gotham that he did not cover. Glickman was on the scene at St. Nicholas Arena in lower Washington Heights for boxing cards. For seventeen years, trotter aficionados enjoyed his trackside reports of harness races from Yonkers Raceway. He even "loved" working at rodeos and even the most déclassé of sports— professional wrestling and roller derby—though he often knew the outcome of the generally fixed "contests" before picking up his microphone. Little children, and especially their parents who regularly tuned in to Glickman's nighttime broadcasts after their kiddies were put to bed, felt very special when Glickman showed up to telecast a marble shooting championship. Glickman believed that the "most difficult broadcast [he] ever did" was his account of "the Ringling Brothers Barnum and Bailey, three ring circus to four hundred blind people . . . on close circuit radio." It has been estimated that he was the voice of two hundred track meets—most notably the Millrose Games from Madison Square Garden—a thousand football games, including sixteen years of high school matches, three thousand basketball games, and fifteen thousand horse races.

Toward the end of his life, Glickman reflected on what he believed made him special: "I actually feel the game as I do the game. When a fellow shoots at a basket and misses you know I miss the hoop." Such sensitivity to players' frustrations, not to mention to their exaltations when they won, came naturally as he analogized from his own playing days. One junior colleague referred to Glickman admiringly as "the first jock announcer" who brought an uncommon expertise from the field or court into the booth. Marty Glickman was not entirely thrilled with that appellation, which smacked of a lack of intellectual seriousness, but he knew that his former student's off-the-cuff moniker was expressed with respect and love.[20]

Mel Allen, né Melvin Allen Israel, voice of the New York Yankees, 1939–64. Credit: Library of Congress, New York World-Telegram & Sun Collection.

7

IDENTITY CHALLENGED

WHILE constant expressions of praise from local fans and scribes warmed Marty Glickman, he was disappointed that throughout his long broadcasting career the sound of his voice was rarely heard outside of Gotham and its neighboring environs. Two undermining factors contributed to his inability to be more than just a renowned New York sports announcer. These difficulties challenged his almost-always optimistic demeanor. He made personal peace with one barrier: the problem of his Jewish-sounding name. A second source of consternation troubled Glickman over the long haul even as he tenaciously continued to move forward with his career. What hurt him most was that he firmly believed fellow Jews had been complicit in keeping him from rising as a foremost national over-the-air personality.

For Jews of Glickman's generation who wanted to move socially and economically beyond their ethnic neighborhood roots and to make it within America's Christian majority, their distinctive last names, which told where they came from, were a considerable handicap. Employment advertisements that indicated that elite companies or firms "preferred Christians" told those who wanted lucrative jobs that their Jewish-sounding names were a problem. Those who did achieve coveted positions, with their origins known, often had to put up with nasty comments and other forms of ridicule on the job. The best colleges and universities screened names as part of their admissions processes. A new last name—and perhaps also a changed first name—helped Jews ascend the walls of the restrictive Ivys. Syracuse University was not among the worst offenders when it came to name shaming, though it made every effort to limit its Jewish enrollees. Marty Glickman was keenly aware of the troubling phenomenon of limits at his alma mater. The Sigma Alpha Mu fraternity delegation had recruited him precisely to counter quotas in what ended up as a failed effort to reverse that trend. This star athlete and his teammate, Al Handler, did not have to change their names. But it is possible other Jewish applicants who could not attain varsity status and make a mark on campus did. Elsewhere, ever-resourceful college officials across the country who were committed to their investigations found additional ways of weeding out the unwanted. One stratagem was to require photographs with applications, meant to detect Semitic features. It also did not help that the students' addresses indicated that they hailed from a Jewish neighborhood. During this era, there were those who seriously contemplated attempting to "pass" but stopped short of making the switch out a sense of loyalty to their family's past and present. Retaining the last name that parents brought with them from Europe was not an affirmation of long-held Jewish religious values but a quiet statement of the importance of retaining an ethnic identity, of belonging to family, community, and neighborhood.[1]

Jews who were in the public eye—like actors and actresses—similarly felt pressure to adopt Christian-sounding names. When Glickman was growing up, the list of movie stars who made the change to "de-emphasize their heritage" included Jacob Garfinkle (John Garfield), Leo Jacoby (Lee J. Cobb), Frederich Weisenfreund (Paul Muni), Melvyn Hesselberg (Melvyn Douglas), Marion Levy (Paulette Goddard), and Emanuel Goldenberg (Edward G. Robinson).[2]

Paul Muni was destined to become one of the silver screen's most distinguished actors. But he did so at the expense of his identity. In rising in the entertainment industry, he became "a paradigm of the tortured . . . actor Jew . . . always dressed in someone else's ethnicity." It made him, according to a friend, "one of the unhappiest men I ever met."[3]

Younger actors who came of age at the same time as Glickman, like Isador Demsky (Kirk Douglas), Bernard Schwartz (Tony Curtis), and Betty Joan Perske (Lauren Bacall), also did what they believed was warranted to avoid problems in advancing their careers. Douglas changed his first and last name several times from his birth as Danielovitch, believing that it was "too unwieldy and too Semitic for Hollywood." Later in life he came close to regretting what he had done when he asserted, "It's more interesting to keep your original name." Nonetheless, he could quip, "Can you imagine 'Issur Danielovitch' on a marquee?"

More often than not the pressure on these performers came from fellow Jews. The instigation for name changes came from the early motion picture moguls who, it has been said, "invented Hollywood." A movieland historian has argued the irony that "as films caught the conscience of the country," industry leaders, the Jews who were largely in charge of studios, not only wanted actors to hide their ethnicity but concealed their own background. "Fear and sensitivity" that they would be found out by anti-Semites who contended that through film Jews were out to control American culture and society underlay that trepidation. The Jew haters delighted in unmasking those who Anglicized their identities. Jewish producers also were unsure whether the general moviegoing public wanted Jewish names and themes in the bright lights. A screenwriter of that era has suggested that these high-profile executives "were accidental Jews, terribly frightened Jews who rejected their background. They would hardly touch a story with a Jewish character."[4]

It was a revolutionary turn within the American movie world when in 1947 Laura Z. Hobson's best-selling novel *Gentleman's Agreement* was made into a film, even if the producers who argued its importance to America were not Jewish. Darryl F, Zanuck, a Protestant of Swedish descent, at 20th Century Fox engaged non-Jewish director Elia Kazan and Jewish screenwriter Moss Hart to adapt this provocative book. That cinematic essay not only called out the multiple dimensions of social anti-Semitism but devoted significant attention to the practice of Jews changing their names, along with the self-hatred that came with it. In the film, the protagonist, a gentile magazine writer, pretends to be a Jew who has adopted a Christian name and finds out what sorts of prejudices a minority group member faced among his fellow Americans. As a theater and movie buff, Marty Glickman knew about the messages of this Academy Award–winning film that hit the screens just as he was striving to advance his own career. While *Gentleman's Agreement* caused many Americans to think deeply about their feelings toward discrimination against Jews, problematic policies did not change overnight. There were still barriers to be overcome.[5]

In Glickman's own corner of the entertainment universe, a Brooklyn-born future radio and television personality named Larry Zeiger, who was just a few years younger than Glickman, changed his name to Larry King. He made this move since he believed "then that was the thing to do. You had to have a name that was immediately recognizable, easy to remember." In King's view, the deemphasizing of heritages was not solely a Jewish problem. He would recall, "I don't know if part of it was anti-Semitic. I think they would have changed the name if it was Gamboli. . . . Any kind of ethnic name wasn't big. You had to change it."[6]

Closest to home when Glickman was starting out, Mel Allen, né Melvin Allen Israel, was already the voice of the New York Yankees. He had come to New York in 1936 from his native Alabama, disappointing his parents who wanted him to be an attorney. He "dropped his last name when CBS felt his name was too Jewish." One radio executive told him, "It was not euphonious enough or easy on the ears for a professional announcer." Until he heard that demand, Mel Allen had not hidden his ethnic background. He once said how back home his original last name did not make a difference. It was pleasant sounding enough. He would joke, "There was a K. K. K. guy in Alabama named Israel." To circumvent the minority group identity quandary, to please his bosses, and to satisfy himself, he would "enunciate the long 'L' in his first name with his accent, which was subtle on the air . . . and said the

'A' in Allen with the same hint of a Southern accent and euphoniously strung the first and last names together as if they were one: 'Melallen.'" For one radio critic, his regional dialect—his southern drawl—was a "perfect fit for the Bronx and became synonymous with baseball's rhythms." An observer of the tenors of life in New York has explained that the welcome accorded Allen and, for that matter, the non-Jew Red Barber, a native of Columbus, Mississippi, with their "lovely cadence," was a tribute to the openness of this polyglot city to out-of-towners, even if these announcers sounded so different from their listeners. An enamored Bronx boy, Christopher Lehmann-Haupt, who grew up to be a notable American literatus, took Allen with him when he was sent packing from Gotham one summer from his hometown to a family farm in Vermont. In foreign territory, he did his utmost to bring in the signal from WHN radio at night so he could listen to "Mel Allen's bronze gong of a voice . . . in the darkness around me with a description of a game hundreds of miles away." For Lehmann-Haupt, what Allen pronounced was "not a description really, for the words didn't call up a picture of reality, they *were* reality."[7]

Glickman's moment of decision occurred when Bill Stern, already a famous senior sportscaster and show business personality, advised his youthful colleague to change his name if he hoped to extend his career geographically beyond New York. Stern, born Bill Sterngold, did not have to convince his father that a non-Jewish name would help him advance professionally. When Bill was a child, his father was head of Michaels-Stern, a firm that Bill said was "the third largest manufacturer of men's clothes in the world." The company failed during the Great Depression. Possessed of a minimal attachment to Jewishness, residing in a small community in Rochester, New York, neither Bill nor Isaac had to explain to a Jewish neighborhood crowd their altered public identities. By the time Stern tendered his firm recommendation to Glickman, he was in the midst of a ten-year run as the "Voice of the Rose Bowl," a most coveted radio slot. He also had to his credit broadcasting the first televised sporting event. In case anyone wondered about his ethnic roots, the surname Stern could easily be construed as non-Jewish.[8]

For Marty Glickman, given his family and neighborhood ties, changing his name to Marty Manning or to Marty Mann constituted a more complicated choice. He knew that his grandparents had given his father and uncle non-Jewish first names as part of their unfulfilled dream that their youngsters might fit into Romanian society and recognized that his dad and uncle had changed their first names as part of their immediate embrace of their new country. But they had retained their surnames. To do otherwise would smack of a desire to separate themselves from the neighborhood and community of which they were part. Glickman's loyalty to his family, who were so supportive of his career choice, trumped any fears that he would lose out because of his name. Marty Glickman would not betray his origins as he sought to advance beyond Brooklyn. He would assert "our name is Glickman, not some phony name so I could get ahead." He would recall that for his folks "it [was] a big deal that their son Marty [was] on the radio," though they did wonder how well he would make a living in that calling. Marty would not want his father to have to explain to neighbors, "Did you hear Marty Manning on the air? That was my son."

By the same token of devotion to family and community, Glickman, who cared little about Sabbath and kosher laws and defined himself as a "cultural Jew," never worked on Yom Kippur because he was concerned how his possible presence would play on his Jewish streets. For him, "the basic reason" for staying away from the booth "is that being known as a Jewish broadcaster, my name is certainly not an Anglican name, it would be an affront to other Jews to have a Jewish broadcaster that did." Though no longer a Flatbush resident, he still felt a special connection to those he left behind, if only geographically. He believed, furthermore, that what he called his "pride in being Jewish" from his upbringing "might have driven [him] to standards that exceed those of people who did not take pride in their race or religion." Grateful for the sparks that his background had given him, Marty Glickman would not turn his back on his ancestry on his faith's holiest day. Beyond his loyalty to his own extended family, the "standard" or "model" for him was Hank Greenberg. Glickman well recalled that in 1934 one of his own sports heroes had sat out a baseball game with the pennant not yet clinched on Yom Kippur. "If he could not play," Glickman would recall, "there was no way I could broadcast." That feeling cohered with his comfort in using some Yiddish phrases during less stressful moments in front of both Jews and some gentiles who liked him and his work.[9]

At the same time that Marty was making a decisive choice, another New York aspiring public figure, Bess Myerson, who grew up in her own largely Jewish neighborhood and who felt strong ties to that community, made a similar decision to retain her family name, come what may. In her case, she demurred when in a private conversation the director of the Miss America pageant advised Myerson that she would be better off with a non-Jewish name to be more "attractive" for a future show business career. For the modest Myerson, it was bad enough that the Atlantic City event would require her to parade around in a bathing suit. She would not deny her roots. This young woman who hailed from the Sholem Aleichem co-ops on Sedgwick Avenue in the Bronx lived "in a building with 250 Jewish families." She keenly desired "everyone to know that I am the daughter of Louis and Bella Myerson." A name change to Betty Merrick would not do. She firmly believed that if she won the beauty contest, "the only people who will really care are my girlfriends from Hunter [College], my friends from camp, my family and the families I've grown up with. And if I win and I'm Betty Merrick, they won't know it's me and I want them to know it's me." She was also willing to deal with the possibility that "a corporate employer couldn't afford to be associated with my slightly Jewish name." Bess Myerson became the one and only Jewish Miss America, winning that crown in 1945.[10]

Myerson's well-known point of pride paralleled Glickman's own determination, and he may have applauded how a Jew who was much like him had ascended so well while affirming her roots. On the other hand, he strongly disdained how he believed another contemporary sports figure, Howard Cosell, dismissed his ethnic background to get ahead. Glickman bought into the widely held allegation that Cosell, in his quest to rise from his Brooklyn neighborhood background, changed his name from Cohen to hide his Jewishness. Truth be told, it is uncertain precisely if and why that switch took place. But Glickman believed that contention about Cosell. Seeing Cosell as a denier of his Jewishness only added to his antipathy of a nemesis who, in his view, epitomized all that was wrong with his profession. Glickman preached that the announcer was merely the vehicle for fans to see and hear what was transpiring. He was apt to say, "The only person who tunes in to listen to an announcer is his mother." In Glickman's view, Cosell believed that he was bigger than the game and was hubristic that those who heard him did so for his long-winded commentaries and caustic criticisms. It troubled Glickman that Cosell delighted in "interposing himself into the event . . . worked at being anathema" and feasted on projecting an image as an antihero. It was a pejorative persona that the friendly Glickman would never embrace. Many colleagues in the sports industry agreed with him. In his darker moments, Glickman may also have been disturbed by how Cosell's nasty approach to broadcasting accrued for him a national audience that liked his negativity, as his career advanced toward the 1970s. His fans seemed to embrace Cosell's constant allegation that, unlike others in the sports media, he "told it like it is." Glickman frequently pointed out that for all of Cosell's self-declared erudition, his most famous tag line was "ungrammatical." Finally, Glickman did not even like that Cosell wore a toupee. That tonsorial decision was all part of what he criticized as his studied disingenuousness. In this regard, Glickman agreed with sportswriter Jimmy Cannon, who also did not think much of Cosell. That boxing journalist once opined, "Cosell's the only guy who ever changed his name and put on a toupee to tell it like it is." Cannon went on to quip, "If Cosell were a sport, he'd be roller derby."[11]

Although Marty Glickman never strayed from his name choice decision even if he understood that it could have a deleterious impact on his own success and may have been bothered that Howard Cohen-Cosell was doing so well, in the case of the disciple whom he would mentor more than anyone else, Glickman fully understood that it made basic linguistic sense for someone like Marvin Aufrichtig later to be known as Marv Albert to make a switch. Talk about euphoniousness—the family name Aufrichtig was difficult to pronounce. Kirk Douglas would have agreed.[12]

In 1953, Marty Glickman suffered a career setback that told him that it was more than just his Jewish-sounding name that would keep him from an esteemed post as a national sports broadcaster. Much like their counterparts in Hollywood, there was an all-too-common belief among high-profile Jewish executives in the early years of the television industry that their growing field was just too Jewish. What ultimately evolved from this attitude was another deleterious form of "self censorship" born of a feeling that as a minority they were "too conspicuous" or worse, that they may be seen in the larger American world as dominant in a public arena. Such was the case generally in the first decades of television when Jews who stood at the helm of networks authorized few Jewish characters and Jewish themes in programming. A "self-protectiveness" against any real or conceivable anti-Semitic charge that Jews were too powerful in that media lay at the core of their decision making.[13]

At first glance, or so he thought, Glickman believed that he was the ideal choice to be the permanent voice of nationally televised professional basketball's "Game of the Week." Who knew more than he that sport's vocabulary—words that were widely identified with him—and he had the proven capacity to bring the excitement of the court into living rooms across the country. He may also have felt that he had earned that desired spot partially in return for his proven commitment to the growth of that sport. He had been there on the scene as the fledgling league made its initial strides in the late 1940s, sometimes in remote, out-of-the-way places. He would recall the night he traveled with the Knicks after a Saturday night game in Syracuse against the Nationals, where they hopped on the Twentieth Century Limited train en route to Fort Wayne, Indiana, for a game the next day against the Pistons. The problem was that there was no stop available for the Limited at Fort Wayne. The team was dumped a mile away at a railroad siding in fifteen-degree weather awaiting a bar-hotel keeper who happened to be a New York fan to fetch them. Then there was the time when he "did a game against the Hawks in Waterloo, Iowa. It was heated by hot air blowers at one end." To help the home team, "they would turn up the blowers when the Knicks were shooting fouls at that end, it would give a knuckleball effect to the shots." Having seen it all, he was warmed when the NBA and the Dumont Broadcasting Network turned to him to be their lead voice. A year later, in 1952, when NBC took over the games from a faltering Dumont operation, Glickman was retained at the microphone. Glickman had been instrumental in the transfer of the rights to the more established and enduring network.[14]

Yet before the 1953 pro basketball campaign, Glickman was sidelined. His replacement was no slouch. Lindsay Nelson, possessed of a smooth Midwestern twang—which came across so different from the hard New York accent—was "literate, personable [and] articulate." He was destined to become "one of the major voices in the history of American sports." Glickman put the onus for his removal on what he called "a faint echo" of Berlin 1936 at the feet of NBA president Maurice Podoloff, his now former friend who had previously referred to Glickman as "the voice of basketball," as well as Haskell Cohen, the league's public relations professional. According to Glickman, Podoloff phoned him and, after hemming and hawing, told him, "Marty, it wouldn't be good if three Jews were in the leadership of the N.B.A. . . . . It would make it a very Jewish league."[15]

Podoloff had a point. Basketball was not only the New York game; it was widely seen as the Jewish game. For decades from the 1920s on, Jews had been prime-time performers. Until the scandal in 1951, CCNY, the most Jewish of college teams, was led by the renowned Nat Holman, who had suited up for the Original (New York) Celtics in the pre-NBA barnstorming years. Jews were the most prominent of those LIU players who decided to skip the Olympics. In 1946, when the Knicks played their first game within the fledgling Basketball Association of America (BAA) the forerunner of the NBA, four of the five starters were Jews. Jews like Sid Hartman, Ben Berger, and Morris Chalfin of the Minneapolis Lakers, Les Harrison of the Rochester Royal, and the so-called Mogul of Basketball, Eddie Gottlieb of the Philadelphia Warriors, were among the first franchise owners. Jews thus had close to controlling interests within this start-up league. However, there is no hard evidence that the American public was troubled by how many Jews were involved in the game as players and stakeholders.

A fearful Podoloff, who for years ran the fledgling NBA out of a one- or two-room office in the Empire State Building, conducted no market surveys to sustain his own nightmare fantasy. Yet he was concerned about how his young league would play in a city like Louisville or Lexington, where college basketball reigned supreme with the University of Kentucky in the lead. It might have been one thing for the Wildcats to come to Gotham to show their mettle. It was another thing for a voice of the "Jewish league" to come regularly into their dens.

Such image considerations—and more than a touch of their own racism—had motivated the officials of the BAA, where Podoloff also served as president, to deny entry to their loop to the New York Rens, the highly talented all-Black team out of Harlem. They were kept out because a majority of owners deemed that their presence could conceivably undermine the association's status among white fans. Paradoxically, the skilled if sometimes "minstrel" teams—like the Harlem Globetrotters—regularly outdrew the Knicks and the Celtics and any other NBA club with white and Black audiences alike. When that traveling African American team was in town for a billed "professional double header," fans were sure to catch the Globetrotters and perhaps left before the NBA fellows took the court.

Be all of this as it may, what Podoloff did do in his conversation with Glickman was to blame NBC executives for the decision. Glickman thought otherwise. For him, it was an unconscionable case of "anti-Semitism . . . from Jews," better described as a virulent form of self-hatred that undermined the career of a fellow Jew. For decades thereafter, Glickman stuck to his belief about "Jewish anti-semitism" and "never quite recovered" from this "severe blow" to his "pride . . . ego . . . and career." Though he "couldn't bring himself to publicly make an issue of the NBA-NBC snub," it darkened his optimistic demeanor.[16]

Those who over the years have speculated why Glickman never became the "dominant voice of TV sports" have offered a collateral narrative. This understanding of what transpired had to have even deepened Glickman's disappointment. It has been suggested that Glickman was passed over not only—or not primarily—because he was a Jew but because he sounded to some ears like a "New York Jew" with the cadences of his hometown. A media critic who deeply appreciated his work would reverently say that "Glickman's voice was not geographically pureed; in the best sense this first-class athlete-turned sportscaster sounded like a New Yorker, Bronx born, Brooklyn raised who had seen the world." But the networks, it has been said, "wanted someone who didn't have such a distinctive regional style . . . a New York style." Glickman believed that he did not possess a "New York accent . . . partly because [he] had gone to school away from New York," even though when he was first on the air in Syracuse a radio listener picked up an "Eastern accented voice." He contended that he was never told that he spoke with that dialect, although both Marv Albert and Spencer Ross, two younger New York sportscasters, found it amusing that in offering advice about their styles and performances, Glickman would begin by calling them "kid," but it sounded like "keed." Albert would reminisce, "He'd call me after games to say, 'Good job, kid' . . . he pronounced it keed." Another journalist and fan of Glickman has recalled how the announcer mispronounced "Tempe, Arizona" as "Tem-pay." Always concerned with accuracy, Glickman later apologized on the air. But Glickman admitted that when he began broadcasting, he "spoke too rapidly at times." But he worked on that element of his presentation from the days when Red Barber influenced him. And in turn Glickman eventually would advise those whom he instructed to slow down too.

However, even though Glickman would be certain not to throw in Yiddish phrases when he was on the air nationally, how he came across in a locale like Fort Wayne was an issue in the executive offices. His audience would be an American group far different from his own New York and Jewish crowd. Later in his career, when he had a rare chance to broadcast a top-flight national game, the Rose Bowl in 1985, a radio critic who also actually liked the way Glickman went about his trade did allow that the announcer was "strictly an Easterner in speech, he gives short shrift to the letter 'r.' He will, for example, say 'quaw-tuh' for 'quarter.'" Still, this columnist from San Diego applauded how Glickman "uses the language with precision and style."[17]

Others who have weighed in retrospectively about the wrong that Glickman was dealt have argued, much like what Marty believed, that it was more than language and intonation that doomed his chances. Rather, wrote one annoyed journalist, "the crusty network executives" said that he was "very New York," but it was an "euphemism" for New York and Brooklyn Jew. Those who made that decision did not appreciate the greatness of Glickman, whose voice is "a Brooklyn Bridge of grace and strength, a blend of concrete and steel." At worst, their choice of announcers was downright prejudice. Another critic of those who ruled the airwaves has charged similarly that "for white bread Anglo-Saxon television executives, he was 'too Jewish and too New York.'" Very likely Marv Albert understood best the intertwined dynamics of discrimination that stymied his mentor's career. In response to an interviewer's suggestion that those at

the network "whispered . . . too Jewish, too New York," Albert
opined, "It was more of a case of the so-called New York label at
that time. Although he had a terrific sports voice and a terrific
style, it was not the mellifluous voice that those particular executives . . . were looking for. It was a completely different landscape"
in the television sports industry in the 1950s, so very different
from the one Albert would thrive in during the decades to follow.
Marty Glickman and Marvin Aufrichtig—both Brooklyn-born—
belonged to different generations of sportscasters and American
Jews. By the time Albert came of age as a national broadcaster,
a New York sports columnist could opine how it had become
acceptable that the younger man "came from the South; South
Brooklyn that is."[18]

After his disappointment at NBC Glickman suffered an additional stinging setback when Roone Arledge, then a rising television sports producer whom he had taken under his wing, showing
him the ins and outs of the sports broadcasting world, did not follow through on the opportunity to advocate for him when ABC
took over the NBC rights to the NBA "Game of the Week." In
his stead, Arledge turned to Chris Schenkel, another young talent
whom Glickman had also mentored. Glickman would recall his
"puzzlement," wondering, was I "too New York"? Decades later,
Glickman, in thinking about this defeat, admitted, "I still don't
know why I didn't get the job. You don't always get the answers
in this business. You just go on." Moving on, figuratively "dust-
ing himself off" when tripped up or pushed down and finding
other outlets for his unquestionable talents, would be his mode
of behavior. Just like his response to the trauma of Berlin in 1936,
Glickman would repeatedly insist that anti-Semitic "factors . . .
never told it all." He would constantly assert, "I have never liked
to believe that I lost a race, lost a job, or whatever because of anti-
Semitism." He didn't make an issue of anti-Semitic rejections
and lived with the disappointment that despite his excellence in
New York, he would not get plum assignments until very late in
his career. Almost two decades later, with the start-up of HBO,

Glickman got his chance to go national. Back home at Madison Square Garden, he was designated as the cable system's initial "one-man sports department." In that position, in 1979, he broadcasted the first nationally televised college basketball "Game of the Week" with another Jewish announcer. That coast-to-coast position only burnished his earned reputation as the premier voice of New York sports.[19]

Sal and Sam Marchiano with their mentor, Marty Glickman. Credit: Courtesy of Sal Marchiano.

8

MARTY AS MENTOR

For fans in the New York area during the 1950s to the 1990s, the national viewing audiences' loss was their gain. Marty Glickman would be a constant in their lives. As one radio/television critic would confirm in the mid-1980s, Glickman "wasn't too widely known in the provinces but sports-minded New Yorkers were crazy about Marty. . . . Mention Marty Glickman's name around town and eyes light up and memories are jogged and stories are related that began with: 'I'll never forget the time. . . .' And these stories will usually involve a Marty Glickman broadcast." His legion of listeners could not have cared if he occasionally said "gonna be" or "marka" or "Warrias" or "attaboy" on the radio waves. When he did that he sounded just like them. By a similar verbal token, they used Glickman's pronunciation of players' names when they spoke about their team's roster, even if an athlete spoke his name differently. They followed the sportscaster's lead. Glickman referred to Erich Barnes, a Giant defensive back of the early 1960s, as "EE-ritch," even as the player called himself "Eric," and his listeners did likewise. Fans also chuckled when the announcer struggled, and yet kept his composure, as he described the actions of a second-string basketball player for North Carolina State, named Bernie Yurin, who entered a game that Glickman announced: "Yurin goes left. Yurin goes right, Yurin is all over the court." Those who tuned in just loved when he spoke excitedly of "the rise and roar of the crowd" or when a great play was made in front of a "hushed crowd" when a crucial foul shot went through the hoop. He was one with the fans in the stands when he would say, "No doubt about it."[1]

Although his greatest claims to well-deserved fame came out of his basketball and football broadcasts, a substantial coterie of fans, natives of his home borough, would not miss tuning in to his pre- and postgame shows before and after Brooklyn Dodger games. Long before sports talk radio shows became ubiquitous all over the country, he along with Burt Lee and Ward Wilson would debate long into the night the strengths and weaknesses of local and national major leaguers. Of the three announcers, Glickman was the "contrarian," sure to voice a "melody" of opinions that were unsung on radio of that day. What kept listeners awake, according to the recollections of one lifelong fan who as a teenager would not miss a show, was how Glickman "did not pull any punches." But ever the gentleman, he never strayed into insults. This Glickman aficionado believed that elsewhere "velvet-toned, eunuch-announcers" would soft pedal athletes' deficiencies to avoid controversies. Not Marty, who "sounded like one of us because he was one of us from Flatbush." Another contemporary has recalled that he would "cherish" those disputatious contretemps as much as "watching and listening to the Dodgers' Robinson, Snider and Reese of the 1950s." For this first call-in sports show, fans joined in on the fun and got to say their piece. Some listeners who were incensed or bemused through what they heard rushed down to outside the studio and playfully accosted the trio, who were anxious to go home after hours on the air. The following day, what Glickman and his colleagues opined and what those who managed to get through via their phone calls had to say provided ample grist for further school lunchroom and street corner debates.[2]

Glickman's many followers likewise got a kick out of his appearance in the 1960s in a skit on *Candid Camera*, a popular early comedy reality show. In that episode, a series of confused customers pick up clothes in a dry goods store and hear Glickman's loud voice announcing a fictitious baseball game, seemingly on the radio, until he comes out from behind a curtain and surprises them. The people upon whom the practical joke was played immediately recognized who had tricked them.[3]

"At the beach in Brooklyn, in Bronx apartments, on Manhattan Streets and in Staten Island homes or under the covers in Queens" this "distinctive voice of New York sports" was a daily companion. "For the generations that grew up next to a radio . . . Marty was at least as big as the players." Older fans who had made it to the Garden on a particular night might vaguely recall what happened to the Knicks. Or the next day, they read highlights in newspapers and magazines. But the "images" that stayed with them "came mostly from the radio" when they were not on the scene at the Garden. "Marty Glickman's voice was [their] sight." Younger fans did their homework while listening to the games and then secreted their transistor radios under their covers after bedtime so as not to miss a moment of the action. One devotee recalled how "each month, [he] took the WHN calendar insert and taped it to the radio next to [his] bed." He was sure not to miss Glickman's descriptions, like that of a Knicks star of the 1950s, "skinny as a rail Carl Braun," or of Joe Lapchick "punctuating his coaching on the sidelines by bouncing and catching a half-dollar off the floor." Though Glickman was careful not to play favorites when he covered the several great New York college teams, his exciting, influential account of the exploits of St. John's caused an allegiance dilemma for one young Orthodox Jewish fan who also "listened . . . in bed with a blanket over the radio." For him, "it wasn't easy to attend yeshiva and root" for a Catholic club.[4]

Since WHN's strong signal reached beyond the immediate New York area, a pair of farm boys growing up in Torrington, Connecticut, likewise "caught the nonpareil Glickman" through their "radio turned low, its speakers muffled by a pillow—impossible for tired parents to detect." Their "duplicity" in staying up late did much to create—through Glickman—their long-standing loyalty to the sport. Nighttime commitments like theirs, they believed, contributed to the "survival" of pro basketball, which was then only "a shaky experiment." Come daytime, all of these youngsters, wherever they resided, replayed the games, first in their minds and then in their schoolyards, shouting the names of players much like Glickman had done.[5]

In 1953, a twelve-year-old young man growing up in Manhattan Beach was likewise listening regularly to the Voice from the Garden, cheering on the Knicks and also imitating the timbre of Glickman's voice when he was chosen for a game at the schoolyard. Already dreaming of a career in sports broadcasting as early as age ten, Marvin Aufrichtig created his own fantasy radio station, which he named WMPA, utilizing his initials, and he walked around his neighborhood "broadcasting" the street games and sandlot sports of his section of Brooklyn to an audience made up of his two brothers. They would also become sportscasters. His game day reports and analyses to his listenership of two were concretized somewhat later when his dad bought him a tape recorder. It was one of those big, bulky models that he carried around with him even to one of his first jobs as a fourteen-year-old office boy in the headquarters of the Brooklyn Dodgers. There, he annoyed the team's owner, Walter O'Malley, when he called the action on the field loudly into his device within earshot of his boss. Soon thereafter, he interacted for the first time with both Howard Cosell and Marty Glickman. In the former case, he had his first real experience on the air when he was a panelist on a Dodger pregame radio quiz show from Ebbets Field that the then-unknown Cosell hosted that featured Little League baseball "experts." There this young man was able to demonstrate how much he knew about the sport. Soon he met up with Glickman when he hung around the Garden. He first gained some notice at the arena when he established a fan club promoting Jim Baechtold, a less than stellar small forward for the Knicks, and then in 1956 he designated himself as the president of the Knicks Fan Club and set out to recruit members. Not long thereafter, he secured a job as a team ball boy.

Upon graduating from Brooklyn's Abraham Lincoln High School, Marvin enrolled at his hero's alma mater. Marty Glickman would say he helped this kid whom he liked from the very start, and whose well-articulated career goals he appreciated, gain admission to Syracuse University, where he studied broadcast journalism within a program that later became known as the S. I. Newhouse School of Public Communications.

Glickman became that prestigious school's prime, if unofficial, student recruiter. Since he had attended Syracuse and went on to achieve such professional success, Glickman was the role model for more than a generation of aspiring sportscasters who sought out that school. A putative chain migration of future star television and radio voices gravitated to this "cradle of sports broadcasting," drawn largely from the New York area but also from other parts of the country in the years after Marv Albert '63 followed in his wise guide's footsteps. This fraternity included Dick Stockton '64, Dave Cohen '72, Bob Costas '74, Sean McDonough '84, Mike Tirico '88, and Ian Eagle '90. The fraternity added a sister in 1986 when Beth Mowins '90 matriculated. Glickman's "influence extended to the [next] broadcasting generations." The issue for those who were part of the second generation was to figure out how to emulate Glickman and, for that matter, "to carry the notes" of their mentors without simply imitating their voices. Ian Eagle realized that it would not be a good strategy to appropriate Glickman's catchphrases of "swish" or "good" or Albert's signature call of "yes." "Book it" became the way Eagle would dramatically emphasize an acrobatic or vital basket.[6]

All of his disciples would gloweringly attest to how supportive Glickman was as they moved forward in their own careers. Albert would speak of his "kindness to everyone he worked with" that he was "very encouraging, always helpful in giving advice." As late as 2008, seven years after Glickman's death, Albert was "still learning from an old master" through a "weekly tutorial" from afar by listening via his computer to old Glickman tapes to upgrade his game. By then, it was more than forty years after Glickman had facilitated his disciple's first big break when he convinced radio management to let the callow twenty-two-year-old substitute for him at a Knicks game when Glickman was stuck in a snowstorm in Newfoundland. Bob Costas would point out that Glickman had "no ego, no pretense and wanted you to be as good as you could be." In an industry that was highly competitive and often cutthroat, where jealousies were so common and destructive, Costas allowed that Glickman "reveled in your success." Sean McDonough would recall the "challenge . . . to live up to his standards" that confronted him when he had the opportunity to work with his "great mentor." For McDonough, "you wanted to be great because he was great."[7]

But Glickman was more than merely a cheerleader who occasionally put in good words with media higher-ups when enviable jobs were in the offing. He was also a teacher who frequently imparted the professional principles that had held him in good stead. Never harsh but always demanding, he sought to have those who followed him to always avoid the broadcasting errors that he had overcome.

Bob Costas was one of those many young people who were attracted to Glickman. Like so many others, as "a kid . . . on Long Island," he would "fiddle with the antenna and pull in some staticky signal from New Haven . . . turn the sound down and listen to Marty Glickman in the radio." The Voice of the Giants was "one of the voices of the soundtrack of [his] youth." When Costas was first starting out in the industry after finishing at Syracuse, and flushed with the "over-eagerness of youth," he turned to Glickman for counsel on how to "sound more mature" on the air; Glickman's response was, "Have you ever heard a middle aged or older person who you respect who speaks so rapidly or tries to get things in to such an extent that it overloads the listener." Remembering much of what Red Barber had told him, even if he did not always follow such wise instruction, Glickman advised Costas to "pull the pace back." When Costas became a national sportscasting celebrity, Glickman would exalt over how his student's "sense of humor, clarity of delivery and intelligence" had brought him to the top of his industry.[8]

In 1965, Glickman articulated an additional set of sportscasting principles in a keynote address to a group of captivated students at Syracuse's first intercollegiate college sports broadcasting conference, which attracted attendees from a variety of eastern schools. There, he stressed two essential points: "do your 'home-work' and speak English." The key to effective broadcasting was nothing less than proper preparation, "knowing everything possible about players including the correct pronunciation of their names." A good announcer also had to "speak in simple and understandable language" and to avoid using jargon and clichés. Glickman believed that when he was on the air he was talking not only to his core fan base but to anyone who might tune in. The speech inspired sophomore pre-engineering major Len Berman, who was working in the production department of the college radio station and who had organized the conference, to aspire to become a broadcaster. He changed his major, over the objections of his parents, who told him "there is only one Walter Cronkite." The family's ultimate compromise was for Berman to major in English and economics while taking public speaking courses and connecting with Glickman through frequent phone conversations. Upon graduation, Glickman assisted Berman in securing a television production and broadcasting slot in Boston. The blossoming Glickman-Berman mentorship took a major step forward in 1979 when the two of them shared a microphone in presenting the college game of the week on HBO.[9]

The ever-available Marty Glickman also found abundant time to help out those who had no connection to Syracuse but who desired to enter his field. For these young people, either through chance or from their intentional reaching out to a man they esteemed, the interaction led to mentorship and ultimately the advancement of their careers. In at least two cases, a Glickman pupil ended up passing on the style and techniques that he learned to a new generation of college students who hoped, too, to be on the sports airwaves. For Marty Glickman the teacher, it was a great source of satisfaction.

As a teenager growing up in the Red Hook section of Brooklyn, Sal Marchiano listened "religiously" to Glickman's postgame show "late into the night in the darkness of his bedroom" and, by day and early evening, tuned in to Knick and Giant broadcasts. "Dead serious" from that early age about becoming a broadcaster, Marchiano, while still a high school student at St. John's Prep in the Bedford-Stuyvesant section of the borough, traveled on Sunday mornings out to Seventh Avenue in Manhattan, where he attended Bert Lee Jr.'s school for broadcasters. The instructor, a young, opinionated sports talk show personality, was emulating his father, who had shared the WHN pre- and postgame mic with Glickman. Bert Lee Jr. had quite a following of his own among young listeners who strained to hear his voice that emanated from a small New Jersey station, WAAT 970. Marchiano wanted to be where the action was. Riding on the D train, he often shared the subway car with Marv Albert, another Brooklyn boy enrollee who had similar dreams. When Marchiano was a senior, due to both talent and perspicacity, Lee Jr. hired him as an intern production assistant. As Lee Jr.'s listener base increased, he moved his show to WATV Channel 13 and brought Marchiano along with him. As fate would have it, one night in 1958 when Lee's guest was Glickman, Marchiano struck up a conversation. Having taken a first step toward establishing a relationship, Marchiano, much like Berman did a few years later, would frequently call Glickman with questions and requests for advice. The mentorship grew further in 1961 when as a junior at Fordham University Marchiano secured a job as a night production assistant at WMGM radio. There he could sidle up next to Glickman as he waited to begin baseball postgame shows and seek his "extravagant wisdom" from the tapes that Marchiano brought with him. By then, Marchiano was a student broadcaster for WFUV radio handling Fordham Rams basketball games and was grateful for "the tough criticism" that was tendered in "a caring way." Upon his graduation, Glickman was instrumental in this disciple, gaining employment with WCBS News Radio 88. It was the beginning of his professional career, which would witness Marchiano on the scene for the next forty years, primarily on television for some of the most memorable baseball, football, basketball, hockey, and boxing events of that era.[10]

Over in the Boro Park section of Brooklyn, at approximately the same time that Marv Albert was growing up a few miles away in Manhattan Beach and Marchiano in Red Hook, Spencer Ross was also listening and watching intently to Glickman on the radio or the television. Although this young man wasn't yet dreaming of a sportscasting career, he also was thoroughly taken with Glickman's style of broadcasting. He could be found sitting on the floor of his apartment in front of the television "doing the game in his head" while "learning the language of 'Glickmanese'" coming across from the announcer. He became such a fan of Marty Glickman that when his bar mitzvah approached, Ross demanded that his father purchase his bar mitzvah suit from Buddy Lee, a clothier in Brooklyn, since Glickman spoke "with such conviction" about the quality of his sponsor's merchandise. However, for almost another decade and a half, Ross would not yet interact with or be helped by his hero, whom he would eventually call his "surrogate father." Spencer Ross would say, "Marty didn't get to know me until I was twenty-seven years old though I first 'met' Marty when I was ten."

A fine basketball player at New Utrecht High School, where a sports reporter from Abraham Lincoln High School named Marv Albert interviewed him after the two schools competed, Ross earned an athletic scholarship from Florida State University. However, after his freshman year in Tallahassee, it was clear to his coach, and to him, that he was not good enough to be elevated to the travel squad. But there was an alternative way for the student-athlete to maintain his scholarship. Local radio station WTNT had approached coach J. K. "Bud" Kennedy about broadcasting FSU games. Having never been in front of a microphone, Ross unabashedly alleged to the coach, and then to the station manager, that he could handle the assignment. He figured that he would use the techniques he had intuited from Glickman. Ross was paid fifteen dollars per game for his expertise. For the next three years, Marty Glickman's broadcasting style would be heard down south through the voice of Spencer Ross. From that point on, Ross's career goal was set.

After graduation, and subsequent to a stint in the army, Ross began doing games and news at a small radio station, WHLI, on Long Island. In 1967, when he heard that the new American Basketball Association was forming and that the New York area had been awarded a franchise, the New Jersey Americans (today the Brooklyn Nets), he "made a pest of [himself]" with the owner-ship and coach angling to be their play-by-play man. It was then that he met Marty Glickman, who was helping the team develop an on-the-air package. During his job interview Ross told Glickman that he "sounded like him" and was hired. Perhaps the meticulous and careful Glickman also reviewed a demonstration tape. It is not known if Ross told Glickman that he had once worked for fifteen dollars a game just like Marty Glickman had earned at Syracuse University twenty years earlier. Had Ross done so, it would have only increased the attractiveness of this candidate to his sym-pathetic interviewer. From that point on, Glickman became his mentor, a refiner of Ross's techniques, and his "greatest advocate and fervent critic." Among his teachings was the advice that when doing a televised game "don't talk too much," let the picture tell the viewer much of the story. Glickman, again repeating a Red Barber admonition, said if after the game you are "hoarse then clearly you talked too much." Twenty years later, Ross would teach this, and many other basics of "Glickmanese," as an adjunct pro-fessor at William Paterson College in New Jersey to another new generation of students of the master sportscaster whose voice long lived on.

In due course, Ross became part of Glickman's own travel squad as he assisted in describing such variegated events as a rodeo in Cowtown, New Jersey, demolition derbies, and amateur wrestling. More important for Ross's professional advancement, when HBO started, Glickman turned to the young colleague to cover New York Islander hockey.[11]

Marty Glickman also gave a gift back to his beloved city in the 1950s and 1960s when he began broadcasting high school sports. Willing, for example, to spend a portion of his Thanksgiving holidays doing the play-by play of a Public School Athletic League football championship game, he proved once again how "he was New York to the bone." His efforts here, in turn, provided a portal for some future announcers whom he helped to follow in his footsteps. In observing a troubling social trend in Gotham's life, Glickman was concerned that so many youngsters were becoming—or were criticized as—in the terminology of that day "juvenile delinquents." In the first postwar decades, youth gangs of the disenchanted terrorized many parts of the city and often set varying and warring ethnic and racial groups against one another. Advertisement posters in subways depicted boys fighting one another on city streets. This frightening phenomenon played its part in motivating Leonard Bernstein to compose the music for the play that would later become the movie *West Side Story*, which spoke about the tragic results of racial hatred. Glickman was similarly deeply concerned about this crisis among New York's youngsters. Always the optimist, his answer was to emphasize to the public much of what was good about the neighborhoods' kids. Recalling what sports had meant to him as a youngster, and the positive excitement it generated in prewar Brooklyn, he found time within his very busy schedule covering every conceivable sport, to head up a weekly and very popular "high school game of the week." Keen to put the best face on the area's teenagers, he did more than just focus attention upon the best football and basketball athletes, many of whom went on to distinguished collegiate and professional playing careers. He also introduced his viewership to off-the-field student leaders who might have starred in a school music group, a debating club, or chorus.[12]

Glickman's endeavor to "capture the flavor of scholastic enthusiasm" was widely praised. After his presentation of the first three high school clashes—one of which incidentally pitted his own erstwhile James Madison crew against Lincoln High School, WOR-TV, which carried the game, received some two hundred phone calls "endorsing the program." There was some concern that players would lose their concentration on the game at hand

and start mugging for the unblinking electronic eye. But the ever-supportive Glickman asserted, "Once a game is under way and a player makes contact with an opponent, he forgets about the camera and just plays." To ensure a high quality of play city-wide, and drawing upon friendships in the wider gridiron world, Glickman, in 1959, organized a football coaches' clinic and lined up "an imposing array of talent for his faculty" that included his former Syracuse assistant coach Bud Wilkinson, who by then was a renowned Oklahoma Sooner coach, and former Orangeman Duffy Daugherty, who was head coach at Michigan State. One reporter's evaluation of the action on the field was that while these schoolboy tilts lacked "the razzle-dazzle" of college matches, the "teams . . . displayed a fine knowledge of football fundamentals" and the video production was of "a professional level."[13]

The most fortunate of the students who attended were those who got the chance to assist Glickman in his broadcasts. Stuyvesant High School's Dave Cohen, who was already thinking of a broadcast career, felt the "thrill" of working as a spotter for Glickman when his club played Far Rockaway. Inspired, much like Marv Albert, who was a high school game statistician, and the others who would make up that chain enrollment pattern, Cohen too went on to Glickman's alma mater in 1968. There he majored in radio and television broadcasting. He stayed in touch, at least figuratively, in 1970 when he rigged up his transistor radio in his dorm room to a reel-to-reel tape recorder to have a record of Glickman announcing a Jets-Giants game. A fan also of Merle Harmon, who was the Jets' announcer, he also recorded his account. Through what he called "a technological achievement," he had "stereo" voices to enjoy and study. In 1980, Cohen and Glickman got back together literally when they combined in presenting a New York State high school basketball championship game. It was a minor event for Glickman to handle a spot on a public broadcasting station where the remuneration—if any—was minimal. But it was a memorable early career moment for Cohen, who deeply appreciated, and long recalled, his very senior colleague's willingness to trek up to Rochester to share a microphone with a novice. Cohen would go on to cover New York Yankees baseball and freelanced over the years for ESPN, broadcasting a variety of sports much like Glickman did.[14]

In 1981, Marty Glickman was tapped to do more than just advise and advocate for those who had long hoped to enter and grow within his industry. Now he was called upon to train individuals basic to American sports—retired athletes. Network executives felt the public wanted to hear these former marquee performers expound based on their on-field experience. But in the minds and words of critics, their inability to articulate properly in front of the microphone mitigated whatever wisdom they may have possessed about the games they had played. Hired with no professional guidance "on a sink or swim basis, quite a few . . . foundered" as they fell back upon clichés and failed to make worthwhile points. Ever the detractor, Howard Cosell led the chorus of naysayers who complained about the power of "the jockocracy" even though, ironically, for several years he shared the television booth of the very popular Monday Night Football with two former NFL stars, Frank Gifford and Don Meredith. For Cosell, the proclivity to invite into the booth ex-jocks not on journalistic merit but because of their name recognition was an unconscionable malaise. Part of his pique had to do with the fact that he was frequently attacked for not having "played the game."[15]

Marty Glickman also strongly believed that trite, overused expressions and jargon led to poor communication and made for bad broadcasting, no matter the announcer's background. He had said as much in his 1965 Syracuse address and probably every time he was interviewed about the talking trade. But unlike Cosell, who relished upbraiding opponents, Glickman was interested in properly inculcating his skills to athletes. As early as the 1950s, he already "had coached informally" Knicks player Bud Palmer and subsequently helped Sugar Ray Leonard handle fight cards. So, when NBC Sports approached him to be their in-house tutor, at the suggestion of former football lineman Merlin Olsen, who was struggling to do well on the air, Glickman readily accepted. Marty was too much of a gentleman to publicly note the irony that the same network that turned him away as the voice of the basketball game of the week in the early 1950s now turned to him as a teacher.[16]

Glickman believed that these students had great potential. They might possibly prove to be better at the trade than many of those who had always wanted to be sportscasters. He allowed that "the jock has two assets over the journalism student; his recognizability and his knowledge of the game." In a subtle swipe at Howard Cosell, he continued, "Why hire the stranger out of journalism school who *never played the game* over the jock who can be taught to broadcast." The trick was to move former players away from those who "patted" them on the back and "glad handed" them and then put them down when they failed. As a demanding teacher, he asserted, "I will tell them I'm going to tell it 'as *it is*,'" another takedown of his nemesis for his oft-repeated ungrammatical catchphrase.[17]

The athletes in training proved to be a very receptive bunch. After all, according to Bob Griese, former Miami Dolphins quarterback, "Athletes are used to constructive criticism. After games you watch films and coaches tell you what you did wrong and how to do it differently next time." He was told to avoid relying upon "footballese," understandable only to the very few who had been in the huddle with him. He was taught some basic Glickman principles, such as "talk into the camera, make eye contact with the viewer," stay clear of clichés, and above all "speak proper English . . . the prerequisite of a good broadcaster." By the time Griese "graduated" he not only was handling his assignments skillfully but was displaying a fine sense of humor. He was comfortable enough "to tell a funny story on the air." Red Barber would have been pleased. In addition to Olsen and Griese, Glickman's successful athlete disciples included John Brodie, Joe Namath, Gene Washington, and Frank Gifford, who worked with Cosell.[18]

During his career as a network tutor, Glickman also showed himself to be ahead of his time in helping some of the first women enter his male-dominated industry. He made himself available even though early in his own career there were some missteps that troubled him when radio executives thought that having a female sit next to him in a booth would be good for ratings and advertising dollars. During Glickman's second year of covering the Knicks, team owner Ned Irish thought female fans would be attracted to the broadcasts if Sarah Palfrey Cooke, a well-known tennis player, would assist Glickman in commenting on the game. Unfortunately, she knew nothing about basketball, and the executive's orders to Glickman to quickly teach her about the sport went awry. When asked during her first effort on the air what she thought of the action on the court, she said, "I'm speechless." Cooke was let go after six regrettable games.

Glickman and the station had a somewhat better experience with tennis player Gussie Moran, who became part of a popular sports talk show crew. When first hired in 1947, she had only "a vague knowledge of baseball as a member of a girls softball team in Southern California." Although Glickman felt that he could do very well without her, he dealt with Moran's weaknesses with a "good natured, amused tolerance." He accepted her "not as a sports expert but as a sports personality." Moran would later admit that without the help of Glickman and his radio sidekick, Ward Wilson, she would not "have lasted a week." She endured for several years and by the late fifties secured a spot on a Yankee postgame show. As with the men he mentored, the issue with women in the industry was not gender but competency.[19]

In 1987, a particular type of qualified woman entered Glickman's "classroom." Gayle Sierens of Tampa, Florida, a graduate of Florida State University with a major in communication, had been working for seven years as a sports reporter for WXFL. On a visit to New York, she found a way of securing an appointment with Michael Weisman, the NBC executive who had agreed with Merlin Olsen's mentoring idea and had appointed Glickman as the teacher to athletes. Fortuitously for Sierens, Weisman was now thinking of promoting his network's brand through adding a woman to their broadcasting operations as a play-by-play sportscaster. Weisman offered Sierens the post with the proviso that Glickman would be her coach too. The "kind, smart" teacher treated her exactly as he had his football player charges. He instructed her, for example, "how to create spotting charts, how to use proper voice inflections etc." In December 1987, on the final Sunday of the NFL's regular season, Sierens became the first woman to do play-by-play when she covered a Seattle Seahawks–Kansas City Chiefs game. Her performance received mixed reviews. A proud Glickman published several of the most favorable newspaper accounts of Sierens's work in his autobiography. Weisman offered her additional opportunities to handle other games. But a combination of family obligations—as a mother she could not see herself "galavanting" around the country—coupled with her ambition to be a news anchor at WXFL kept her from doing another game. She would maintain her television post handling straight news for a quarter century. In retrospect, Sierens, although a pioneer, did not see herself as a trendsetter. She would say, "We"—she, Glickman, Weisman, and former NFL defensive tackle Dave Rowe, who did the color commentary—"may have kicked down the door, but no one else came in," at least for a long time thereafter. Twenty-two years would pass before another woman, Beth Mowins, would call an NFL game. Mowins was a Syracuse graduate who was born professionally into that university's "cradle of sports broadcasting." Nonetheless, Sierens's big moment meant a lot to an unidentified high school girl whom she encountered at a Florida football game while preparing for her NBC gig. The young woman, busy speaking into a tape recorder, did not recognize Sierens, but she did say, "Now that NBC is giving this woman a chance to be a play-by play broadcaster, I'm hoping that someday I can do that too."[20]

Growing up, Susan Anne Marchiano, known professionally as "Sam," had the same dreams as that Florida girl and possessed a greater chance that her hopes would be realized. She was Sal Marchiano's daughter, and her supportive dad introduced her to the world of sports news and broadcasting within which he had become a well-regarded figure. After graduating from Columbia, she worked for a while in print media before catching on at New York's Sports Channel, where she was a sideline reporter and a pre- and postgame personality for a number of local teams. To up her game in "describing events" that were passing so quickly on the field and rink, she followed the request of her station manager to have Marty Glickman work with her much like he had done with her father decades earlier. These tutorials, with a second-generation disciple, included recitations of those lines from Edgar Allan Poe's "The Raven" that he had frequently used to warm up for his broadcasts. Though Sam Marchiano was initially "intimidated" to be a student in the presence of the "great man," as her father always reverently referred to Glickman, she found this "natural teacher" to be "kind, patient and unhurried." Sam Marchiano would go on to be a national correspondent for Fox Sports and an anchor person for mlb.com, before becoming an adjunct professor within NYU's Institute of Global Sports.[21]

In 1988, Marty Glickman became Professor Glickman when he was called to Fordham University as an adjunct within the communications program. He was tasked with teaching and advising the school's sportscasters-in-training. These men and a few women were already working in the student-run sports department of WFUV radio covering Ram basketball and football games and hosting a Sunday evening talk show called *One-on-One*. Every Tuesday the students presented recordings of their performances in front of their professor, who responded with "realistic, tough and demanding criticism, but also with supportive encouragement." During one memorable class, Glickman told a young woman who admitted that she was fearful every time she was about to go on the air, "Honey, the day you are not nervous is the day you should retire. You should always have jitters, cause if you don't you have lost your passion." Glickman had in the back of his mind how he felt right before stepping up to the mic in Syracuse some fifty years earlier. He also advised her, and the other attentive listeners, to ignore the brickbats that the ignorant might throw at them. His message was that while announcers should be respectful of those who differed with them and remember that "always someone is listening for the first time . . . you [must] realize you can't please everyone." In 1997, Glickman relinquished his position at Fordham.

Much like the disciples at Syracuse whom he inspired, many of the Fordham students who benefitted from Glickman's hands-on efforts became well-known local and national sportscasting personalities. In one case, a graduate, just like Spencer Ross, went on to teach Glickman's style and "philosophy focusing on the fundamentals . . . considering the listener and viewers first . . . no *shtick* [gimmicks], no cuteness just accurate descriptions" to his own new generation of aspiring announcers. In 1998, after finishing school where he was the sports director at WFUV, Rick Schultz interned at WFAN, the nation's first 24/7 sports talk outlet. His broadcasting career led him to "stints with Army athletics, two minor league baseball teams and an ESPN affiliate" as well as working back at his alma mater. Even as he progressed, he stayed in touch with his teacher and frequently showed up at Glickman's apartment for refresher sessions with his tapes in hand. Over the years, he taught "Glickmanese" at Marist College and the Connecticut School of Broadcasting before creating his own private mentoring and tutoring service.[22]

While words of appreciation have rolled off the tongues of all those whom Glickman mentored, without a whit of a dissenting word, when Bill Walton spoke about the man whom he would say "was a little, short guy who turned out to be a giant amongst people," he did so with the word "love" on his lips and in is heart.

Walton was the star basketball center for the almost perennial national championship UCLA Bruins, leading them to titles in 1972 and 1973 and garnering for himself three national player of the year awards. In 1977, three years into his pro career, he won the NBA's most valuable player award as he steered the Portland Trail Blazers to their only professional championship. Amid all of these triumphs, he rarely spoke publicly about his exploits because of his problem with stuttering, which had afflicted him from his early youth. As a "very shy and reserved young man," he "took refuge in the things that [he] did well—most notably athletics," which "shielded the deficiencies that limited [his] overall growth and development. . . . It was a convenient way of avoiding [the] responsibilities of developing human relation skills." At college, to avoid "disasters," he relied upon his coach, John Wooden, and his teammate, point guard Greg Lee, to handle interviews. Walton suffered that frustration until he met Glickman at a Los Angeles charity function. Upon hearing that he could not speak without stammering, Glickman risked confronting Walton with advice designed to remedy the troubling disorder that he himself had successfully overcome as a young man in Brooklyn. Glickman believed that one of Walton's problems, much like "other people who stutter," was that "Bill was full of information in his head and worried he might forget it and had to say it right away." He was told to "corral and line up his thoughts." This basic tip, and other more detailed pieces of advice that were first given in the corner of that banquet hall, would, according to Walton, "change his life" and constituted his "greatest accomplishment," more than all of his on-court victories. While staying in touch for guidance and in friendship, Bill Walton would become a television commentator and public speaker. His success in that arena was a "wonderful surprise" for Glickman. In an attempt to be as "concerned and selfless" as his teacher, Walton volunteered to be a spokesperson for the National Stuttering Foundation. When Glickman died, John Wooden told an obituary writer, in an ironic way, that notwithstanding his regard for all of the athlete-announcer's manifold achievements, within and without the confines of sports, the coach was angry with Glickman. He explained to the perplexed reporter that Glickman was the one who taught his great player to speak without any problems but "did not teach him how to stop." It was a fitting tribute to the American sportscaster mentor par excellence.[23]

Left to right: Marty Glickman with John Woodruff and Margaret "Gretel" Bergmann Lambert discussing the 1936 Olympics. Credit: Courtesy of the United States Holocaust Memorial Museum.

9

OLYMPIC MEMORIES

WHILE Marty Glickman crafted a celebrated career over five decades after World War II, assisted the next generation of sportscasters with reaching their professional goals even as he chafed, and coped over his own unrealized hope of being a national sports television personality, he kept his deep and painful feelings about his trauma in Berlin in 1936 to himself. He rarely talked about the "meeting," and when he did his explanation for all that had gone wrong was "politics," a vague euphemism for nepotism. He did not identify Avery Brundage as the prime instigator of his sidelining. He did not speak in explicit terms about Olympic anti-Semitism for fifty years. This longue durée of silence was exemplified early on when he was invited to address, in the months following his return to Syracuse, both "Jewish and non-Jewish groups" in venues close to campus. Reportedly, "despite his lack of maturity"—the young college sophomore was but nineteen years of age—he "spoke easily and thought well on his feet" before crowds that were interested in his account of what had happened the previous summer. In his presentations, he reiterated what he had said while still in Germany that anti-Semitism was not at the root of the infamous meeting that had kept him from participating. Appearing, for example, at a gathering at Temple Beth El in Rochester, he asserted that "racial prejudice had nothing to do with it. I was tremendously disappointed at being kept off the Olympic team at the last minute. But I want everyone to know that I was proud to be there in Germany as a United States representative. It was just too bad that I didn't get a chance to show that the German philosophy of so-called Aryan supremacy is a myth." The ever-upbeat runner, "still an Olympic rooter," revealed that he looked forward to being able to "take another crack at place on [the] 1940 Olympic squad." In the meantime, he would fulfill his football promise as "one of the toughest backfield men in the country to catch."[1]

In July 1948, Glickman appeared to have put the incident in Berlin much further behind him when he was referred to as the "mastermind" behind the gala send-off of the U.S. Olympic "squad of 260" as they boarded the S.S. *America* on their way to the London games. The former Syracuse University sprinter, who was identified as an athletic alumnus who had "made the trip to Berlin in 1936," shared the festivities with the president of the AAU, a representative of the New York Athletic Club—which was still off-limits to Jews—and with none other than Avery Brundage.[2]

While these athletes were taking off for Europe, *New York Times* sports columnist Arthur Daley wrote a retrospective about controversies that had often swirled around the Olympic games prior to World War II. For him, the problem with these gatherings always began because "as soon as personal opinions, instead of performances on the track are permitted to enter the picture, bickering and discontent are sure to follow." The story of how Glickman and Stoller were excluded was offered as a prime example of an unwarranted dispute. But Daley offered no indication that anti-Semitism motivated Brundage and his compatriots. While asserting that the "switch" to Owens and Metcalfe was "obviously . . . a certain guarantee of victory," he also allowed that the two Jewish runners— their ethnicity was not noted—probably could have done almost as well as their replacements. The banning was projected simply as an unexplained "arbitrary decision" that "the Olympic coaching staff has not lived down yet."[3]

In 1956, when writing his own Olympics retrospective, Jesse Abramson, who in 1936 had come as close as any journalist on the scene to imply that anti-Semitism was involved in the exclusion, only repeated his questioning of American Olympic Committee motives from twenty years earlier. He again wrote, "We won the 400-meter relay in record time but Sam Stoller and Marty Glickman were somehow left off the quartet and no one ever satisfactorily explained why."[4]

An ongoing regnant lack of attention in newspapers, which even recalled the 1936 Olympics concerning why the Jewish runners were left out, was exemplified in 1961 within a profile of Glickman, who was by then gaining much attention as a broadcaster. As television critic Bert Burns walked his readers through "the glib sportscaster's" life, he noted only that the former "gridder and trackman" who had been a member of the U.S. team "suffered the misfortune in the Berlin games of being a sprinter in the same events as Jesse Owens."[5]

Media amnesia about the prejudices that beset Glickman and Stoller reached its peak in 1966 when a film titled *Jesse Owens Returns to Berlin* appeared on American television. Commemorating thirty years since the great Olympic champion triumphs, the show, produced by Bud Greenspan, a close friend of Glickman's, was the first of several large-scale documentaries and movies that would appear about Owens's triumphs in the 1936 games. The script followed the sprinter step by step as he came back to the Olympic Stadium and was greeted by an adoring crowd. However, as the show took viewers back to Hitler's era, it offered a highly sanitized account of what transpired, devoid of almost all references to controversies. It offered little more than a retracing of how Owens won his gold medals with abundant detail about the athletic challenges he overcame, the opponents whom he defeated, and his crowning moments on the podium as the "Star-Spangled Banner" was played in front of over one hundred thousand spectators who chanted his name at the "magnificent" Olympic Stadium. Much was also said of the friendships he made with participants from all over the world. Owens noted sadly that it turned out to be the last time the best athletes in the world would gather as comrades before the calamitous World War II. Special note was taken of how a great German long jumper named Lutz Long helped him win that event when the two men were in competition. Long advised Owens on how to avoid fouling on his third and final qualifying leap. Had Owens stepped over the line, he would have been disqualified. No mention was made in the documentary of how the heartwarming sight of the African American and the German walking arm in arm after the track meet played within the Nazi hierarchy box in the stadium. For his show of brotherhood, Long would become persona non grata within Hitler's circles. He died in combat during the Italian campaign.

As far as Jews were concerned, Owens did allow pleasantly that "the Jewish population of Germany was given a reprieve" from Nazi attacks due to "the protests of many nations. There would be no persecutions during the games." When it came to the 4 × 100 meters relay, Owens did not mention Glickman or Stoller, nor the "meeting" where, according to so many prior accounts, he had courageously spoken up on behalf of his Jewish teammates only to be told bluntly to sit down and shut up. His narrative was that "due to the quality of the opponents from Germany and Holland," who demonstrated impressive and troubling skills, a "real scare" was put "into our team" and "convinced [us] that the race would not be a walk-over." This account came awfully close to affirming Cromwell's fallacious idea that the Germans had some secret champions ready to win for Hitler. But Owens was proud that Metcalfe, Wykoff, Draper, and he carried the day for America and shared the glory of having laurel wreaths placed on their heads in front of hero-worshipping fans. Finally, concerning the allegation that Hitler snubbed him, refusing to shake his hand after he won—a rebuff that did not take place—Owens reflected that back in 1936 he "lost no sleep" over whether Hitler might congratulate him. However, he was greatly flattered that twenty-five years later, when he came back to Germany to run a commemorative lap of the Olympic Stadium, the mayor of West Berlin warmly embraced him.[6]

Nine years later, in 1975, Greenspan noted the Glickman-Stoller controversy only as a small part of one of the episodes in a much larger, twenty-two-segment project then underway called "Olympiad." The focus of this particular filming was the career of Ralph Metcalfe, who, along with Owens, replaced Glickman and Stoller on the 4 × 100 meters relay team in Berlin. In discussing that controversial race, the narrator, David Perry, reading Greenspan's words, stated in passing how on the day prior to event a switch was made; two Jews were left out, and reports circulated within Berlin that the Nazis had pushed for the change and U.S. officials had complied. Within Metcalfe's own sound bite, he identified the victimized runners and asserted that due to his displeasure with the decision, he was motivated to run his fastest race. The episode stopped short of mentioning who among the leaders of the AOC went along with the Germans' alleged demands as the full, detailed story of the instigators of the "meeting" and its aftermath remained to be told.[7]

Growing up in the 1950s and 1960s, Marty and Marjorie Glickman's children were well aware that their father had been an Olympian. The youngest of the four Glickman youngsters reached her majority at the end of the 1960s. There was a signed photograph of the 1936 U.S. track team on a wall in their home. David and Nancy Glickman also have both recalled that every four years their father was approached to comment on some or another controversy surrounding the always-political international games. But their father did not flash back to them about Berlin 1936. When he responded to reporters' questions about present-day Olympic entanglements, during the era of the highest Cold War tensions that constantly pitted the United States against the Soviet Union, he always stopped just short of mentioning his personal Jewish angle. Marty Glickman was on the record as quite opinionated about how government leaders and their propagandists used the Olympics as their forum, undermining the purity of the games. He was particularly chagrined about how those in charge, on the American athletic side, contributed mightily to this wrong emphasis.

For example, prior to the 1956 Winter Olympics in Cortina, Italy, Glickman was troubled that AOC leaders were so worried that America would lose to the Russians. It was the first time the Soviets were competing in the Winter Games. The word within the sports world was that they came out from behind the Iron Curtain with a stellar squad. For Glickman, the worry among the "badge-wearers" was much like at Berlin 1936: "It's the same old story the officials keep botching things up." The problem, both then and now, was that "officials just get too officious and too patriotic. All the brass . . . is concerned because the U.S. may not win a single gold medal. What does it matter? America is here to compete, not to win. When you get hungry for medals you kill that spirit" of friendly competition. "Chauvinism" and the "win at all costs" philosophy undermined Olympic ideals and would continue to trouble Glickman as he witnessed subsequent quadrennial gatherings. As it turned out, in 1956 the Soviet Union finished first in those Nordic and Alpine events, with sixteen medals. The United States garnered seven medals and finished sixth in the ranking of nations.[8]

As the 1980 Moscow games approached and President Jimmy Carter ordered an American team boycott of the Olympics to protest the Soviet invasion of Afghanistan, Glickman was among the minority of commentators and former athletes who differed with the decision. He didn't want "politics," his long-standing code word for his problems in 1936, "to destroy the dreams of some other Olympic athletes." He did not mention that his dream had been turned into a nightmare, as he asserted how "I still believe very very strongly about Olympic participation and the Olympic ideals." He continued, "I still love it, if the Olympics aren't good, what the hell is?"[9]

Glickman's love for the international gathering of athletes was severely tested when, in 1972, the "serene games," as the Munich Olympics had been advertised, were shattered when Palestinian terrorists murdered eleven Israeli athletes. The use of the Olympics as a political forum had now turned violent. Years later, Glickman would recall how "I never felt more Jewish than in 1972 at Munich. . . . It was one of the most emotional experiences

I ever had."Yet, at no point did he connect Berlin 1936 to Munich 1972. Although angered at the behavior of the IOC, he was not surprised that this "self-perpetuating body," which claimed that they "lived by the Olympic ideal . . . fell short, very short" during this terrible time. Avery Brundage was not only still around but now the international organization's president. Unchanged in his attitudes, after one day of mourning where Brundage in his "memorial" speech linked the murdering of the Israeli athletes to "commercial and political pressures" that threatened "to destroy this nucleus of international cooperation and goodwill we have in the Olympic movement," the IOC head reassured the world that "the games must go on."[10]

Glickman's upset was magnified when he observed the actions of athletes from around the world and the behavior of some of his broadcasting colleagues to the euphoria demonstrated during the closing ceremonies. He would never forget that "horror" that brought him to "tears" when he saw participants "singing and dancing" after those "marvelous Israeli athletes had been murdered." He was deeply troubled that a U.S. announcer "with a shit-eating grin on his face and a smirk" referred happily to "Munich the City of Lights" as he reported on the final festivities as if "there's another automobile race going on or another basketball game." He would be forever sorry that he had helped Chris Schenkel enter the "business," as he showed no "sensitivity, no emotion" to what had occurred just days earlier. In the back of his mind, Glickman had to have recalled how thirty-six years earlier the media had blissfully moved on after his sidelining, but he did not publicly connect the events in Munich and Berlin. Taking to the airwaves on the radio back in New York, he dealt with this "tough time" through "emotionalizing it, particularly the lack of Olympic support for Israel and Jews." He would say: "what are they so gay about after what happened?" Yet as a true believer in what a pristine amateur Olympics could be, while years later he was annoyed when professional athletes, like the 1992 NBA Dream Team, were recruited to win for America, he remained supportive of international games. For Glickman, though, the "true amateurs were the boys and girls playing in the school yards" much like he had done as a young boy in Brooklyn. Still, he would never call for the abolishment of the games.[11]

Clearly, Marge Glickman and their children knew how their husband and father felt about the Olympics. However, growing up, the four youngsters knew nothing about his exclusion in 1936. That was until Nancy, then in junior high school, watched "a documentary about Jesse Owens" and inquired of her dad for more details about the Berlin games. To her utter surprise, Marty took her upstairs to the attic, which had become a master bedroom, opened a dresser, showed her his Olympic uniform, and then related the story of his and Stoller's sidelining. However, according to David Glickman, his "always upbeat" father never "dwelled on the negative." If and when stories of Brundage and the ordeal ever came up in subsequent family conversation, his father was sure to note that 1936 was not 1972: "no one was killed" when Stoller and he had their problems. He would make that tragic comparison again and again when he publicly addressed the anti-Semitism that he endured; but not yet.[12]

Among those outside of his family who would become very close to him, including in particular the first generation of those announcers whom he would mentor, the sad saga of Glickman-Berlin was barely known and not widely discussed. Marv Albert has recalled that "as a young Jewish boy, growing up in the Brooklyn area it was more of a legendary thing that I heard about. It wasn't something that touched me because it happened many years before I was born." As youngsters, Spencer Ross, Len Berman, and Dave Cohen all knew about Jesse Owens's triumphs but had "no awareness" of what had happened to Glickman. Many years later, Ross would reflect on the irony that if his mentor had not been kept out of the race, "there would have been a parade" in Brooklyn celebrating Glickman's victory, where he would have proudly worn his gold medal and then "no one would have known him" as an athlete.[13]

As a kid, Hollywood-born Wayne Norman did not know any-thing about Marty Glickman. Living on the West Coast, this future sportscaster's role models were the iconic Vin Scully and Chick Hearn, providing play-by-play for the Los Angeles Dodgers and Lakers. He became acquainted with Glickman only in the early 1980s when late in Glickman's career the senior sportscaster signed on to broadcast University of Connecticut football and basketball games. It was a great acquisition for the small radio station. Like almost everyone else in the industry, Norman learned from this mentor. In his case a valuable lesson was to never use foul language, even when preparing for an event. Such verbiage might inadvertently carry over to the live broadcast, and always remember "your voice is what people hear" and the wrong words "will reflect poorly upon you." The twosome trav-eled together for four and a half years, swapping sports stories, with Norman picking up much more of Glickman's wisdom. It remained for a chance encounter with a veteran sportswriter who reported for the *Portland Daily News* in a cheap hotel room that the two travelers shared on the road in Maine for Norman to overhear a "jaw-dropping account" that caused him to "put down his notes and became glued" to the conversation as Glickman responded to the question of whether he still harbored a "grudge" against Hitler, Brundage, and his coaches. His consciousness raised, Norman mused that he has wondered when and how he otherwise would have learned of what had happened to his cir-cumspect colleague. Norman would long remember family man Glickman's one enduring grievance: "I don't have a gold medal to show to my grandchildren."[14]

In 1979, ready to detail his entire life for posterity, Glickman met privately with an interviewer working for the American Jewish Committee's oral history project. In his multihour discussion—the transcript runs close to 250 pages—Glickman made abundantly clear for whomever might eventually read his account that he firmly believed that American anti-Semites and not "politics" had removed Stoller and him from the relay team. Without a hint of equivocation, he testified, "In order to save the Nazis from more embarrassment . . . the Jews were kept off the team by an American Nazi named Avery Brundage with the help of Dean Cromwell." It was bad enough that Hitler, Goebbels, and Von Ribbentrop had to endure watching Owens win his gold medals. Glickman recalled seeing them in the chancellor's box. The AOC head, he asserted definitively, was "a Nazi sympathizer," and both he and the track coach were members of the America First Party. "The American Nazis couldn't do much about" Owens et al. "because there were so many blacks of such prominence" but they could avoid "embarrassing" their German friends.[15]

Speaking of Jew hatred, Glickman recalled the hurt that the New York Athletic Club's behavior caused him and had much to say about pressures placed on him to change his name along with the prejudices that had kept this New York Jewish broadcaster from reaching a national audience. Glickman was also unsparing of Maurice Podoloff and Haskell Cohen for their weakness. His many recollections, which began with his account of a boyhood in Brooklyn, continued with his collegiate years in Syracuse and followed his career in radio and television, would form the basis for his memoir, *The Fastest Kid on the Block*, published almost twenty years later, in 1996.[16]

In 1980, a year after he sat for that extended private discussion, Glickman began to move away from this long-standing guardedness and to speak openly to journalists about the nefarious opponents and the discriminations that had troubled his life, starting with Berlin. In the larger context of explaining why he opposed a boycott of the Moscow games, Glickman, for the first time in a published interview, explicitly asserted that Cromwell's explanation of why Stoller and he were kept from running was "obviously a lie" and that the so-called politics of 1936 meant, without question, that he was prevented from running because he was Jewish. He also identified Brundage, by name, as the force behind the AOC desire not to "embarrass" Hitler and that his antagonist was deeply involved with the America First group. But he did stop short of calling Brundage an American Nazi, as he had done in the unpublished interview a year earlier.[17]

A year later, in 1981, Bud Greenspan, who fifteen years earlier did not include the Glickman-Stoller incident when he produced *Owens Returns to Berlin* and in 1975 noted the controversy over Jews only in passing, now made clear, with and on behalf of his friend, who were the culprits. Utilizing Marty Glickman's own words, he explained in the *New York Times* how Owens ended up with four gold medals. Greenspan detailed the "meeting" and the exclusion and quoted the victimized runner as certain that "the decision to keep the only Jewish athletes out of the competition was made by *American Nazis.*"[18]

In 1984, a second full-length documentary on Owens, running four hours, appeared on American television, titled *The Jesse Owens Story*. Although journalist, and later historian, William L. Shirer, who was on the scene in Berlin in 1936, praised the film for capturing "color and excitement . . . through the use of actual newsreel footage" of the stadium triumphs of the African American over Hitler, it set back the telling of a complete true story of what happened to the Jewish runners in Berlin. While unlike *Jesse Owens Returns to Berlin* this movie portrayed the all-important track team meeting, the depiction was rife with errors when compared with Glickman's recollections of his whole Olympic experience. One scene has the American Olympic team on a bus to the Olympic Village where two Jewish athletes, baseball player Herman Goldberg and a fictitious "American sprinter" named Dave Levitt, notice a sign in German that, when translated, read "Dogs and Jews Not Wanted." Goldberg and Levitt then jump off the bus, assert that they want no more of the Nazi games, and demand to be taken back to the boat and to immediately return to America. It remained, in the docudrama, for a heroic Owens to step up and convince them that the Jewish sportsmen and he were in Berlin to disprove the myths of Aryan racial superiority. The immediate problem is resolved in the film only when a young boy, a member of the Hitler Youth, appears, whitewashes the sign, asserts how Hitler had told his people to treat their visitors well, and then asks for Goldberg's and Levitt's autographs. Glickman is identified only in the subsequent "meeting" scene, where he does tell Cromwell that the Germans have no great hidden runner and that the world will know that this move is but a ruse. However, the screenwriters grant Levitt the major speaking part where he accuses Brundage of being a Nazi sympathizer. "Levitt" was most likely a theatrical stand-in for Stoller. It is not known why this switch in characters was made. In Glickman's account, Stoller was silent. All told, the depicted chronology and behavior presented of Glickman was all wrong. It cannot be determined how Marty Glickman reacted when the film was shown.[19]

It remained for a return trip to Berlin in 1985 for Glickman to totally come to grips with what had befallen him almost five full decades earlier. He had returned as a member of the Jesse Owens Foundation to the then-divided capital of Germany to plan a track meet memorializing his friend who had died five years earlier. Owens's return in 1966 had been a moment of triumph for the African American Olympic champion as a packed stadium cheered for him. But Glickman was filled with painful memories and profound anger as he walked alone down the track in an empty stadium and peered to the grandstands where Hitler and the rest of his evil entourage had been seated. Subsequently, he would pen a poem that constitutes the prologue to his autobiography, which would be published eleven years later.

In a few compelling verses, he identified the Nazis both in Germany and in the United States who had spurned Stoller and him with unmitigated opprobrium, expressing, without equivocation, his greatest hatred for Avery Brundage: "The huge brooding stadium surrounds me. . . . Just like the day almost fifty years ago. The distant echoes of 120,000 voices reverberate around the empty stadium. The anger swells within me, Rage. What might have been. Those dirty sons of bitches. Hitler, Robertson, Cromwell and Brundage. . . . That Brundage, especially Brundage. That was 1936. This is 1985. . . . The anger is spilling out. An anger I stored up all those years. Those dirty bastards, evil Nazis. American Nazis."[20]

Several months later in 1986, after returning to America, he would tell a *New York Times* reporter how his "anger was overwhelming when I walked out of the tunnel. . . . I started to shake, I found myself wanting to shout out at the people who took away my chance. . . . I almost passed out with the rage." At that point, he would clearly state that "religion was the reason he and Stoller were denied their chance." Previously, in private conversations with this friendly interlocuter, he had mused about how and when Brundage had directed orders to Cromwell and Robertson to turn back the Jews. But until his return to Berlin, Glickman did not identify Brundage by name for public consumption as the prime instigator.[21] Writing his own guest op-ed for the *Times* in 1994, Glickman would emphasize, "Being there visualizing and reliving those moments caused the eruption which had been gnawing at me for so long and which I thought I had expunged years ago."[22]

Although Glickman's passionate pique would not always be expressed as definitively in his subsequent accounts of Berlin 1936, the saga of Brundage versus Glickman became his dominant narrative during the final fifteen years of his life. More often than not, Brundage was identified as his prime enemy.

For example, in 1992 in response to a question from an audience member at a media seminar who was interested in knowing more about his full life story, Glickman would absolutely assert that "two Jewish boys were prevented from running because we were Jewish, prevented by an American Nazi aided and abetted by a track coach." After his second trip back to the Berlin stadium in 1994 he reiterated that "I believe that Avery Brundage . . . told Robertson and Cromwell to drop us from the relay to save Hitler from further embarrassment by having two Jews standing on the winning platform. . . . Brundage was an American Nazi." A film producer reported that when interviewed for another documentary two years later, Glickman made clear that "he was removed . . . in

1936 because he was Jewish. And when Glickman says 'Nazi,' he literally spits the word out."[23]

Marv Albert would recall how, after 1985, his mentor's demeanor changed toward recounting "the meeting" and its aftermaths. Decades earlier, back at the time when Glickman gave his disciple his "start . . . he would talk about it from time to time. But I felt as the years went by, particularly" after "he took a trip to Berlin to actually honor the memory of Jesse Owens' participation in the '36 Olympics he became more embittered about it later on as there were various TV specials were made about it." After he "looked up at the area where Adolf Hitler was sitting . . . he was constantly thinking about it later on. I think it really upset him."[24]

As to why Marty Glickman's hatred for those who denied him Olympic glory remained for so long inside of him, away from the public, residing within the recesses of his soul, until that searing moment in Berlin 1985, those closest to him have suggested several additional factors were in play. Some have noted affectionately that his silence bespoke "this upbeat" fellow's preternatural optimistic mien and an ability to transcend negative circumstances that would have embittered and waylaid lesser people. By disposition, he was "not an angry person" who "loved his job covering his games" and was content to hold whatever residual grief he had "inside." Commenting on Glickman's problems with prejudice after 1936 in the early world of television, one admiring writer noted that "he integrated well as a New Yorker comfortably separated" from "the great WASP America." For himself, Glickman repeatedly said, as a point of emphasis if not of honor, that he would never explain away a setback as due to anti-Semitism: "I felt I could overcome it, no matter what. I had not let the 1936 Olympics incident discourage me. I couldn't bring myself to publicly make an issue of the NBA-NBC snub." Others among his friends, family, and disciples have pointed out differently, albeit with abundant understanding, to underlying occupational and financial insecurities that abridged his responses to enemies, be they Brundage or, later on, Arledge or even Podoloff.[25]

That latter sensibility about succeeding in a wider non-Jewish world possesses a ring of verisimilitude. Marty Glickman, once again as with so many episodes in his life, had much in common with so many Jewish men and women of his generation. When people of his age group were confronted with opposition to their professional or social quests during the interwar and early postwar times within which they lived, they believed the best course of response was to find unobtrusive ways of dealing with their relegation to the margins of American life. They stopped short of proclaiming how un-American anti-Semitism was. On that score, Sal Marchiano may have explained that common behavior best when he opined, "Marty was pragmatic, he understood that he had to make a living and there were forces too strong to buck. . . . Until the 1960s, no voices of protest were raised in America everything was accepted that's just the way it was." No one wanted to hear troubling reminders of the past or the issues of the present. Marty understood "those realities" concerned as he was with job security.

This proud Italian American's sensitivities may be attributed to his own ethnic-based dilemmas that he faced up to early in his own career. When he was starting out as a weekend reporter for a local New York outlet, his station manager wanted him to change his name to "Sam March." Marchiano refused, and it took the intercession of former football star and All-American Frank Gifford, who had become a broadcaster, to stick up for Sal for him to secure his job. Ten years later, Marchiano knew he had made the right decision when Frank Sinatra told him how he was following his career and was very proud that a fellow who had grown up in the Italian American neighborhood of Red Hook, Brooklyn, had stood tall about his ancestry. This renowned entertainer hailed from a comparable ethnic enclave in Hoboken, New Jersey.[26]

In any event, by the time Glickman let loose with his feelings about his experiences with anti-Semitism, a new era of American Jewish self-confidence was well underway as this minority group increasingly felt accepted within American society. For the younger generation who grew up in the 1960s and later, the dilemmas of social and occupational anti-Semitism were problems that their parents had faced. Unlike their elders, who worried either to themselves or out loud "what will the Gentiles think?" about how they looked, sounded, or behaved, these youngsters intuited that the answer to that once-troubling question was that their Christian counterparts, colleagues, or coworkers just liked them. They would not let those who would marginalize them get away with their prejudices.

This period of unparalleled integration within this country and the feeling among Jews that they were truly at home in America did not happen overnight. But in the few decades after World War II—even if nasty anti-Semites would still be around—prior barriers started to fall and openness trended upward. Slowly but surely, elite colleges and universities unlocked their doors to high-achieving Jewish students. Much like it was important to so many for America to beat the Soviets at the Olympics, it was even more crucial to have bright young people, no matter their ethnicities, outdo the Russians in the areas of science and technology. Laboratories became a playing field, and smart Jews were seen as among those who could help win the fight for democracy. On another high-level front, prestigious banks, law firms, and large corporations began to value their Jewish associates' abilities. In most places in America, when workdays were done, Jews were able to find new suburban housing among their fellow citizens as the days of residential restrictions were ending.

Marty Glickman might not have been totally attuned to all of these positive developments, but he understood the significance of what Sandy Koufax did, or did not do, on Yom Kippur of 1965. When the star southpaw for the Dodgers announced that he would not pitch in the opening game of the World Series on the holiest day of the Jewish calendar, his decision in an incipient culturally pluralistic America was widely praised. Glickman knew that thirty-one years earlier, in a far less tolerant time and place, the owners and managers of the Detroit Tigers, amid a contentious pennant race, had pressured Glickman's sports hero, Hank Greenberg, to play on the High Holidays. For Jews, America was changing for the better.[27]

As of the 1980s, the heady times for Jews in America were in even fuller swing. They were able to rest assured that they had the respect, friendship, and even admiration of most Americans among whom they lived so comfortably. By that decade, not only did Jewish students inundate Ivy League schools, but each of those institutions could boast of a Jew as a president, law school dean, or other major academic officer. When surveyed, less than one in ten gentiles reported having any problems with Jews as neighbors. A study of the attitudes toward Jews in New York executive suites showed "by the end of the 1980s" that though discrimination had "not totally disappeared . . . it was on the verge of extinction."[28]

While not as widely chronicled, but indicative of the new status quo, within the world of New York sports, which Glickman knew best, Jewish fans of the Mets once showed how empowered they had become. During the 1986 baseball postseason, as supporters of the national pastime, they had the chutzpah to protest the scheduling of a crucial game on Yom Kippur. At that juncture, there were no Jewish players on the Mets nor on their opponents, the Houston Astros, although some of the Mets owners were Jews. Why, however, they argued, were the "Lords of Baseball" so insensitive to Jewish religious traditions? If Marty Glickman followed this brief kerfuffle, which was editorialized in favor of the protesters in an op-ed piece in the *New York Times*, he might have smiled ruefully about how far Jews had come from his day in their relationship to a powerful American institution, in this case a sports establishment. He could now sense that what he had to say about the totality of his and the Jewish people's recent horrible past could find receptive audiences among the younger generation of Jews and other Americans too.[29]

For instance, in 1988, when interviewed for a book of memoirs of famous America Jews, Glickman not only reiterated his "belief" that he said had been his narrative "for many years now, that we were replaced to save Hitler and his entourage and the Nazis generally from further embarrassment by having Jews compete and stand on the winning podium" but also pointedly said, "I have to explain to younger people that 'thirty-six' was different from 'forty-four' or 'forty-five' or any of the later years. Nineteen thirty-six was still two years before Kristallnacht. It was three years before the outbreak of the war and five years before we got into the war." But it was a prejudicial step toward the Jewish catastrophe. This explanation, which initially he had shared only with his family, would now be articulated publicly and widely. He had become not only a mentor to sportscasters but also a teacher to the next generation of Americans and this country's Jews about what his negative experience ultimately meant.[30]

By the 1990s, Glickman's public Berlin 1936 narrative, replete now with its anti-Semitic dimensions, intersected with the ever-growing interest among American Jews in not only bearing witness to what had befallen European Jewry during the Holocaust but also criticizing their government, American society, and even their own communal leadership's performance during those dark days of 1939–45. In the decades that immediately followed the end of World War II, most American Jews did not actively memorialize the Holocaust nor draw weighty contemporaneous lessons from that calamity. It has been said that "American Jewry suffered from an almost-two-decades self-imposed amnesia" regarding the consummate evils the Nazis had inflicted upon their people, "pushing" memory of the catastrophe "to the hidden corners and, indeed under the rug of their communal lives." Students of the FDR administration, who were already writing so much about his presidency, did not dwell in their research on the behavior of his administration toward the existential crisis that the Jews faced under the Nazis' heels. This other quiet, circumspective period ended at the close of the 1960s. At that juncture, those who examined Roosevelt's presidency began to question provocatively what Washington did, or failed to do, in response to the issue of rescue.

A new widespread consciousness of the realities of the Holocaust was initially raised to some degree when American Jews basked in the Israelis' audacious capture of Adolf Eichmann in 1960 and his testimony in a Jerusalem courtroom about his complicity in the murder of one-third of the Jewish people. But it took dramatic events in 1967, first the fear that the Jewish state would be destroyed and then the exaltation when after six days of battle in June they soundly defeated Arab armies that threatened them from all sides, for American Jews to shout "Never Again." Then they began to think deeply and to speak without reservations, about a tragic and powerless past. In the flush of victory "American Jewry became transformed and could then, at last bring the Holocaust out of the recesses of its cultural shame into its public display."[31]

The marching orders of "Never Again" would bring masses of Jews to the streets and their leaders confidently to seats of government in what ended up as a successful fight to free Soviet Jewry, who were long threatened with cultural extinction under communism. By the time that Marty Glickman returned to Berlin in 1985, the Holocaust had become both a retrospective and proactive "symbol central to the identity of American Jewry."[32]

At precisely the same time that 1967 witnessed this new activism among American Jews, the country's reading public, Jews and gentiles alike, would become engrossed with the first powerful indictment of their government's flaccid response to the refugee crisis of the late 1930s and the dilemmas of rescue once the war began. Journalist Arthur D. Morse's *While Six Million Died*, aptly subtitled *A Chronicle of American Apathy*, exposed and documented for the first time "how America ducked chance after chance to save Jews." Although the harshest accounts of callousness were directed at anti-Semitic State Department officials and at a too-long-unconcerned FDR as Jews were murdered, Morse was also unsparing in his attacks relating to the prequels to the Holocaust, including a chapter titled "The Olympic Spirit." There Avery Brundage was identified and criticized for ensuring that the American team showed up in Berlin to the satisfaction of his friends in the Third Reich. Glickman and Stoller's problems once the games began did not gain Morse's attention as he described the contemptible manipulations of the AOC. However, the German propagandists' use of sports was, for Morse, an important step toward murder at Auschwitz. It is not known if Glickman read this book, though it did appear initially as "an advance feature in the *New York Times*" and serialized excerpts found their way into *Look* magazine, a weekly that was then blessed with a national circulation of close to eight million readers. Nonetheless, Morse's "sensational" reportage did add wide gravitas to Glickman's recitations of his experience, even if he would always note that what happened to him paled in comparison to what befell the six million victims of the Nazis.[33]

Although Marty Glickman added his preamble to the Holocaust narrative relatively late in the accretion of testimonials, discussions, and debates, when he did so, it allowed this mentor to be in effect a teacher too with a public educational mission and opportunity. His classroom would be Jews and Christians both, starting with those within the younger generation who may have been sports fans and including audiences from coast to coast. The United States Holocaust Memorial Museum became a prime venue for his testimony.

This institution, chartered by Congress in 1980, set as its goal to "advance and disseminate knowledge about this unprecedented tragedy," to memorialize its victims, and to call upon visitors to the museum in Washington, D.C., to ponder "the moral and spiritual questions raised by the events of the Holocaust." In the decade after its opening in 1983, among its many weighty concerns, exhibits portrayed not only the road to the Final Solution during World War II and "collaboration and complicity in the Holocaust" but also the historical roots of Jew hatred as well as the courageous attempts by Jews to survive in the ghettos of Eastern Europe and the failed Allied attempts at rescue of the doomed.[34]

As the 1996 Olympic Games, awarded to Atlanta, Georgia, approached, museum professionals intuited that they could "capitalize" on the excitement of the games again coming to America as "a soft way to introduce Americans to the Holocaust" through a focus on the Nazis' use of propaganda within the aegis of sports. Exhibit curator Susan Bachrach explained, "Nazi Germany wanted to show the world that it was ready to rejoin the community of nations after its defeat in World War I. Hosting the Olympics presented the Nazi leadership with an extraordinary opportunity to project the illusion of a peaceful, tolerant Germany under the guise of the Games' spirit of international cooperation."[35]

It made abundant sense to have athletes, Jewish and non-Jewish, who were caught up in this triumph of Hitler's disinformation campaign speak about how the games affected their lives. Thousands saw excerpts of Glickman's four-hour interview, placed in a prominent spot in the exhibit, as he shared the spotlight with three other sports people whose experiences underscored the complexity of the Berlin 1936 moments in time. His video colleagues included Milton Green, who related how he decided after much soul searching to join the boycott of the games, and John Woodruff, an African American who won gold in the 800 meters. Woodruff was a stand-in for the late Jesse Owens as the museum wished visitors to understand how Nazi racism was applied to Black athletes as well as to Jews. For many people, Margaret "Gretel" Bergmann Lambert's account of Nazi duplicitousness was the most striking. Her story paralleled Glickman's in many ways. The Nazis had told the world before the 1936 Olympics that this Jewish athlete, a world-class high jumper, would be on their nation's team as evidence that the Reich was "unbiased in its selections," only to tell Bergmann weeks before the games that "she had not qualified."[36]

Glickman directed his primary attack on the evildoers within the American team with Brundage, whom he now clearly identified as his prime adversary, as the focal point of his staunch condemnation. He testified, "Avery Brundage, I believe, head of the American Olympic Committee, was the basic reason . . . that Sam and I didn't get to run. Adolf Hitler was being humiliated by the great success of the Black American athletes and I think he wanted to see to it that Jewish athletes did not stand on the winning podium and further humiliate Adolf Hitler. . . .

My experience in the Olympic games . . . soured me on Avery Brundage, certainly soured me on anti-Semitism and the Nazis as well." It is not known if Glickman was aware that even as he was now anxious to speak out, others—including some historians of the 1936 Olympics who then looked back at the story of Stoller and his removal—wondered if nepotism, and not anti-Semitism, ultimately was in play at that crucial "meeting." What is certain is that Marty Glickman was resolute and unflinching in telling the many people, who he believed were ready to hear him, that he was victimized by Jew hatred.[37]

A year after its premier in Washington, D.C., museum officials created a traveling exhibit that, over the succeeding nineteen years, was welcomed to twenty-one cities all over the country. The venues included local Holocaust museums, Jewish and local sports halls of fame, and the very prominent Naismith Memorial Basketball Hall of Fame in Springfield, Massachusetts. All of these places were connected to Glickman's life. In 1991, he had been enshrined at the Naismith center in recognition of his broadcasting career. On at least four occasions, Glickman was tapped to keynote the opening of the exhibit, which gave additional national exposure to his account and afforded him a profound teaching moment to Jewish and non-Jewish audiences. Now firmly on the stump, Glickman offered even more details about what he believed was Brundage's perfidy. At the very first stop on the exhibit's tour, in Grand Rapids, Michigan, he told his audience in no uncertain terms that "his offense was that he was a Jew" and that Nazi propaganda minister Joseph Goebbels, under unqualified orders from Hitler, told Brundage that "Jews could not run." It was an explicit demand from Berlin that Brundage, that American Nazi, in turn transmitted loyally to the coaches. In 2008, concomitant with the Beijing Olympics of that year, the exhibit was remounted in D.C., before being taken again on the road in 2010.[38]

In October 2016, fifteen years after Marty Glickman's death, the exhibit found its way to the California African American Museum in Los Angeles's Exposition Park. It was mounted under the auspices of the Southern California Committee for the Olympic Games and was located near the campus of the University of Southern California. For those who followed Glickman's life story, close by where Dean Cromwell had once held sway, the sagas of his track coaches, their AOC superior Avery Brundage, Adolf Hitler, Jesse Owens, and even Wilmeth Sidat-Singh came to a final triumphant conclusion.

Marty Glickman receives an award from the United States Olympic Committee, with Howard Cohen. Credit: Howard Cohen.

CONCLUSION

An Award from the United States Olympic Committee

WHEN Marty Glickman returned to the Berlin stadium for his second visit in 1994 and realized that he had outlived all of his Nazi tormentors, including Avery Brundage, who had died in 1975, he felt that his "Olympic story" had "come full circle." However, the United States Olympic Committee (USOC) was still unrepentant about how it had treated him so many decades earlier. The governing body's name but not its orientation was changed several times beginning in 1940. In 1996, before the games commenced in Atlanta, Georgia, the German Olympic Committee invited Margaret "Gretel" Bergmann Lambert to be its "guest of honor during the . . . Centennial Games." Sixty years after what Lambert called a "charade," the Olympic leaders of a new Germany were out to make amends. At that point, the USOC broached the idea that in commemoration of the hundredth anniversary of the first Olympics, it might be appropriate to have some of the "old timer U.S. Olympians" march into the stadium arm in arm with the contemporary American team. For friends and associates of Glickman, this projected parade would be a worthy opportunity for American sports officials to follow the lead of their German counterparts and, in a sense, apologize through honoring the man whom they had sidelined sixty years earlier. The suggestion to the USOC was for "Glickman [to] have a moment alone to bask in the cheers of the crowd maybe even holding the American flag."

The "USOC suits," as one outraged critic called them, rejected the proposal with the flaccid explanation that "they didn't want to do anything that would be perceived as 'political.'" While

Glickman did not comment on the pungent choice of the ironic word "political" to explain this renewed turndown of a Jewish athlete, he did remark, "I'm still an embarrassment to them. Only once in the 100 year history of the Olympics have any athletes who were fit and qualified not been allowed to compete for the American team. And that was the two Jews." In effect, Glickman attested that then, as it had been in 1936, he was a victim of anti-Jewish animosity.[1]

Two years later, in 1998, the USOC formally recognized the errors of its ways when, due to the initiative of the National Jewish Sports Hall of Fame, the committee bestowed on Glickman—and posthumously on Sam Stoller—its inaugural Douglas MacArthur Awards. The general had been the AOC president in the 1920s. When Howard Cohen of the Jewish group approached William J. Hybl, president of the USOC, his plan was to have the committee award a "replacement medal" for the one Glickman most likely would have won had he not been sidelined. Cohen had been moved to action after seeing a video of Glickman's second trip back to Germany for that 1994 Giants football game. After reviewing the facts that Cohen presented to Hybl, an attorney, asserted that he "was used to looking at evidence [and] the evidence was there." He and his organization determined that the "USOC isn't afraid to tackle things to have wrongs corrected."

When contacted about a projected public ceremony of presentation and celebration, Glickman demurred about accepting a medal. For him, a real Olympic medal had to be earned and what would be given to him now would not be the one that he had long wanted to show, and ultimately will, to his grandchildren. Still, he recognized how the MacArthur award was "really remarkable" for it represented the USOC finally apologizing for the injustice that Brundage had perpetrated so many decades ago. At the same time, in response to Hybil's tribute, Glickman did remark in a light-hearted yet semiserious manner, "What took you so long?"[2]

The IOC, unlike the repentant German sports contingent and even then the contrite USOC, would show, for the longest time, how far it had to go toward rectifying the misdeeds of Brundage. It will be remembered that in 1972 the Olympic movement's president barely memorialized the murder of Israeli athletes. In 2012, as the London games approached, the Israeli delegation and members of the local Jewish community called on the IOC to observe a moment of silence during the inaugural ceremonies in recognition that forty years had passed since the slayings in Munich. The IOC denied the request, citing that "it had honored the victims on other occasions." The IOC did not want to deal with potential pushback from Arab delegations. Politics were in play once again. The most the organizers would do in response to Jewish pressure, and other sympathetic voices, was to observe a moment of silence within the Olympic Village but not at the Olympic Stadium. Bob Costas, who was set to anchor the television coverage of the game's opening, was "baffled" by the "insensitivity" of this decision. Then as the Israelis marched into the stadium he took it upon himself to proclaim that "for many tonight with the world watching is the true time and place to remember those who were lost and how and why they died." He then remained silent for five seconds before NBC went to its commercial. It is reasonable to presume that had Marty Glickman still been around, he would have been very proud to witness how a foremost disciple understood so well what that atrocity had meant to Israelis and to him as a Jew. At the Tokyo games of 2020, forty-eight years after Munich, the IOC paid specific tribute to the eleven athletes along with those "lost during the pandemic and throughout Olympic history."[3]

In July 2015, fourteen years after Glickman's passing, the organizers of the Fourteenth European Maccabi Games—the international Jewish Olympics—invited Nancy Glickman to join them at their opening ceremonies and athletic events in Berlin. Upon visiting the Olympic Stadium, where her father was not allowed to compete, "clutching the red-white and blue striped singlet of his uniform, she waved it at the box where Hitler presided" and called out, "We're here Dad!" She echoed Marty's shout-out to the Nazi leader's ghost, "I am still here and you are not."

After that emotional moment, Nancy turned to her daughter and said that if she would have children of her own—the next generation of the Glickman family—it would be fitting if the family would pilgrimage to this memorable site. Her daughter "nodded at the idea of a new family tradition in honor of her grandfather who taught her to sprint in the hallways of his Manhattan apartment building." In the end, such a sacred journey might be more significant than even the missing gold medal.[4]

★ ★ ★

Approximately a quarter century ago, in 2000, the American Jewish Historical Society (AJHS) desired to add its voice to those many sports and Jewish organizations that were publicly appreciating Marty Glickman's multiple achievements. In that spirit, the athlete-sportscaster-mentor-teacher and Jewish historical figure was invited to speak to a gathering of sports and history buffs. He had already sat for an extensive interview for the society's oral history sports archive. Given the AJHS's mission to elevate the sagas of well-known Jewish personalities in this county well beyond celebratory and heroic narratives, I was tapped to introduce our guest and to respond to his remarks. At that point, I held the dual posts within the society as chair of its Academic Council and as associate editor of *American Jewish History*. This is the scholarly journal that I had helped shepherd and that had published in 1989 Peter Levine's article, primarily based on Glickman's long interview with the American Committee's own oral history project, called "Marty Glickman's Olympic Odyssey," also titled "My Father and I, We Didn't Get Our Medals." I was known to both my professional colleagues and the lay associates as their "sports guy," and I was then working on a book, *Judaism's Encounter with American Sports*, that would be published in 2005. Among that book's central themes was the concept that the Jewish sports experience in the United States can be used as a metaphor for narrating how Jews, their culture, and their religion have progressed and have been challenged within American society. For me, a critical barometer for determining degrees of acceptance or rejection of Jews as equal citizens is whether they have been "chosen in" or kept out within our country's games. Sports define communities. From what I already knew of Glickman's quests on the track and among broadcasters, his life spoke to this phenomenon. I believed his experiences could be projected beyond the sports venues as archetypal of the life story of a whole generation of Jewish children of immigrants who came of age beginning in the 1920s. That morning, Marty Glickman was too ill to attend the session, and the disappointed audience had to listen only to me. Now, through this work, I have been privileged to get a second chance to speak largely about a man whom I, like millions of New York fans, had listened to and enjoyed as a youngster—and, more important, to use what happened to him over eight decades ago to illuminate basic elements in the American Jewish experience. Although Marty Glickman never did get his medal to show his grandchildren, his legacy lives on.

ACKNOWLEDGMENTS

I T is a pleasure to thank the many people who assisted me in writing this book. In researching for this biography, I was gratified by the interest of so many outstanding contemporary sportscasters whom Marty Glickman influenced and the distinguished newspaper writers who reported upon and analyzed his activities to share their reminiscences of Glickman with me. I thank Dave Halberstam, Dave Cohen, Jim Freedman, and Gerald Eskenazi for putting me in contact with their colleagues. My search for primary source materials was aided immensely by Nancy and David Glickman, who granted me access to the Glickman family scrapbooks, as well as by their willingness to be interviewed about their unforgettable father. The background information on the Glickman family's early years in America was provided by genealogist extraordinaire Karen Franklin. I am warmed by her long-standing interest in my work.

The arduous task of poring over decades of newspaper and magazine accounts of Glickman's life was accomplished due to the impeccable efforts of Ayelet Marder, my student at Yeshiva University's Stern College for Women and researcher assistant. I am grateful for her contribution to and enthusiasm for the project. Our ability to consult secondary sources was facilitated through the indefatigable work of Yeshiva University's crack interlibrary expert Rebekah Shoemake. I am also pleased to acknowledge the university's support of the project through its Chelst-Schreiber-Zwas Book Grant.

As the manuscript moved toward completion, I turned to some members of Glickman's erstwhile fan base for their impressions and criticisms of my work. I am thankful to Douglas Marino, Steven Matthews, Jonathan Halpert, and Rabbi Avi Weiss for their help in trying to get the broadcaster's story straight for a wide audience. Professors Benjamin R. Gampel and Marc Lee Raphael provided their own expertise on the penultimate version of this study, as did the several outside readers whose comments were greatly appreciated. Needless to say, as always, any errors of fact and interpretation are mine alone.

At New York University Press, I am blessed to have as my editor, now of long standing, Jennifer Hammer. Although by her own admission she is not a "sports person," she understood how, if properly "pitched," this work could be more than just a sports book. She gracefully challenged me to deepen its reach as a volume accessible to readers of all walks of life, including those who never set foot in stadiums or tune in to game broadcasts.

Finally, I am thrilled to dedicate this book to our latest grandchild, Charlie. He and his older siblings and cousins and their accomplished parents are sources of great pride and joy to me and to Pamela, who is the bedrock of the Gurocks.

Riverdale, New York, 2023

NOTES

INTRODUCTION

1 On Marty Glickman's admonition to drivers and former New York Yankee president Mike Burke's recollection of cars pulling off the road, see Marty

Glickman, "Oral History Memoir October 3–4, 1979," Oral History, 220. See also Dave Cohen's comparable memory in "Glickman: Q and A with Dave Cohen and Jim Friedman" (Newhouse Sports Media Center, Syracuse University, November 13, 2013), https://youtube.com/watch?v=EknUPvFF100. See also interview with Len Berman, April 13, 2022, about listening to Glickman from out of town. On another occasion where Glickman made a similar statement about motoring safety when he was at the mic, see *Fastest Kid*, 123. See also Lou Bergonzi, "Glickman Hasn't Lost His Touch," GFA. Note that many newspaper and magazine articles cited throughout are from the Glickman Family Archive (GFA), as I have called it. Many of these references are incomplete because the articles come from family scrapbooks that do not always indicate the source or exact date.

2 On this "stunt," as Glickman described it, see *Fastest Kid*, 132. For Glickman's statement about his being a New Yorker, see Oral History, 11. On the qualities of Glickman's New York voice, see George Vecsey's comment in the HBO documentary titled *Glickman*.

3 On Glickman's staccato style of broadcasting, see William N. Wallace, "Marty Glickman, Announcer and Blocked Olympian," *NYT* (January 14, 2001). For Glickman's own description of his approach to broadcasting, see Oral History, 60, 61, 64. See *Fastest Kid*, 77, for his positioning at the Garden. See also Jack Kerouac, *On the Road* (New York: Viking, 1957), 237.

4 Don Freeman, "Point of View," *San Diego Union* (January 1986) (GFA). For Friedman's remark, see "Remembering Marty Glickman," *Insight* (February 14, 2014), WCNY Connected. For Levine's opinion, see *Fastest Kid*, 7.

5 Oral History, 17, 20, 199.

6 *Fastest Kid*, 2.

7 *Fastest Kid*, 2–3.

8 *Fastest Kid*, 173. For the museum's mission statement, see United States Holocaust Memorial Museum, "Mission and History" (n.d.), https://ushmm.org.

1. RUNNING THROUGH THE STREETS OF THE BRONX AND BROOKLYN

1 For statistics on Jewish movement in New York City in the 1920s, see C. Morris Horowitz and Lawrence J. Kaplan, *The Jewish Population of the New York City Area, 1900–1975* (New York: Federation of Jewish Philanthropies, 1959), 49, 234, 251, 257. On the rise of new neighborhoods that attracted Jews, see Deborah Dash Moore, *At Home in America: Second New York Jews* (New York: Columbia University Press, 1981).

2 Abraham Cahan, "The Commercial Advertiser," republished in Irving Howe and Kenneth Libo, eds., *How We Lived: A Documentary History of Immigrant Jews in America, 1880–1930* (New York: Marek, 1979), 117.

3 For a comprehensive examination of Jewish life in new neighborhoods in the 1920s, see Moore, *At Home in America*. On the decline in observance among Brooklyn Jews in the 1920s and beyond, see Jeffrey S. Gurock, "Jewish Commitment and Continuity in Interwar Brooklyn," in *Jews of Brooklyn*, ed. Ilana Abramovitch and Sean Galvin (Hanover, N.H.: University Press of New England, 2002), 231–41.

4 Jenna Weissman Joselit, "Jewish in Dishes: Kashruth in the New World," in *The Americanization of the Jews*, ed. Robert M. Seltzer and Norman J. Cohen (New York: New York University Press, 1995), 248, 250.

5 On the problems Jews and others faced during the Great Depression, see Beth S. Wenger, *New York Jews and the Great Depression; Uncertain Promises* (New Haven, Conn.: Yale University Press, 1996). On the interethnic battles in New York during the same period, see Ronald H. Bayor, *Neighbors in Conflict: The Irish, Germans, Jews and Italians of New York City, 1929–1941* (Baltimore: Johns Hopkins University Press, 1978).

6 Joseph Kissman, "The Immigration of Rumanian Jews up to 1914," *YIVO Annual of Jewish Social Studies* (1946/1948): 61–63; Lucian-Zeev Herşcovici, "Iaşi," in *The YIVO Encyclopedia of Jews in Eastern Europe* (2010), https://yivoencyclopedia.org.

7 On Romanian educational policies toward Jews, see Carol Iancu, *Jews in Romania 1866–1919: From Exclusion to Emancipation*, trans. Carvel de Bussy (New York: Columbia University Press, 1996), 117–20.

8 For examples of the often told saga of the Jassy race, see *Fastest Kid*, 4, 36; Oral History, 8–9; Peter Levine, "'My Father and I, We Didn't Get Our Medals': Marty Glickman's American Jewish Odyssey," *American Jewish History* 78 (March 1989): 421. Glickman also referenced the event in the documentary film on his life.

9 On the migration of Hermann to America, see the ship's manifest for the "S.S. Blucher Arriving from Hamburg on the 20th of December 1910," in *New York, U.S. Arriving Passenger and Crew Lists (Including Castle Garden and Ellis Island), 1820–1957* (2023), https://ancestry.com. The dates of the arrival of his parents are not extant. On the languages in the Glickman home, see *Fastest Kid*, 37.

10 "New York State Certificate and Record of Marriage, Bureau of Records, Borough of the Bronx, June 24, 1916," in *New York, New York, U.S. Marriage Licenses Indexes, 1907–2018* (2023), https://ancestry.com. On the differences between a salesman and a factory worker among Jews of this era, see Thomas Kessner, *The Golden Door: Italian and Jewish Immigrant Mobility in New York City, 1880–1915* (New York: Oxford University Press, 1977).

11 On the family story of Harry and Molly's prior acquaintance in Jassy, see *Fastest Kid*, 36. For a comprehensive study of the social connections among Jews through these societies, see Daniel Soyer, *Jewish Immigrant Associations and American Identity in New York 1880–1939* (Cambridge, Mass.:

Harvard University Press, 1999). On Molly's occupation before marriage, see "1915 New York State Census," in *State Population Census Schedule, 1915, New York State Archives* (2023), https://ancestry.com. On the Glickman's residences in the Bronx and the people among whom they lived, see "New York State Marriage Certificate," in *State Population Census Schedule, 1915, New York State Archives* and "14th Census of the United States" (U.S. Census Bureau, January 1920), https://census.gov. Glickman's *Fastest Kid,* 36, states inaccurately that he was born on Fox Street. In fact, he lived in the vicinity of Fox Street in the South Bronx.

12 There is a lack of clarity as to the peregrinations of the family before 1930 and their life at 763 Coney Island Avenue. Glickman has his family moving around Brooklyn neighborhoods from Brownsville to Bensonhurst to Flatbush. It is certain from the time Marty attended elementary and junior high school that he went to PS 217 on Newkirk Street in Bensonhurst and Montauk Junior High School on Sixteenth Avenue, also in Bensonhurst. However, he asserts that the family also lived in a building owned by his maternal grandfather in Brownsville across the street from Thomas Jefferson High School, far away from where he attended school. It is possible that the grandfather owned two different apartment buildings. What is certain, as per the 1930 census, is that as of that year the family lived with his grandfather and other relatives in Flatbush, very close to the Ocean Parkway Jewish Center, which the family sometimes attended. The neighborhood designations are not legal ones and are defined largely by residents who lived there. On neighborhood geography, see Kenneth T. Jackson and John B. Manbeck, eds., *The Neighborhoods of Brooklyn* (New Haven, Conn.: Yale University Press, 1998), 10, 16, 118.

13 On the nature of housing in Flatbush in the 1920s comparable to 763 Coney Island Avenue, see Jackson and Manbeck, *Neighborhoods of Brooklyn,* 117. For Glickman's statements on where he lived, see Oral History, 30, 44–45. On the residents of 763 Coney Island Avenue, see "15th Census of the United States" (U.S. Census Bureau, April 1930), https://census.gov. On the death of Morris Glickman, see his military death certificate, Form No.724-SAGO, dated October 20, 1918. On the location of Harry Glickman's business, see "Bankrupt Fraud Sends Glickman to Jail 18 Months," *BE* (June 16, 1931). On automobile ownership as a sign of affluence among immigrant Jews when public transportation was the way to get around, see Moore, *At Home in America,* 58.

14 On Harry and Molly Glickman's religious values, Marty's Glickman's Jewish education, and his later feelings about his religious training experience, see Oral History, 28–29, 237–38. See also Glickman's videotaped interview with Mark Aaron at the AJHS, May 16, 2000.

15 For statistics on the Jews' population in Flatbush as of 1930, see Horowitz and Kaplan, *Jewish Population of the New York City Area,* 235. On the

interaction among white ethnic groups, as recalled by Glickman, see Oral History, 37.

16 On Glickman's youthful sports activities and running with his father, see AJHS. See also Lesley Visser, "Past, Present Meet as Glickman Talks," *Boston Globe* (January 16, 1983) (GFA).

17 Stephanie Credno and Darlene You, "The Golden Age of Sports," in *The Roaring 20s: An Era of Change* (February 17, 2017), https://20sroaringhistory.weebly.com.

18 On Harry Glickman at the Dempsey-Firpo fight, see *Fastest Kid*, 64.

19 Gerald Eskenazi, "When Jewish Boxers Were Lords of the Ring," *Haaretz* (June 1, 2016). See also Paul Berger, "The Rabbi Boxer," *Observer* (May 25, 2010), https://observer.com.

20 Ari Sclar, "Basketball and the Jews: A Street Game Goes Professional" (My Jewish Learning, n.d.), https://myjewishlearning.com; Jon Entine, "When Jews Had Game," *Jewish Journal* (June 14, 2001), https://jewishjournal.com. For Parker's statement, see "Sports Slants," *JTAB* (January 21, 1935).

21 Irving Howe, *World of Our Fathers: The Journey of the East European Jews to America and the Life They Found and Made* (New York: Simon & Schuster, 1976), 182.

22 On Jews and Boxing, including name changes, see Peter Levine, "'Oy Such a Fighter': Boxing and the American Jewish Experience," in *Ellis Island to Ebbets Field: Sport and the American Jewish Experience* (New York: Oxford University Press, 1992), 144–69. See also Douglas Century, *Barney Ross* (New York: Schocken, 2006), 25, and Colin Tatz, "The Secret Jewish History of Boxing," *Forward* (March 14, 2017).

23 On the Glickman parents' attitude toward recreation for their children, see Oral History, 31. On Harry Glickman's support of Marty's athletics, see also *Fastest Kid*, 38–39.

24 Burt L. Standish, *Frank Merriwell at Yale; or, Freshman Against Freshman* (repr., Alpha Edition, 2018), esp. 2, 32, 56, 99, 137–38, 226. On Glickman's recollections of the Merriwell books' impact on him, see Oral History, 11, 100.

25 "Bankrupt Fraud Sends Glickman to Jail 18 Months," *BE* (June 16, 1931).

26 On Glickman family problems, see *Fastest Kid*, 39; Oral History, 44–45, 50. See also David Glickman email to Gurock, October 10, 2021.

27 On Marty Glickman's lack of early contact with anti-Semitism, see "Interview with Marty Glickman for the Great Depression" (Washington University Film and Media Archives, December 23, 2013), https://youtube.com/watch?v=7BpERC8rrmI.

28 For the most comprehensive study of 1920s–1930s American Jewish problems with exclusion and political anti-Semitism, see Henry L. Feingold, *A Time for Searching: Entering the Mainstream* (Baltimore: Johns Hopkins University Press, 1992), esp. chaps. 1 and 7.

29 On Bund and Christian Front activities in New York, see Bayor, *Neighbors in Conflict*, 97, 163.

2. A JEWISH FRANK MERRIWELL AT A COLLEGE-BOUND HIGH SCHOOL

1 On praise for Glickman as a student, athlete, and friend and the prediction that he would become a physician, see the brochure "The Milestone" (New York, 1935), 66 and *The Log* (1935): 91, 93, 106.

2 Harold G. Campbell, "Hails Pioneering of Erasmus Hall," *NYT* (October 3, 1937): A6; John L. Hess, "Madison High Alumni Mark 50 Golden Years," *NYT* (June 6, 1974): 41; Beth Sherman, "Class of '35 Recalls Glory Days at James Madison," *NYT* (October 14, 1985): B5.

3 On the economic difficulties Jewish and non-Jewish students faced in pursuing higher education during the Great Depression, and the differing rates of attendance between the two groups as well as the proclivity of Jewish women to go to work while their brothers went to college, see Beth S. Wenger, *New York Jews and the Great Depression; Uncertain Promises* (New Haven, Conn.: Yale University Press, 1996), 62–63; Nettie Pauline McGill, "Some Characteristics of Jewish Youth in New York City," *Jewish Social Service Quarterly* 14 (1938): 256–58; Leonard Dinnerstein, "Education and the Advancement of American Jews," in *American Education and the European Immigrant 1840–1940*, ed. Bernard J. Weiss (Urbana: University of Illinois Press, 1982), 47. On the post office as an alternative to college, see Betty Rizzo and Barry Wallenstein, eds., *City in the Center: A Collection of Writings by CCNY Alumni and Faculty* (New York: City College of New York, 1983), 67.

4 Madison school records do not indicate the religion of students. The determination of the high proportion of Jews at the school was based on the Jewish-sounding names (e.g., Cohen, Goldberg, etc.) as opposed to the non-Jewish names (e.g., Connelly, O'Brien) derived from the school yearbook *The Log* (1932–35) and from memoirs of students.

5 On the proportion of Jews at CCNY and Hunter in the 1930s, see Dinnerstein, "Education and the Advancement of American Jews," 50, and Stephen Steinberg, *The Academic Melting Pot* (Berkeley, Calif.: Carnegie Foundation, 1974), 9. See also Sherry Gorelick, *City College and the Jewish Poor: Education in New York, 1880–1924* (New Brunswick, N.J.: Rutgers University Press, 1981), on professorial efforts to break Jewish students from their pasts.

6 On the introduction of Hebrew into public schools but not at Madison, see Judah Lapson, "A Decade of Hebrew in the High Schools of New York City," *Jewish Education* 13 (April 1941): 34–45. See also "May Teach Hebrew at Madison High," *BE* (March 25, 1935): 5; interview with Donald Fleishaker, January 24, 2021.

7 On the history of sports at CCNY, see Arthur Taft, "125 Years of Sports at City College," *City College Alumnus* (June 1973): 917. The statistics on the performance of several teams were derived from the files of the CCNY Archives.

8 See *The Log* (1935) for a listing of the school's James Madison graduates of 1935 who sought to attend outside of New York. On out-of-town Jewish student college choices, see Lee J. Levinger, *The Jewish Student in America: A Study Made by the Research Bureau of the B'nai B'rith Hillel Foundation* (Cincinnati: B'nai B'rith, 1937), 20. This study of Jewish college choices suggested that "perhaps . . . studying elsewhere [was] due to the limited number of educational institutions in New York City and their frequent overcrowding" as well as "the quotas which exist" in some of the best schools "which lead Jews in that great Jewish center to seek opportunities elsewhere." On the undesirability of New York students at out-of-town universities, see Marianne Sanua, "'We Hate New York': Negative Images of the Promised City as a Source for Jewish Fraternity and Sorority Members, 1920–1940," in *An Inventory of Promises: Essays on American Jewish History in Honor of Moses Rischin*, ed. Jeffrey S. Gurock and Marc Lee Raphael (New York: Carlson, 1995), 237.

9 On Glickman's academic record, see Oral History, 54. On his overwhelming desire to race in the Olympics, see Oral History, 82. For the teacher's statement in his junior high school yearbook, see also United States Holocaust Memorial Museum, "The Nazi Olympics: Berlin 1936" (n.d.), https://ushmm.org. On his feeling about leaving New York, see Oral History, 83.

10 Lew Zeidler, "City Champions Get Four on First Team and Two on Second," *BE* (December 9, 1934): 43. On Glickman's position in the single wing offense, see *Fastest Kid*, 41. For Glickman's sense that ultimately he had become in high school like Merriwell, see Oral History, 83.

11 *BE* (January 10, 1932): 39; *The Log* (June 1932): 73.

12 *The Log* (June 1933): 83; *The Log* (June 1934): 88; *The Log* (June 1935): 114.

13 *The Log* (June 1934): 88.

14 Arthur E. Patterson, "Erasmus Hall, Madison Card Extra Games," *HT* (October 5, 1933): 25; Patterson, "Luckman Scores Twice as Erasmus Hall Routs James Madison in Annual Game by 19–0," *HT* (October 15, 1933): B6.

15 "A High School Flash about Marty Glickman," *JTAB* (June 4, 1934).

16 Patterson, "High School Sports," *HT* (October 10, 1934): 26.

17 "Erasmus and Madison Show Power," *New York American* (September 25, 1934) (GFA); Patterson, "High School Sports," *HT* (October 10, 1934): 26.

18 *BE* (October 13, 1934): 9; "Luckman-Glickman in Duel as Erasmus Meets Madison," *Brooklyn Times* (October 11, 1934); "An Angle of Interest," *BE* (October 16, 1934): 10.

19 Patterson, "James Madison Trounces Erasmus, 25–0, Shackling Luckman Before 20,000 at Ebbets Field," *HT* (October 13, 1934): 15; "Erasmus Set Back by Madison, 25–0," *NYT* (October 13, 1934): 18; "Glickman's Surprising Move Speeded Madison," *Brooklyn Times* (October 13, 1934) (GFA); "Slants on Sports," *JTAB* (October 22, 1934); Harold Parrott, "Wrecking Crew in Fall of Erasmus, *BE* (October 13, 1934) (GFA); Ira Berkow, "I Remember It All as if It Were Yesterday," *NYT* (December 2, 1994): B12.

20 Patterson, "Madison Gets into P.S.A.L. Final by Blanking Manual, 12–0 for Sixth Straight," *HT* (November 25, 1934): B4; Zeidler, "Madison Gridiron Team Makes Gallant Fight to Reach Title Heights," *BE* (November 26, 1934): 22; Patterson, "High School Sports," *HT* (November 28, 1934): 27; Kingsley Childs, "Madison Sets Back Roosevelt 12 to 0 on Two Long Runs," *NYT* (December 2, 1934): S1. See also the untitled newspaper account of Glickman's telegram dated November 17, 1934 (GFA).

21 Patterson, "Miami Invites James Madison to Game Dec 25," *HT* (December 4, 1934): 25; "P.S.A.L. Puts Ban on Miami Contest," *NYT* (December 6, 1934): 29.

22 Zeidler, "Madison Gridiron Team"; "Four Aces in the Backfield," *JTAB* (December 5, 1934); "Headliners of the Year," *BE* (December 30, 1934): 68.

23 "Glickman Back in His Former Running Stride," *BE* (February 23, 1935): 9; "Glickman's Dream Realized in Breaking Schoolboy 'Century Record,'" *BE* (March 30, 1935): 10.

24 "New Utrecht High Takes Track Meet," *NYT* (January 13, 1935): S1; Patterson, "High School Sports," *HT* (March 14, 1935): 26; Childs, "Track Crown Kept by New Utrecht," *NYT* (March 30, 1935): 21; "New Utrecht Wins Ninth Consecutive P.S.A.L. Track Title," *HT* (March 10, 1935): H7.

25 "Ellison to Settle 'Sprint Dispute' with Marty Glickman," *BE* (April 20, 1935): 6; "Glickman Confident He Can Take Ellison," *BE* (April 22, 1935): 10; "Team Honors Go to Hill School and Union High in Track Meet at Princeton," *NYT* (May 5, 1935): S5.

26 "Marty Glickman, Star Sprinter Sets Mark," *BE* (May 12, 1935): 41; *The Log* (1935): 114.

27 "James Madison High: The View from the Loyal Class of '35," *NYT* (November 19, 1995): CY10. On Salpeter, see also "Sevens Elect New Grade President" (GFA).

28 *The Log* (1935): 114.

3. RECRUITED TO FIGHT QUOTAS AT SYRACUSE UNIVERSITY

1 Zeidler, "Scholastic Highlight," *BE* (December 7, 1934): 20; "Have You Heard That . . . ," *JTAB* (December 2, 1934); Zeidler, "Scholastic Highlights," *BE* (January 14, 1935): 12; Patterson, "High School Sports," *HT* (January 4, 1935): 21; Zeidler, "Scholastic News," *BE* (February 25, 1935): 10; "Glickman's Dream Realized . . . ," *BE* (March 30, 1935): 10.

2   Heywood Broun and George Britt, *Christians Only: A Study in Prejudice* (New York: Vanguard, 1931), 74.

3   On Yale's restrictive policies, see Dan A. Oren, *Joining the Club: A History of Jews at Yale* (New Haven, Conn.: Yale University Press, 1985), 48–57. On Yale's athletic achievements, see "Timeline of Yale Football" (n.d.), https://studylib.net, and "Yale Athletes Who Have Participated in the Olympic Games" (Yale University, July 19, 2012), https://news.yale.edu/2012/07/19.

4   On Glickman turning down Yale, his relationship with Dorman, and her early career, see *Fastest Kid*, 55, and Oral History, 82.

5   Interview with Nancy Glickman, January 17, 2022.

6   On Little's tribute to sports at Madison, see "The Milestone" (New York, 1935). See also Sid Luckman, *Luckman at Quarterback: Football as a Sport and Career* (Chicago: Ziff-Davis, 1949), 15–16.

7   On the mission and curriculum at New College, see George W. Lucero, "New College, Teachers College, Columbia University: A Demonstration Experimental Teachers College (1932–1939)" (Ed. D thesis, Illinois State University, 2009), 321–24. See also Luckman, *Luckman at Quarterback*, 19, 45.

8   Luckman, *Luckman at Quarterback*, 9–10. On Glickman's recollections of his relationship with Luckman, see AJHS.

9   On the alumni recruitment trip, see *Fastest Kid*, 41–42, and Oral History, 82–84, 90.

10 Harvey Strum, "Discrimination at Syracuse University," *History of Higher Education Annual* 4 (1984): 104. See also Strum, "Anti-Semitism at Syracuse University," *American Jewish Archives* (April 1983): 4.

11 Jay Cox, "The Original Orange Olympic Champ" (Syracuse University, June 22, 2020), www.syracuse.edu.

12 Strum, "Anti-Semitism at Syracuse University," 5; Strum, "Discrimination at Syracuse University," 104; Broun and Britt, *Christians Only*, 114.

13 Irving Rosenfeld, "Syracuse University, Syracuse, N.Y.," *AH* (December 19, 1924): 199–200.

14 On the restrictive numbers and ultimate change, see Strum, "Discrimination at Syracuse University," 106–7, 113. On the hope of the Jewish journalist, see A. Margolin, "Jewish Sport and American Intellect," *Daily Jewish Courier* (April 5, 1923) noted in Peter Levine, *Ellis Island to Ebbets Field: Sport and the American Jewish Experience* (New York: Oxford University Press, 1992), 202.

15 *Fastest Kid*, 41–42. It is not possible to determine the three schools, other than Yale, West Virginia, Columbia, and Syracuse, that the Jewish Telegraphic Agency said were after Glickman. On Glickman's feeling years later that others were more privileged than he "for a reason I still do not know," see Oral History, 87. On the question of athletic scholarships in the 1930s, see Ronald A. Smith, *The Myth of the Amateur: A History of College*

Athletic Scholarships (Austin: University of Texas Press, 2021), and interview with Smith, February 2, 2002.

16 *Fastest Kid*, 42.

17 *Fastest Kid*, 47. On Handler on the trip to Syracuse, see Oral History, 89. See also, for the names of the Madison alumni who attended when Glickman was there, *The Log* (1935). On Morton Handler, see *The Log* (1935): 106.

18 Herb Braverman, "Colgate Frosh Sole Barrier on Yearling '11' Schedule" (GFA).

19 *Fastest Kid*, 8, 43–44. On Luckman sitting out his freshman year, see Columbia University Athletics, "Sid Luckman" (August 5, 2006), https://gocolumbialions.com, and Oral History, 91.

20 Oral History, 92.

21 On Glickman's memories of how he fit in as a Jew on campus, see Oral History, 88–89.

22 Broun and Britt, *Christians Only*, 77, 80, 97. See also *AH* (November 13, 1925) and "On College Campuses," *AH* (December 16, 1932).

23 Broun and Britt, *Christians Only*, 91, 121.

24 For a most recent use of Gallico's oft-quoted sentiments, see Jeffrey Goldberg, "Scheming Oriental Hebrew Basketball Players," *Atlantic* (January 22, 2010).

25 On Glickman's Jewish holiday incident, see AJHS. On Hank Greenberg and the High Holidays, see, for example, William Simons, "Hank Greenberg: The Jewish American Sports Hero," in *Sports and the American Jew*, ed. Steven A. Riess (Syracuse, N.Y.: Syracuse University Press, 1998), 192–200.

26 On Glickman avoiding fights, see AJHS.

27 On Syracuse policies toward exemptions for Jewish holidays, see Strum, "Discrimination at Syracuse University," 107.

4. WELCOMED IN GERMANY

1 On the send-off from New York, see "Good Bye Olympians and the Best of Luck to All of You," *New York American* (July 16, 1936) (GFA). For an account of life aboard the S.S. *Manhattan*, see Arthur J. Daley, "U.S. Olympians Obey All Rules Heeding Warning by Committee," *NYT* (July 20, 1936): 19; "Nazi Poison Spread on Eve of Olympics," *AJW* (July 24, 1936): 15; and "Nazi Gab-Fest at Heidelberg," *Sentinel* (July 23, 1936): 32.

2 On de Coubertin's views, see Monique Berlioux, ed., *Olympism* (Lausanne: International Olympic Committee, 1972), 1; see also Allen Guttmann, *The Games Must Go On: Avery Brundage and the Olympic Movement* (New York: Columbia University Press, 1984), 12–13.

3 On the awarding of the Berlin games to Germany, Hitler and Goebbels's attitudes toward sports and the Olympics, and the decision of the IOC, see Guttmann, *The Games Must Go On*, 62, 63, 65–66, 68.

4 On Nazi activities against Jews in sports after agreeing to abide by IOC rules, see Richard E. Lapchick, "A Political History of the Olympic Games," *Journal of Sport and Social Issues* 2 (1978): 2. On the evolution of the Third Reich's anti-Jewish policies, see Karl Schleneus, *The Twisted Road to Auschwitz: Nazi Policy toward German Jews 1933–1939* (Urbana: University of Illinois Press, 1970). See also Moshe Gottlieb, "The American Controversy over the Olympic Games," *AJHQ* 61 (March 1972): 182–84.

5 Gottlieb, "American Controversy over the Olympic Games," 183–88.

6 On Sherrill's views, see "A General Warns Jews to Lay Low or Else," *AH* (October 25, 1935). See also Ted O'Reilly, "Charles H. Sherrill, Hitler and the 1936 Olympics," *From the Stacks* (October 19, 2016), https://blog.nyhistory.org.

7 Gottlieb, "American Controversy over the Olympic Games," 189–91; Guttmann, *The Games Must Go On*, 78–79.

8 Guttmann, *The Games Must Go On*, 71, 73; Gottlieb, "American Controversy over the Olympic Games," 196–97.

9 For Untermyer's statement, see Gottlieb, "The American Controversy over the Olympic Games," 191. For reports on Jewish athletes and their associations being punished for not coming to the games, see "Sportsmen Not to Participate in the Olympics," *AH* (July 17, 1936): 76; "Refuses Olympics, Viennese Swimmer Disqualified," *AH* (July 31, 1936): 124.

10 On the alternate games in New York, see Edward S. Shapiro, "The World Labor Carnival of 1936: An American Anti-Nazi Protest," *American Jewish History* 74 (March 1985): 255–73.

11 Rafael Medoff, "Americans Who Stood Up to Hitler," *Arutz Sheva* (December 4, 2010).

12 *Harvard Crimson* (May 20, 1936): 1, www.ushmm.org.

13 Rafael Medoff, "A Basketball Team That Stood Up for the Jews," *Jewish Standard* (August 8, 2008), https://jewishstandard.timesofisrael.com.

14 "Great Hall Meeting Climaxes 'Boycott Olympics' Campaign," *The Campus* (October 18, 1935): 1; "5,000 Students to Mobilize in Peace Assembly Today," *The Campus* (November 8, 1935): 1.

15 For the CCAA position, see *Microcosm* (1936): 140. On President Robinson's stance, see "'Boycott Olympics' Petitions to Circulate through College," *The Campus* (October 11, 1935): 1.

16 "Olympics Fencing Aspirant Berlin-Bound if Selected," *The Campus* (December 6, 1935): 1; "Olympics to Be Played with Guns Says Fencing Coach Joseph Vince," *The Campus* (December 10, 1935): 3.

17 On Ornstein's largesse, see "Berlin Bound," *AJW* (July 24, 1936): 5.

18 Carrie Kahn, "My Jewish Grandpa's Triumph at Hitler's Olympics," NPR (August 8, 2008), https://npr.org. See also Seymour E. Smith, "Olympic Boycott Plan Revives Berlin Memories," *Sun* (January 27, 1980) (GFA).

19 For a recollection about what Glickman felt about the boycotters, see AJHS. On Glickman's awareness of the Nuremberg Laws, see United States Holocaust Memorial Museum, "The Nazi Olympics: Berlin 1936" (n.d.), https://ushmm.org. For Glickman considering fighting in the Spanish Civil War, see Oral History, 119.

20 "U.S. in Olympics in '36—O'Brien," *DO* (September 23, 1935): 8.

21 H. B., "The German Olympics," *DO* (September 28, 1935): 8; Robert Shulenberger, "Bryan Favors Transfer of Berlin Olympic Site," *DO* (November 11, 1935): 1.

22 Bill Evans, "Olympic Board Gives Mastrella Welter Position," *DO* (April 23, 1936): 3; Art Heenen, "Time Trials Give Locals Opportunity," *DO* (April 23, 1936): 3; "Shea to Begin Sports Review at WSYU at 8," *DO* (May 13, 1936): 4.

23 For Glickman's recollections that the boycott had no impression upon him, see undated *Washington Post* article (GFA). On Glickman's unequivocal feeling to go to Berlin and that there was bigotry back home in the United States, see *Fastest Kid*, 13. For Glickman family statements to Marty about being as good as anyone and the idea that he would show through running the fallacy of the Aryan myth, see Oral History, 35, 101. See also AJHS for Glickman's retrospective feelings about responding through victory to Nazism.

24 On Glickman qualifying for the Olympics, see *Sentinel* (August 6, 1936): 23; *AJW* (February 7, 1936): 2. For the controversy over his finish in the qualifying event, see *Fastest Kid*, 10–11.

25 For Glickman's arrival in Berlin and communication with his parents, see *Fastest Kid*, 14–15. For a reporter's observation, see Harold Parott, "Sportspourri," *BE* (July 23, 1936): 16.

26 "No Boosts for Olympic Ace," *AH* (August 7, 1936): 153; see also "Some Knife and Fork, Exercise by Lads and Lassies of the U.S. Olympic Team," *New York Evening Journal* (n.d.) (GFA).

27 Rabbi Louis I. Newman, "Tell It in Gath," *Sentinel* (August 6, 1936): 12. See also "Our Sport World," *Sentinel* (August 6, 1936): 23.

28 "Nazis Organize to 'Sell' Reich to Olympic Guests," *AJW* (July 10, 1936): 3. See also "Nazis Training Amateur Guides for the Games," *WT* (August 11, 1936): 6.

5. SIDELINED IN BERLIN

1 On American team behavior at the opening ceremonies, see "'This Flag Dips for No Earthly King': The Mysterious Origins of an American Myth," *International Journal of the History of Sports* 25 (2008): 142–62. On preparations for the race, see *Fastest Kid*, 17–18.

2 For Glickman's account of when and how he and Stoller were removed from the race team, see *Fastest Kid*, 17–23. On Glickman musing about

Cromwell's intentions and other possibilities, see AJHS. What Glickman never referenced was that while still on the S.S. *Manhattan*, Cromwell and Robertson were seriously considering replacing Glickman with Mack Robinson. This brief Associated Press dispatch filed while the team was still at sea was not widely noted at the time and was not mentioned in any later discussion of what happened to Glickman. But it did indicate that the coaches wanted Robinson to join Draper, Wykoff, and Stoller on the relay team. Bill Bingham, in his capacity as manager of the track team, overruled them, and at that point the squad remained to consist of Stoller, Glickman, Draper, and Mack Robinson. If this report is accurate—which complicates the narrative of the sidelining—not only were the two Jewish athletes bumped from the event, but so was Mack Robinson, another Black runner. But then again, Robinson had already medaled in the 200 meters. His seeming exclusion from the relay group was not at issue, though he was annoyed that he did not get a chance for an additional medal. This Associated Press dispatch, which references the possible discussion among AOC officials, was found tucked away in the GFA, which suggests that after the fact Glickman may have known about this early discussion. It is not known which newspaper(s) carried this story. What might have happened on the boat was not noted in subsequent reporting on the sidelining. See "Put Glickman on Relay Team, July 20, 1936" (GFA). On Robinson's disappointment, which was noted decades later, that he was not designated as a possible member of the relay squad but with no reference to the possible early discussion on the boat of Robinson as a replacement for Glickman, see Bob Raisman, "A Sad Footnote to Jesse and Jackie," *DN* (GFA).

3 *Fastest Kid*, 17–23; Peter Levine, *Ellis Island to Ebbets Field: Sport and the American Jewish Experience* (New York: Oxford University Press, 1992), 408. See also "Hitler's Games Took Glitter Off Golden Moments," undated article (GFA).

4 William O. Johnson Jr., *All That Glitters Is Not Gold: The Olympic Game* (New York: Putnam, 1972), 184. See also "Hitler's Games Took Glitter Off Golden Moments," where Glickman, decades after the fact, recollected that Robertson also apologized to him without indicating why the remorse, in his case, while the runner and coach were still in the Olympic Village.

5 "Pro-Nazi Speech by USC Track Coach Stirs Ouster Demand," *AJW* (September 25, 1936): 24; "Avery Brundage at German Day Rally at Madison Square Garden," *AH* (October 9, 1936): 422.

6 Johnson, *All That Glitters Is Not Gold*, 184; On Rice's statement, see *Fastest Kid*, 24; John Kiernan, *The Story of the Olympic Games: 770 B.C. to 1936* (New York: Lippincott, 1936), 267. For Mahoney's response, see "Strictly Confidential," *Sentinel* (August 27, 1936): 4.

7 For Abramson's report, see *Fastest Kid*, 21.

8 Phil Berube, "Disappointed but Happy" (GFA).
9 J. P. Abramson, "Clark and Parker Trail Denver Star in Sweep of 3 Places by America," *HT* (August 9, 1936): C1; J. P. Abramson, "250,000 See Marathon Go to Son, Japan," *HT* (August 10, 1936): 1.
10 On *New York Times* coverage, see "Owens Out of Relay," *NYT* (August 5, 1936): 27; "Brundage Expels Mrs. Jarret Anew," *NYT* (August 9, 1936): S1; "Japanese Smashes Olympic Mark," *NYT* (August 8, 1936): 1; "Stoller Declares He Will Quit Track," *NYT* (August 10, 1936): 13; "An Open Letter to Avery Brundage . . . ," *NYT* (August 11, 1936); "'Best Sports' Code Is 'Don't Get Mad,'" *NYT* (August 11, 1936): 23. See also Peter Levine, "'My Father and I, We Didn't Get Our Medals': Marty Glickman's American Jewish Odyssey," *American Jewish History* 78 (March 1989): 416.
11 "Brundage Issues General Holm Ban," *DN* (August 9, 1936): 80.
12 Jack Micey, "Public Ennui No 1," *DN* (August 10, 1936): 58. See also "Holm Cashes in in Fame Heave Ho," *DN* (August 9, 1936): 33; "Malone Offers to Help Holm," *DN* (August 10, 1936): 58.
13 Jimmy Powers, "The Powerhouse," *DN* (August 9, 1936): 36; Associated Press (August 11, 1936): 47; "Dropped in Relay, Glickman Blames Olympic Politics," *DN* (August 9, 1936): 82.
14 On the *World Telegram*'s coverage of the Olympics, especially Williams's reports and comments, see Joe Williams, "Big Day for Germany . . . ," *WT* (August 1, 1936): B1. There he noted that the Americans did not drop their flag. See also Williams, "Negro Stars Shine at games," *WT* (August 4, 1936): 32; "Negro Star Toast of Berlin," *WT* (August 5, 1936): 36; Williams, "America Bows in Distance," *WT* (August 8, 1936): 9; "AAU Drops Eleanor Holm . . . ," *WT* (August 8, 1936): 1; Williams, "U.S. Pretty Fair at Sports," *WT* (August 11, 1936): 24.
15 "Mrs. Jarrett Defiant under Permanent Ban," *BE* (August 9, 1936): 1; "Permanent Ban on Mrs. Jarrett Raises Her Ire," *BE* (August 9, 1936): 28; Alan Gould, "Highest Honors for U.S. So Far since '12 Games" *BE* (August 10, 1936); 2. The *Herald Tribune* continued to cover the Holm Jarrett incident. See "Mrs. Jarrett Returns, Determined on Fighting to Keep Amateur Status," *HT* (August 13, 1936): 19.
16 George Currie, "1936 Olympic Squawks Still Reverberate," *BE* (September 2, 1936): 23.
17 Louis E. Cohen, "Glickman at Syracuse," *BE* (September 16, 1936): 40.
18 Zeidler, "Luckman vs. Glickman," *BE* (November 11, 1936): 20.
19 "Good Luck," *AJW* (July 7, 1936): 4; "Jews Preparing to Flee Germany-Fear Perils after the Games," *AJW* (July 17, 1936): 2. See also an untitled article, *AJW* (July 31, 1936): 1.
20 "Did Nazis Force 2 Jewish Runners from the U.S. team," *AJW* (August 14, 1936): 5.

21 "Marty Glickman," *AJW* (September 4, 1936): 1; Bernard Postal, "Favoritism Not Prejudice," *AJW* (September 4, 1936): 4; Harry Conzel, "It Looks Like a Big Year for Our Football Heroes," *AJW* (October 30, 1936): 5; "Three from Midwest Named to Jewish All-American Team," *AJW* (December 3, 1937): 3; "1938 Jewish All-American Team Chosen," *AJW* (December 2, 1938): 5.

22 "Olympic Story," *AJW* (August 20, 1948): 5.

23 "The Berlin Olympics," *Sentinel* (August 13, 1936): 4; "Sportgossip," *Sentinel* (August 20, 1936): 14; "Our Sport World," *Sentinel* (August 27, 1936): 23; "Our Sport World," *Sentinel* (January 4, 1937): 24. See also "Stoller Declares He Will Quit Track," *NYT* (August 10, 1936): 13.

24 "The Nazi Laugh," *AH* (July 31, 1936): 135; "Non-Aryans at the Olympics," *AH* (August 14, 1936): 170; Ed Sullivan, "Blackbird: A Timely Parable Inspired by Certain Happenings at the Olympics in Germany," *AH* (August 14, 1936): 175.

25 "Two Notes on Sportsmanship," *AH* (August 21, 1936): 194; Haskell Cohen, "Jewish Griders Aplenty," *AH* (October 23, 1936): 454.

26 "Syracuse Three Olympians Relate First Hand Stories," *DO* (September 22, 1936): 5; Herb Braveman, "Shades of Red Grange Appear as Marty Glickman Sports No. 77," *DO* (September 24, 1936): 4.

27 "Owens Scores Pros, Heils Hitler," *BE* (August 24, 1936): 1–3.

28 "Untermyer Urges Anti-Nazi Boycott," *NYT* (April 14, 1933): 15. For a comprehensive treatment of the larger-than-sports boycott, see also Gottlieb, "The Anti-Nazi Boycott Movement in the United States: An Ideological and Sociological Appreciation," *Jewish Social Studies* 35 (October 1973): 198–227.

29 Louis Minsky, "The Policy of Aggressiveness," *Menorah Journal* (April–June 1935): 1–17. On Jews "overplaying their hand" in response to anti-Semitism, see also Henry L. Feingold, *A Time for Searching: Entering the Mainstream* (Baltimore: Johns Hopkins University Press, 1992), 210.

30 Michael J. Socolow, *Six Minutes in Berlin: Broadcast Spectacle and Rowing Gold at the Nazi Olympics* (Urbana: University of Illinois Press, 2016), 153. Interestingly, broadcasters also did not discuss the Jarrett problem.

31 On Harry Glickman's response, see "Glickman Father Bitter," undated newspaper article (GFA). See also *Fastest Kid*, 29, and AJHS.

32 On Graham's racist attitude toward Sidat-Singh, see interview with Strum, January 18, 2022.

33 *Fastest Kid*, 50–51. For the article that notes "white hope," see "Outstanding Speeder . . . in Training," January 3, 1937 (GFA).

34 On the NYAC incident, see Oral History, 40–41; *Fastest Kid*, 52–53.

6. NEW YORK'S BROADCASTER

1 "Hill Sprint Star Show Magic Eye Camera How He Gets Off to a Flying Start," *Syracuse Herald Journal* (May 2, 1937): 24 (GFA).

2 On Syracuse's mediocre football record of 11–12–1 between 1936 and 1938, see "A Century of Orange," *Syracuse Herald Journal* (September 3, 1989): 1, 3, 6; *Fastest Kid*, 42–43. As was often the case with these Jewish all-star teams, Ambrose Schindler, a gentile with a Jewish-sounding name, was named as the fourth member of the honored backfield.

3 On Glickman's performance, see Harry Cross, "Syracuse Beats Cornell as Glickman Stars, 14–6" (GFA) and an untitled report on the game from apparently a Brooklyn-based fan in GFA. For Glickman's own recollection of the game, see *Fastest Kid*, 44–45. On Glickman's size, see Jack Tucker, "Still an Olympic Rooter" (1936) (GFA).

4 On Glickman's initiation as a broadcaster while still a student, see Jack Matthews, "Olympic Gold Eludes Broadcast Legend," *Chippewa Herald-Telegram* (August 14, 1986): 3 (GFA); Jack Craig, "Glickman Tells it Like it Was . . ." (GFA). See also *Fastest Kid*, 48–49.

5 On Glickman dating Christian sorority sisters and Marge and Marty's mutual understanding that they might date other people, see Oral History, 89. For examples of telegrams between Marty and Marge, Marty's comments on show programs, and announcements about their marriage and Elizabeth's birth, see GFA. On Marge's visit to Syracuse, see telegram dated April 21, 1936 (GFA).

6 On Glickman's early career strides, see *Fastest Kid*, 55–63. See also William Juengst, "Radio Dialog," *BE* (November 16, 1942): 14.

7 *Fastest Kid*, 52, 90. On Glickman's relations with other soldiers, see Oral History, 167–68, and AJHS. See also "Pacific Isle Gets Sports Broadcast" (October 28, 1943) (GFA).

8 Oral History, 149, 154; *Fastest Kid*, 92, 121.

9 On the array of sports broadcasters performing in New York at that time, see David J. Halberstam, *Sports on New York Radio: A Play-By-Play History* (Chicago: Masters Press, 1999); see also *Fastest Kid*, 66–70.

10 On that benefit game, see *Fastest Kid*, 72, and Halberstam, *Sports on New York Radio*, 192.

11 Glickman, "When Garden Was the Place for Basketball-Wise," *NYT* (November 25, 1984): S2; "Sid Bakal on Radio," *HT* (February 26, 1961): H50.

12 On Barber's influence on Glickman, see Oral History, 142–44; Red Barber, *The Broadcasters* (New York: Dial Press, 1970), 249; Charles Friedman, "Off the Backboard," *NYT* (December 22, 1946): 55; James Tuite, "From Playing Field to Announcing: Then and Now," *NYT* (August 11, 1963): 101. See also interview with Dave Cohen.

13 Halberstam, *Sports on New York Radio*, 65–66.

14 "Madison Square Garden," *Variety* (February 7, 1951): 27 (GFA); Bill Modoono, "UConn's Mikes" (GFA). See also Halberstam, *Sports on New York Radio*, 200.

15 For the best study of the 1951 scandal with references to Glickman, see Matthew Goodman, *The City Game: Triumph, Scandal and a Legendary Basketball Team* (New York: Ballantine Books, 2019), 53; Richard Sandomir, "When Hoop Dreams Became a Nightmare," *NYT* (March 22, 1998): TV51; Friedman, "Off the Backboard," 55. See also *Fastest Kid*, 75–77, 79–81.

16 On Glickman handling multiple sports in a given day and his preparation, see Halberstam, *Sports on New York Radio*, 199. See also Tony Marcano, "At the Mike with the Guru of Glib," *NYT* (November 26, 1995): CY3.

17 On Glickman's relationship with Husing, see Halberstam, *Sports on New York Radio*, 101.

18 On Glickman's football broadcasting style, see Halberstam, *Sports on New York Radio*, 111; on his use of Yiddish, see Oral History, 15; interview with Spencer Ross, April 1, 2021. On DeRogatis, see Sal Marchiano, *In My Rear View Mirror* (New York: 11:22 Publishing, 2007), 111. See also Gerald Eskenazi, "Schmalz Is Man on the Spot for Jets," *NYT* (October 8, 1976): A2. On Glickman's yardage terminology, see interview with Douglas Marino, May 6, 2022. On Glickman's use of a curse word, see MBSS2.

19 *Fastest Kid*, 120–21. On his removal from the Giants, see "WOR Signs Glickman for Jet Broadcasts," *NYT* (March 31, 1973): 71; "Observer Thrown for Loss by Glickman's Departure," *NYT* (March 4, 1979) (GFA); Vecsey, "Glickman Is Back Where He Belongs," *NYT* (December 18, 1988): S3.

20 On the range of sports that Glickman covered, see *Fastest Kid*, 5, 58–59, 96–97, 144, 146. See also HBO *Glickman* for Glickman's sense of his own abilities and a colleague's referring to him as the first "jock announcer."

7. IDENTITY CHALLENGED

1 On the phenomenon and rationale for Jewish name changing during the interwar and early postwar periods, see Kirsten Fermaglich, *A Rosenberg by Any Other Name* (New York: New York University Press, 2018).

2 Lester D. Friedman, *Hollywood's Images of the Jews* (New York: Frederick Ungar, 1982), 64.

3 Neal Gabler, *An Empire of Their Own: How the Jews Invented Hollywood* (New York: Crown, 1988), 302.

4 Ale Russian, "Kirk Douglas Wished He Had Kept His Original Name Issur Danielovitch: 'It's More Interesting,'" *People* (February 6, 2020), https:// people.com; Friedman, *Hollywood's Images of the Jews*, 64. On anti-Semites arguing that Jews controlled Hollywood, see Steven Carr, *Hollywood and Anti-Semitism: A Cultural History up to World War II* (Cambridge: Cambridge

University Press, 2001): 124. See also Jack Nagourney, "Film Museum Fills History Gap," *NYT* (March 22, 2022): C4.

5 Elliot Cohen, "Mr. Zanuck's 'Gentlemen's Agreement': Reflections on Hollywood's Second Film about Anti-Semitism," *Commentary* (January 1948). See also Gabler, *Empire of Their Own*, 349.

6 Howard Simons, *Jewish Times: Voices of the American Jewish Experience* (New York: Knopf Doubleday, 1990), 126.

7 Richard Sandomir, "Mel Allen Is Dead at 83; Golden Voice of the Yankees," *NYT* (June 17, 1996): B9; Mel Allen and Ed Fitzgerald, *You Can't Beat the Hours: A Long, Loving Look at Big-League Baseball Including Some Yankees I Have Known* (New York: Harper & Row, 1964), 6; Stephen Borelli, *How About That! The Life of Mel Allen* (Campaign, Ill.: Sports Publishing, 2005), 40; Benjamin Ivry, "100 Years on Radio: A Century of Jewish Announcers," *Forward* (August 17, 2021); Christopher Lehmann-Haupt, *Me and DiMaggio: A Baseball Fan Goes in Search of His Gods* (New York: Simon & Schuster, 1986): 18. See also interview with Vecsey, April 13, 2022.

8 David J. Halberstam, *Sports on New York Radio: A Play-By-Play History* (Chicago: Masters Press, 1999), 54–56. In Stern's autobiography, he made no mention of his family's original name and almost no reference to his family's Jewish roots. See Bill Stern and Oscar Fraley, *The Taste of Ashes: An Autobiography* (New York: Henry Holt, 1959).

9 On Glickman's decision, see Oral History, 199, 236–37; *Fastest Kid*, 60; Sal Marchiano, *In My Rear View Mirror* (New York: 11:22 Publishing, 2007), 107. On Glickman referencing Greenberg, see Oral History, 191. On Glickman defining himself as a "Cultural Jew," see *Fastest Kid*, 86. On Greenberg's decision, see William Simons, "Hank Greenberg: The Jewish American Sports Hero," in *Sports and the American Jew*, ed. Steven A. Riess (Syracuse, N.Y.: Syracuse University Press, 1998), 192–200.

10 Kevin Eckstrom, "Bess Myerson on Being the First (and Only) Jewish Miss America," *Religion News Service* (January 6, 2015), https://religionnews. com; Elaine Woo, "Bess Myerson, Miss America Who Rose in Politics and Fell in Scandal, Dies at 90," *Los Angeles Times* (January 5, 2015), www. latimes.com. See also Susan Dworkin, *Miss America, 1945: Bess Myerson's Own Story* (New York: Newmarket Press, 1987), 92–94.

11 On the argument over whether Cosell changed his name to hide his Jewish ancestry, see John Bloom, *There You Have It: The Life, Legacy and Legend of Howard Cosell* (Amherst: University of Massachusetts Press, 2010), 20–21; Dave Kindred, *Sound and Fury: Two Powerful Lives, One Fateful Friendship* (New York, Free Press, 2006), frontispiece, 21. For Glickman buying into the view that Cosell wanted to downplay his Jewishness, see *Fastest Kid*, 157. See also Marcano, "At the Mike with the Guru of Glib," CY3. For Glickman's negative comments about Cosell, see MBSS1. On Cannon's

negative view of Cosell, see Tom Callahan, "Direct from the Stands, the Bad Seed," *Washington Post* (May 2, 1993).

12 On Glickman's views of Albert's name change, see *Fastest Kid*, 87.

13 David Zuwarik, *The Jews of Prime Time* (Hanover, N.H.: Brandeis University Press, 2003), 5–9.

14 On Glickman efforts within the early NBA, see Halberstam, *Sports on New York Radio*, 199, and interview with Spencer Ross, April 14, 2022. On the transfer to NBC, see also *Fastest Kid*, 85.

15 Maury Allen, *Voices of Sport* (New York: Grosset and Dunlap, 1971). On the difference between a midwestern and a New York sound, see also MBSS2. On Podoloff's fears, see Oral History, 161, and *Fastest Kid*, 86.

16 On the prominence of Jews in basketball and the Jewish presence as players and owners in the beginnings of the NBA, see Gurock, "Boys from the City: New York's Jewish Basketball Stars," in *City Game: Basketball in New York*, ed. William H. Rhoden (New York: Rizzoli Electra, 2020), 31–37. See also Rich Westcott, *The Mogul: Eddie Gottlieb, Philadelphia Sports Legends and Pro Basketball Pioneer* (Philadelphia: Temple University Press, 2008). On how Jewish basketball may have been seen in Kentucky back in the 1950s, see interview with Vecsey. On the exclusion of the New York Rens, see also "Lapchick and Sweetwater: Breaking Barriers" (MSG Network, 2008). On Glickman's reaction to the "snub," see *Fastest Kid*, 86, and Oral History, 160–61.

17 Gerald Eskenazi, "It's the Best, Like Glickman" (GFA); Freeman, "Point of View" (GFA); interview with Spencer Ross, April 14, 2022; Richard Sandomir, "A Precise, Animated Diction That Captivated the Listener," *NYT* (January 7, 2001); Richard Sandomir, "Many Lessons Still to Be Taught by an Old Master," *NYT* (January 25, 2008): D4; Eli Dunn, "The Glickman Years at UConn" (2022), www.wili.com.

18 Vecsey, "Glickman Can't Stick to a Career," *NYT* (December 23, 1992); B9; Marchiano, *In My Rear View Mirror*, 107; ESPN, "Outside the Lines: Marty Glickman," *Page 2* (2001), www.espn.com. See also Stan Isaac's comments about the South and South Brooklyn, MBSS2.

19 *Fastest Kid*, 29, 88–90, 137–39. On Glickman dealing with rejection, see Marchiano, *In My Rear View Mirror*, 109–11.

8. MARTY AS MENTOR

1 Freeman, "Marty Remembers 'Feel of the Game,'" *TV Week* (November 17, 1984): 5. On the sound of Glickman's New York voice, see "Pittsburgh Steelers at New York Giants 12-15-63" (Classic Sports Radio Network, July 6, 2017), https://youtube.com/watch?v=6oUnSwkIco8. This rare audio is, of course, a version of his football call, but arguably the same words were used for basketball. See also interview with Gerald Eskenazi, May 5, 2022; interview with Wayne Norman, April 11, 2022; and Vecsey, "Glickman Can't Stick to a Career," *NYT* (December 23, 1992): B9. See also, for a different version of the "Yurin" call, *Fastest Kid*, 78.

2 Sal Marchiano, *In My Rear View Mirror* (New York: 11:22 Publishing, 2007), 105. See also Gerald Eskenazi, "Finding Enlightened Talk on the Air," *NYT* (March 19, 1985): B11; *Fastest Kid*, 63.

3 "Candid Camera Classic: Baseball Broadcast Talks Back" (Candid Camera Classics, July 5, 2017), https://youtube.com/watch?v=QLUW_OGWMmU.

4 Steve Jacobson, "Three Books Worth Spending Time With," *Newsday* (December 17, 1996) (GFA); see also Vic Ziegel, "Glickman, Garden's Voice" (GFA); Marchiano, *In My Rear View Mirror*, 105.

5 Owen Canfield, "It's Hard to Grow Tired of NBA," *Hartford Courant* (November 12, 1996) (GFA).

6 Dennis D'Agostino, "Remembering Marty Glickman" (NBA, January 5, 2017), www.nba.com; Bryan Curtis, "How NBA Announcers Inspire Their Successors," *The Ringer* (June 11, 2021), www.theringer.com.

7 For retrospective accolades offered by disciples, see the following YouTube videos: "Newhouse Sport Media Center: Tribute to Marty Glickman '39" (YouTube, August 11, 2015), www.youtube.com/watch?v=PwC6brHB4nk, and "Mike Tirico '88 Receives Marty Glickman Award for Leadership in Sports Media" (YouTube, November 16, 2017), www.youtube.com/watch?v=zMTPVrfUUZo. See also Richard Sandomir, "Many Lessons Still to Be Taught by an Old Master," *NYT* (January 25, 2008) D4, and Dave Anderson, "The Voice," *NYT* (June 24, 1973): I95.

8 On Costas's need to slow down tempo, see ESPN, "Outside the Lines: Marty Glickman," *Page 2* (2001), www.espn.com. See also Richard Sandomir, "A Precise, Animated Diction," and Glickman's comments on Costas's later abilities, MBSS1.

9 Interview with Len Berman, April 13, 2022.

10 Marchiano, *In My Rear View Mirror*, 7–13, 293–95; interview with Marchiano, April 13, 2022. For another poignant example of Glickman advising a young broadcaster, see Barry Kipnis, "A Lifetime's Lesson in a Single Session with Marty Glickman: Meeting the Legendary Broadcaster," *Sports Broadcast Journal* (February 6, 2018), www.sportsbroadcastjournal.com.

11 David J. Halberstam, *Sports on New York Radio: A Play-By-Play History* (Chicago: Masters Press, 1999), 218; interview with Ross, April 1, 2022.

12 On youth gang violence in New York City in the decades after World War II, see Eric C. Schneider, *Vampires, Dragons and Egyptian Kings: Youth Gangs in Postwar New York* (Princeton, N.J.: Princeton University Press, 1999). On Bernstein's feelings about youth violence and *West Side Story*, see Burton Bernstein and Barbara G. Haws, *Leonard Bernstein: American Original* (New York: HarperCollins, 2008), 6–7; *Fastest Kid*, 147–48; Marchiano, *In My Rear View Mirror*, 106. On Glickman's willingness to broadcast high school sports, see also William Doino Jr., "Marty Glickman's Triumph," *First Things* (September 2, 2013), www.firstthings.com.

13 Howard M. Tuckner, "Fledgling Football," *NYT* (November 9, 1958): X19; Irving T. Marsh, "Kiphuth's Swim Career Coming to Close at Yale," *HT* (February 1, 1959): B5.

14 Interview with Dave Cohen.

15 Lawrie Mifflin, "A Tutor Refining Athlete-Broadcasters," *NYT* (September 18, 1984): B15. See also "The Jockacracy," *Sports Curmudgeon* (September 13, 2018), https://sportscurmudgeon.com.

16 Tony Marcano, "At the Mike with the Guru of Glib," *NYT* (November 26, 1995): CY3; "Glickman Tells It Like It Was," *Boston Globe* (November 2, 1984): 80. See also *Fastest Kid*, 149.

17 Cosell's rejoinder articulated in two of his books, significantly titled *Like It Is* (Chicago: Playboy Press, 1974) and *I Never Played the Game* (New York: William Morrow, 1985), was that sports was dominated by "the Jockocracy," a term that he acknowledged was coined by Robert Lipsyte, and that his never having played the game was not a barrier to him. Rather, he claimed three decades of work "pounding the beat as a sports commentator was his claim to fame." To be sure, Cosell rarely patted athletes on the back. See *I Never Played the Game*, 15, 17.

18 Mifflin, "Tutor Refining Athlete-Broadcasters," B15. On Glickman as tutor, see also Gene Duffy, "Meet the Coach of NBC's Football Analysts," *Times-Union* (September 14, 1984): 50; Morgan Hughes, "Glickman a Sharp Critic of Announcers," *Sporting News* (January 7, 1985): 33; "Broadcasting Legend," *Chippewa-Herald Tribune* (August 14, 1986): 9; Freeman, "Marty Remembers 'Feel of the Game,'" 5.

19 *Fastest Kid*, 63, 158; Sid Bakal, "On Radio," *HT* (June 19, 1960): H50.

20 Interview with Gayle Sierens, May 3, 2022; Richard Sandomir, "First Woman to Call N.F.L. Play-by-Play, and the Last," *NYT* (January 28, 2009): online ed. See also Isaacs, "Pioneer, Yes—Promising, No," *Newsday* (December 28, 1987): 77.

21 Interview with Susan Anne Marchiano, May 4, 2022.

22 "Who Was Marty Glickman?," *Sportscaster's Club* (November 2, 2021), http://sportscastersclub.blogspot.com; Phil Giubileo, "A Couple or Three Stories about Marty Glickman," *PlaybyPlay.biz* (November 21, 2021), www.playbyplay.biz; "At WFUV Sports, a Passing of the Torch," *Fordham News* (November 16, 2017), https://news.fordham.edu; interview with Rick Schultz, May 10, 2020.

23 Interview with Bill Walton, May 3, 2022; Untitled, undated essay on stuttering written by Bill Walton, made available to Gurock, May 3, 2022. On his problem, see also Richard Sandomir, "The N.H.L. Wins One by Avoiding Face-Off," *NYT* (June 4, 1996): B15.

9. OLYMPIC MEMORIES

1 Jack Tucker, "Still an Olympic Rooter, Glickman Says at Beth El" (1936) (GFA).

2 Doug Kennedy, "Festivities Mark Departure of U.S. Squad for London Games," *HT* (July 15, 1948): 23.

3 Arthur Daley, "In Pursuit of Olympic Glory," *NYT* (July 9, 1948): 14.

4 J. P. Abramson, "60 Years of Olympics," *HT* (November 7, 1956): B 4.

5 Bert Burns, "Monitor Rules Marty's Gab" (February 1961) (GFA).

6 "Jesse Owens Returns to Berlin" (IMDB, 2022), https://imdb.com. In actuality, after Hitler refused to greet a different Black American runner, Cornelius Johnson, he was told by the IOC to greet either all the winners or none of them. See Hyde Flippo, "Did Hitler Really Snub Jesse Owens at the 1936 Berlin Olympics?," *ThoughtCo* (May 30, 2019), www.thoughtco.com.

7 "Olympiad: The Big Ones That Got Away" (Paley Center for the Media, n.d.), www.paleycenter.org.

8 Interview with Nancy Glickman, interview with David Glickman, February 3, 2022. "Glickman Encourages Athletes to Compete with Olympic Spirit," *Stars and Stripes* (February 1, 1956) (GFA). For statistics on the Cortina Games, see "1956 Winter Olympics" (Olympedia, n.d.), www.olympedia.org. On Glickman's subsequent statements about the undermining of Olympic ideals, see MBSS1.

9 "Victim in '36 Games Is Against '80 Boycott," *Boston Globe* (January 12, 1980): 12; "Olympics: To Compete," *Bulletin* (January 20, 1980) (GFA).

10 Jack Ellis, "'Games Must Go On,' Says Brundage," *Stars and Stripes* (September 7, 1972).

11 On Glickman's reaction to Munich, see Oral History, 112–14, 196, 201. On Glickman's additional negative feelings about Schenkel, see *Fastest Kid*, 190–91. For Glickman's critical views of the professionalization of the Olympics, see MBSS1.

12 Interview with Nancy Glickman; interview with David Glickman. Although Nancy Glickman has not recalled the title of the documentary that spurred her to inquire of her father, given her age and the year of the appearance of the film, most likely the date is ca. 1967–68. See also "Glickman: Q and A with Dave Cohen and Jim Friedman" (Newhouse Sports Media Center, Syracuse University, November 13, 2013), https://youtube.com/watch?v=FknUPvFF100.v, where the Nancy Glickman and Marty Glickman discussion is referenced. As indicated in chapter 5, in 1948 there was a brief note in the *American Jewish World*, characterized as an "interesting sidelight" to an article about Owens, where it was reported how Harlem Globetrotter owner Abe Saperstein, who was traveling with Owens to Yankee Stadium, told a reporter how Glickman related his problems with AOC officials in Berlin to his listening audience.

13 On Albert's memories, see ESPN, "Outside the Lines: Marty Glickman," *Page 2* (2001), www.espn.com; see also interviews with Ross, Cohen, and Berman.

14 Interview with Wayne Norman, April 12, 2022.

15 Oral History, 102–3.

16 Oral History, 183–85, 199.

17 "Victim in '36 Games Is Against '80 Boycott," *Boston Globe* (January 12, 1980): 12; "Olympics: To Compete," *Bulletin* (January 20, 1980) (GFA).

18 Bud Greenspan, "Why Jesse Owens Won 4 Gold Medals," *NYT* (August 8, 1981): W2.

19 "The Jesse Owens Story," www.youtube.com/watch?v=MkOj-2wNG; William L. Shirer, "Recreating the 1936 Olympics in Berlin," *NYT* (July 8, 1984).

20 *Fastest Kid*, prologue.

21 Arthur Pincus, "50 Years Later, Bitter Memories of the Berlin Games," *NYT* (August 10, 1986): S9; interview with Pincus, June 7, 2022.

22 Marty Glickman, "For Glickman, Berlin Memories Still Tinged with Regret," *NYT* (August 7, 1994): S9.

23 MBSS1; Glickman, "For Glickman, Berlin Memories Still Tinged with Regret; Richard Sandomir, "When the Olympics Were about an Ideal," *NYT* (June 2, 1996): H32. On Glickman's statements about his sidelining and Brundage late in his life, see also Robert Lipsyte, "After This Station Break, the Olympic Ideal Will Be Right Back," *NYT* (May 19, 1996): S2; Robert Lipsyte, "Tug of War Emerging over the 2000 Games," *NYT* (August 1, 1993): S2; "Jewish Heritage: Anti-Semitism Stole His Olympic Medal," *Public Exponent Press* (June 2, 1995): 8 (GFA).

24 ESPN, "Outside the Lines." Despite Glickman's public statements, the full truth of what happened to Stoller and him was not universally known. For example, when interviewed in 1988, Herman Neugass, who, it will be recalled, absented himself from the 1936 Olympics and arguably had greater interest than most in the outcomes of the games that he stayed away from, said, "I only know that they didn't run. When I talked to one of them, Sam Stoller, . . . he told me he was told by one of the coaches on the way back [to America] that the reason they were withdrawn was that the German authorities had come to the coaches and advised them that they were not in a position to protect any athletes in case there was a riot or something of that matter. That's what they told me I don't know anything more than that." See Howard Simons, *Jewish Times: Voices of the American Jewish Experience* (New York: Knopf Doubleday, 1990), 335.

25 On Glickman's optimism, see interview with Eskenazi; interview with Vecsey. Vecsey has additionally commented trenchantly on the trauma of his own returning to the Olympic stadium. When, as a reporter, he covered the FIFA

World Cup in that same venue in 2006, Glickman "was constantly on [his] mind" and he comprehended that "until you go physically into the stadium and smell the sulfur of the devil you don't understand." On Glickman refusing to blame anti-Semitism for his problems, see *Fastest Kid*, 86.

26 Interview with Sal Marchiano; interview with Pincus. On Glickman "sublimating" and "suppressing" his anger, "putting it out of his mind," see interview with Ira Berkow, April 8, 2022. David Glickman remembered that while his father never "dwelled on the negative," he was always concerned about supporting his family through broadcasting. See interview with David Glickman.

27 On the chronology of the process of decline in anti-Semitism in postwar America, see Edward S. Shapiro, *A Time for Healing: American Jewry since World War II* (Baltimore: Johns Hopkins University Press, 1992), 28–59. On Koufax's significance to Jews and other Americans, see David Kaufman, *Jewhooing the Sixties: American Celebrity and Jewish Identity—Sandy Koufax, Lenny Bruce, Bob Dylan and Barbra Streisand* (Waltham, Mass.: Brandeis University Press, 2012).

28 Shapiro, *Time for Healing*, 51. See also Nathan Perlmutter and Ruth Ann Perlmutter, *The Real Anti-Semitism in America* (New York: Arbor House, 1982), 75, for data on acceptance of Jews as neighbors.

29 On the dilemmas and resolutions of the High Holiday issues and American sports, see Jeffrey S. Gurock, "Baseball, the High Holidays and American Jewish Status and Survival," in *What Is Jewish about America's "Favorite Pastime"? Essays and Sermons on Jews, Judaism and Baseball*, ed. Marc Lee Raphael and Judith Z. Abrams (Williamsburg, Va.: College of William and Mary, 2006), 27–34.

30 Simons, *Jewish Times*, 336–37.

31 For an alternate view of American Jewry's early memorialization of the Holocaust, see Hasia Diner, *We Remember with Reverence and Love: American Jews and the Myth of Silence after the Holocaust, 1945–1962* (New York: New York University Press, 2010). See her analysis of the voices that argue for inactivity on pages 2–9.

32 On the periodization of the fight for Soviet Jewry and the use of the "Never Again" slogan, see Henry L. Feingold, *"Silent No More": Saving the Jews of Russia, the American Jewish Effort, 1967–1989* (Syracuse, N.Y.: Syracuse University Press, 2007), esp. 54, 104. On the Holocaust as a symbol of Jewish identity by the mid-1980s, see Michael Berenbaum, "The Nativization of the Holocaust," *Judaism* (Fall 1986): 447.

33 Arthur D. Morse, *While Six Million Died: A Chronicle of American Apathy* (New York: Random House, 1967), 142–53. On the appearance of excerpts of the book in the *Times* and *Look*, see David S. Wyman Institute for Holocaust Studies, "While Six Million Died" (n.d.), https://enc.wymaninstitute.org/?p=539.

34 United States Holocaust Memorial Museum, "Mission and History" (n.d.), https://ushmm.org.

35 United States Holocaust Memorial Museum, "United States Holocaust Memorial Museum Press Release Template" (n.d.), https://ushmm.org.

36 Interview with Susan Bachrach, June 10, 2022; Ira Berkow, "Margaret Bergmann Lambert, Jewish Athlete Excluded from Berlin Olympics, Dies at 103," *NYT* (July 25, 2017).

37 For Glickman sound bites, see United States Holocaust Memorial Museum, "The Nazi Olympics: Berlin 1936" (n.d.), https://ushmm.org. Notwithstanding Glickman's firm belief that Brundage was the source of the sidelining, which late in his life he fully expressed, Susan Bachrach has pointed out that scholars of the Olympics are uncertain whether anti-Semitism as opposed to favoritism was at the root of the sidelining. On this alternate view that "accusations of vicious prejudice hung over the American coaching staff for years. Whether or not the accusers are justified, the substitutions were badly timed," see Richard D. Mandell, *The Nazi Olympics* (Urbana: University of Illinois Press, 1987), 165.

38 Information on the venues where the exhibit appeared outside of D.C. was provided by Susan Bachrach. See Bachrach to Gurock, June 13, 2022. For accounts of Glickman's stump speeches, see Lonny Goldsmith, "The Olympics Dark Side," *Detroit Jewish News* (December 12, 1997); Dennis Anstine, "Nazi Olympics: An Old Story Worth Being Told Eternally," *Portland (Ore.) Business Journal* (January 14, 1999).

CONCLUSION

1 Ira Berkow, "Margaret Bergmann Lambert, Jewish Athlete Excluded from Berlin Olympics, Dies at 103," *NYT* (July 25, 2017); *Fastest Kid*, 3; Bob Raisman, "No Reprieve for Marty's Olympic Pain," *DN* (July 17, 1996): 79; Ira Berkow, "The Return of the Old Sprinter," *NYT* (December 3, 1996): B13.

2 Gerald Eskenazi, "Glickman, Shut Out of 1936 Games, Is Honored at Last," *NYT* (March 29, 1998); interview with Alan Freedman, June 8, 2022; interview with Howard Cohen, June 9, 2022.

3 On Costas's actions, see "Bob Costas Speaks of Munich Attack Controversy during Olympic Broadcast," *Guardian* (July 12, 2012). See also "After 49 Years, Israeli Victims of 1972 Massacre Honored at Tokyo Opener," *Times of Israel* (July 25, 2021).

4 Melissa Eddy, "In Berlin, Remembering Jewish Feats Well Beyond the Track," *NYT* (July 28, 2015): A10.

INDEX

AAU. *See* Amateur Athletic Union
ABC, NBA rights of, 146
Abraham Lincoln High School, 152, 157
Abramson, Jesse, 97; Olympics retrospective of, 170–71
Abramson, Marty, 46
Academic Council, of AJHS, 196
Acme, 22
African Americans: integration of, 11; Jews compared to, 96, 121; museum for, 190–91; racism against, 11; segregation effect on, 14, 24
AJCong. *See* American Jewish Congress
AJHS. *See* American Jewish Historical Society
Albert, Marv, 141, 156, 182; on Glickman, Marty, style, 144–46; on Olympic sidelining, 176; Ross interviewed by, 157; at Syracuse University, 152–53
Alexander, Thomas, 53
Allen, Mel, 122, *132*; name change of, 136–37
Amateur Athletic Union (AAU): AJCong relation to, 75–76; AOC relation to, 74; Jewish Welfare Board in, 77; at U.S. Olympic team send-off 1948, 170
America, S.S. (ocean liner), 170
America First Party, 178
American Basketball Association, 158
American Hebrew (publication), 106–7
American Jewish Committee, 55; oral history project of, 177

American Jewish Congress (AJCong), 74, 110; AAU relation to, 75–76
American Jewish Historical Society (AJHS), 196
American Jewish History (journal), 196
American Jewish World (publication), 104; "Jewish All-American Team" of, 105, 117
American Olympic Committee (AOC), 70, 71; AAU relation to, 74; Abramson, J., questioning motives of, 170–71; Brundage report to, 96; chauvinism in, 174; fair play canon violated by, 98; O'Brien on, 108–9; Sherrill relation to, 75; subservience to, 109
Der Angriff (Nazi publication), 88, 107
anti-Semitism, 11, 14, 74–75; of Christian Front, 31; of Cromwell, 105; Glickman, Marty, on, 109–10, 146; in Hollywood, 134–36; from Jews, 144; Jews fighting, 110–11; of Nazi regime, 69, 177–78; of NYAC, 114, 178; occupational, 183–84; at Olympic Games, 5, 7–8, 9, 10, 67, 169, 177–78, 181, 182, 185–86, 225n37; in Romania, 16–17; at Syracuse University, 56–58, 63–64, 66, 67; at universities, 55, 59–60; in U.S., 30; in U.S. Olympic leadership, 7, 96–97; in U.S. state department, 187
AOC. *See* American Olympic Committee
Arizona, Tempe, 145
Arledge, Roone, 146

227

Madison Highway (school newspaper), 46
Madison Square Garden, *116*; basketball
    at, 36–37, 122–23; "Game of the Week"
    at, 147; German Day rally at, 95;
    Knicks at, 2–3; Kuhn renting, 31; Mill-
    rose Games at, 62, 84, 131; Olympic
    qualifying games at, 79, 81; protests in,
    110; WHN radio coverage at, 120
Mahoney, Jeremiah T., 37, 76, 77, 96–97,
    111
Major League Baseball, 24; Greenberg
    in, 67
Manhattan, New York City, 13–14, 20, 21
Manhattan, S.S. (ocean liner), 69, 85
Manual Training High School, 44
Marchiano, Sal, *148*, 155–56, 157, 164–65;
    on Glickman, Marty, pragmatism, 183
Marchiano, Susan Anne "Sam," *148*,
    164–65
Marines, 120–21
Marist College, 166
Marshall, Louis, 55–56
Maryland, University of, 112
Massachusetts, Springfield, 4, 190
Mays, Willie, 5
McCarthy, Clem, 122
McDonough, Sean, 154
Mendelson, Sid, 57
Menorah Journal, 110
Mercersburg Academy, 51
Meredith, Don, 161
Merner, Carl, 50
Merriwell at Yale (Standish), 28
Merson, Leo, 78–79
Metcalfe, Ralph, 96; in Olympic 400
    meter relay, 92, 170, 173
Metropolitan Championships (NYC), 62
Micey, Jack, 99
Michaels-Stern, 137
Michigan: Grand Rapids, 190; University
    of, 66, 95
Mikan, George, 125
Miller, Leon "Chief," 80

Millrose Games, 62, 84; Glickman, Marty,
    as broadcaster for, 131
Minnesota Vikings, 1
Minsky, Louis, 110–11
Miss America pageant, 139
mlb.com, 165
"Mobilize for Peace Assembly," 79
Monday Night Football, 161
Montauk Junior High School, 28, 34,
    204n12
Monticello, New York, 22
Moran, Gussie, 162
Morse, Arthur D., 187–88
Mowins, Beth, 164
Mullin, Willard, 100
Muni, Paul, 134
Munich, Olympic Games in, 174–75, 195
Myerson, Bess, 139

Naismith Memorial Basketball Hall of
    Fame, 4, 190
Namath, Joe, 5
name changes, of broadcasters, 133–36,
    183; of Albert, 141; of Cosell, 140; My-
    erson on, 139; of Stern, 137–38
National Football League (NFL), 1–2
National Invitational Tournament (NIT),
    126
National Jewish Sports Hall of Fame, 4
National Stuttering Foundation, 167
"Nazi Olympics: Berlin 1936" (exhibit),
    8–9
Nazi regime, 6, *90*; *Der Angriff* of, 88;
    anti-Semitism of, 69, 177–78; Poland
    invaded by, 9; propaganda of, 88–89,
    188–89, 190; racism of, 72–73, 100, 104,
    189; in U.S., 180–82
NBA, 127; Dream Team of, 175–76;
    "Game of the Week" of, 141, 146, 147;
    Jews in, 142–43
NBC, 142; ABC relation to, 146; Podoloff
    blaming, 144; Weisman at, 163–64
NBC Sports, 161–62

ABOUT THE AUTHOR

JEFFREY S. GUROCK is the Libby M. Klaperman Professor of Jewish History at Yeshiva University. He has written or edited twenty-five books, including *Jews in Gotham* (NYU Press), honored in 2012 as the book of the year by the Jewish Book Council.